The Marketing Workbench

Using Computers for Better Performance

D0067830

The Marketing Workbench

Using Computers for Better Performance

John M. McCann
Fuqua School of Business
Duke University

DOW JONES-IRWIN
Homewood, Illinois 60430

ISBN 0-87094-763-X

Library of Congress Catalog Card No. 86–70518

Printed in the United States of America

1 2 3 4 5 6 7 8 9 0 K 3 2 1 0 9 8 7 6

To Ann

It is now technically possible to wire up the nation so that a corporate marketing executive can get instant reports on sales as they happen. And that leads to a fantasy view of the future brand manager, sitting like Captain Kirk on the bridge of the Starship Enterprise, getting reports on sales and then directing the specialists in his marketing crew to pour on instant consumer incentives where competition demands.[1]

Perhaps this "fantasy" contains some elements of the actual future. If so, the marketing manager will be sitting at the marketing workbench (MWB).

The ideas that led to *The Marketing Workbench* can be traced to my work with Data Resources, Inc. (DRI). In the mid-1970s, I took a leave of absence from my assistant professorship at Cornell University to join DRI, where, as a consultant, I was responsible for a major portion of that firm's interaction with consumer products firms. I became deeply involved in the development of model oriented decision support systems for use by the brand groups at firms such as Olympia Brewing, R. J. Reynolds, and General Foods.

In those applications, the marketing workbench that resulted was a computer terminal tied to the DRI computer in Lexington, Massachusetts, via telephone communication lines. Toward the end of my stint at DRI, IBM introduced a small desktop computer

---

[1] Philip H. Dougherty, "Market Research, At a Scan," *New York Times,* June 20, 1984.

(the 5100) whose econometric and planning software package provided much of the functionality of the DRI mainframe, particularly for the class of problems important to my consulting clients. This configuration was the "germ" for the idea of distributing managerial computing between the desktop and the mainframe. When I left DRI and joined the faculty of Duke University, I continued to be interested in the idea of supporting marketing managers via a distributed-processing network.

Next, I participated in the development of a computing philosophy for the Fuqua School of Business at Duke University. In 1981, the school was designing a new building that would include a computer center. I became intrigued with the possibility of substituting personal computers for the traditional time-sharing computers in use at most leading business schools. The school's acquisition of an Apple computer and an Osborne computer convinced me that the future of managerial computing would involve the strong participation of personal computers. I wrote a memo to the school's dean, Tom Keller, outlining my views about the future of computing and recommending that Fuqua adopt a network of personal computers. He, in turn, asked me to serve as the chairman of a committee to further develop the idea.

In 1982, I became Fuqua's director of academic computing, which meant that I had to design and implement the personal computer (PC) approach to management education. By this time, the IBM PC had been introduced and electronic spreadsheets were being used for many business applications. We built our computer facility around the IBM PC, adopted Lotus 1-2-3 as the primary language for business students, and networked the personal computers to an IBM System 38, with an IBM 4341 running the virtual machine (VM) operating system. The System 38 provided a "virtual diskette" facility that permitted the PC user to store data and programs on the System 38 without having to be concerned about the transferral process.

All of the above made it possible for me to observe the reaction of M.B.A. students to personal computers and spreadsheets. It was overwhelmingly positive! The students quickly saw the potential of spreadsheets as vehicles for applying the theories and methods they were being taught, and they became quite creative in using these new tools.

My next experience involved the teaching of a Management Information System (MIS) course titled Management Information and Control Systems. I decided on a highly applied course in which I would teach the development of small information systems on the PC using KnowledgeMan, an integrated system for MIS application development. My 50 students showed that they had the ability and motivation to grasp and apply the concepts of screen management, relational databases, nonprocedural commands, and a procedural language. By the end of the course, they could use KnowledgeMan to build workable and sometimes innovative applications.

These experiences suggested that individuals who aspire to become business managers or business specialists (e.g., financial analysts or brand managers) can take control of their own information needs: they can use high-level packages to build relatively powerful applications that support the activities of individual "knowledge workers."

This background was enhanced when I undertook consulting assignments with two package goods firms that involved designing computer systems to support marketing and sales management. The rapid adoption of the idea of networked personal computers by the management of these firms indicated a willingness on the part of practicing managers to adopt the new technologies. Also, just as the students were quick to use the personal computers in their work, the line marketing and sales managers in the two firms soon found creative uses for these computers.

Perhaps the strongest motivating event I experienced occurred during a dinner conversation I had with the vice president in charge of one of the divisions of a major package goods firm. The conversation involved the use of computers in marketing and the role they might play in the future. The following dialogue occurred:

Vice President: You may take my desk, my secretary, and my phone, but you may not take my personal computer.

Professor: What do you do with the PC that makes it so valuable?

Vice President: I use it to think!

The vice president went on to explain that he used it to "find the root cause" of a problem, to ascertain the causes of this situation, and to explore potential solutions. He said he used an IBM PC and the Lotus 1-2-3 electronic spreadsheet for this exploration.

The PC's friendliness, coupled with its ability to do "feedback learning" seemed to be the two aspects that most attracted him to this computer. He had tried and rejected a similar approach on mainframe computers.

The notion that the computer can add an additional dimension to management was expressed by Owen Butler, chairman of the board of Procter & Gamble, during a speech at MIT.

> If a computer is a device to store, retrieve, and manipulate information of all kinds, then it does the same things that the mind does. If a computer can do those things with almost infinite speed, accuracy, and capacity, then clearly it is a mind expander.[2]

He went on to say that the most important minds in the corporation are the top managers, and hence those minds should be expanded the most.

These notions of using the computer as a mind expander and an assistant in creative work led to the realization that managerial workstations should contain knowledge as well as information.

Interest in the knowledge management aspect of the MWB flows from recent successes in the use of computers to augment a specialist's ability to do productive work. Systems that use the notions and approaches of the artificial intelligence field have been successful in both synthesizing and syndicating the knowledge that resides in the minds of professionals and experts. This success is beginning to make managers aware that the computer can do more than extract, summarize, display, and print numbers.

Exposure to work in artificial intelligence has heightened my interest in computers for marketing management. Discussions with artificial intelligence researchers at IBM, Control Data, and Xerox indicated that it was possible to computerize expertise, and that marketing knowledge workers could play a strong role in this work. This view was strengthened when I attended New York University's 1983 "Symposium on Artificial Intelligence Applications in Business," and the 1984 meeting of the Association of Computing Machinery. The last meeting was dedicated to the "Fifth-Generation Challenge," to denote the computing ac-

---

[2] Owen Butler, "A Computer Is a Mind Expander," *Business Computing Systems* 3, no. 2 (February 1984), pp. 74–75.

tivities generated by the Japanese government's Fifth-Generation project, a major R&D endeavor involving artificial intelligence.

A sabbatical leave from the Fuqua School of Business at Duke University afforded me the opportunity to undertake a study of how computers are being used to support marketing managers in one industry. One of the members of the Fuqua School's board of visitors, IBM senior vice president and group executive C. B. Rogers, Jr., thought enough of my research ideas to request a research outline and plan, and to then locate a sponsor for my study within the IBM corporation. Erich Baumgartner, industry marketing manager, was interested in understanding the use of computers by brand managers and agreed to sponsor the study.

This book was written for those executives, managers, professionals, and students who are interested in how computers are currently being used by marketing managers and for those who are concerned about the future role of computers in marketing management. It discusses these topics and the issues and opportunities involved in moving from today's relatively simple computer systems and workstations into tomorrow's marketing workbench.

John M. McCann

CONTENTS

Management: *The Knowledge Tree. Expert Systems. Expert Systems and Marketing Activities. Personal Support Environment for Promotion Specialist. A Promotion Management System of Advisers. Dynamic Promotion Reports. Summary.*

Impact of Specific Trends and Developments: *Data Explosion. Expanded View of Data. Regional Marketing. Sales Force Computerization. Merger of Sales and Marketing. New Ways to Understand and Exploit Information. Marketing Group Computerization. Knowledge Management. Summary.*

Evolution of the MWB: *First Generation. Second Generation. Third Generation. PC and Mainframe Data.* Network-Based Marketing Workbench: *The Network Philosophy. The Data Architecture Viewpoint. The Data Warehouse. Network Design Approaches.* Cooperative Processing Approach: *Cooperative Processing Concept. An Evolutionary Approach to Cooperative Processing. Multiple Systems. The Key Element: Program-to-Program* Communication. Current Implementation of Cooperative Processing: *Cooperative Processing Hardware: 3270 PC. Program-to-Program Communication: API. Stand-Alone MWB. Summary.*

Introduction. Management Services: *The Systems Philosophy. The View of the Future. The Strategy. Specific Growth Paths.* Information for Marketing Management: *Marketing Research Department. Market Analysis. Marketing Management Information System. Current Situation.*

PART ONE

Today's Computing Environment

The first part of the book is devoted to a discussion of the computing environment confronting marketing managers in the mid-1980s. Chapter One serves to (1) introduce the topics in the book, (2) provide a glimpse of its major findings and conclusions, and (3) present the organizational structure of the manuscript. Chapter Two looks at the computer oriented activities that most companies are undertaking. It includes short descriptions of three companies and describes those practices and procedures common to all or most of the firms in the study. Chapter Three takes a different perspective as it looks at those elements that are different among the firms. This chapter introduces the notion of an intellectual technology and uses this notion to differentiate among those firms that encourage and support direct computing by the marketing managers from those that tend to place computer support in he hands of "computer experts."

Chapter Four discusses a generic computer system that will support the needs of today's managers. In addition, it presents specific recommendation about hardware and software that will allow a firm to implement the generic computer description. The final chapter in Part One describes the use of computers by marketing managers at Pillsbury. Pillsbury was selected because the firm had recently adopted a mainframe-based marketing management information systems (MMIS) that provides most of the functions described in Chapter Four.

These five chapters give the reader a grasp of the issues involved in using the current round of computer technology in the support of marketing managers. In addition, they provide a good introduction to some of the organizational and philosophical aspects of the computerization of marketing management.

CHAPTER ONE

Background

INTRODUCTION

This book contains three themes or "stories." The first theme, which is based on interviews with marketing managers and MIS professionals in a sample of companies, involves a description of the current computer related activities of marketing managers. Its purpose is to introduce the reader to the topic of marketing oriented computing and to a provide a background on the current status of the marketing workbench.

This view of the current status of computer use in marketing was obtained by visiting consumer goods firms and speaking with four different groups:

- Senior management involved in managing the marketing functions and the firms' information systems.
- Marketing managers who make use of computers.
- Management information system (MIS) professionals who build systems for use by marketing managers and analysts.
- The key person who acts as a liaison between marketing and MIS, usually called the manager of marketing systems.

The interviews with these managers and professionals were totally unstructured. The purpose of the study was explained and each person was asked to talk about his/her views of the role of computers in marketing within the firm, both from a company perspective and from personal experience.

The consumer packaged goods industry was selected for study because it is undergoing rapid change due to the pending explosive growth of data generated by (1) UPC scanners at retail outlets, and (2) marketing research data collected by new electronic-measuring devices. Since marketing analysis and management are similar across many types of businesses and product categories, the findings of this study should be applicable to managers and professionals in almost any company.

Having gained a view of today's computing environments and the organizational issues involved in selecting a direct-computing philosophy by marketing managers, the reader is then confronted with a description of an array of developments on the technological and marketing fronts that will change the status quo. Discussion of these developments and their implications for the marketing workbench constitute the second theme.

The third theme involves the marketing workbench itself, explored in terms of the philosophical and architectural decisions that a company must make in evolving from its current computer situation into a world that has been buffeted by the "revolutions" identified earlier.

OVERVIEW OF CONCLUSIONS AND FINDINGS

Current marketing practice can be supported by a mainframe and personal computer combination built around packages such as:

- Acustar, EXPRESS, or ANALECT for the marketing management information system.
- Lotus 1-2-3® or Framework® for the PC-based analysis and reporting.
- Multimate or Display Write for word processing.
- PROFS for communication and office automation.

These and similar components are evolving in the direction of better user comprehension. This evolution will permit more and more computer-naive marketing managers to incorporate the marketing workbench into their daily activities.

But, the marketing and computer worlds are dynamic, and major changes are imminent. Technology is evolving in the following directions:

- Personal computers are becoming more powerful; the new IBM AT can handle three megabytes of main memory, which is about five times more than the current IBM PC. And the underlying microprocessor is capable of using much more memory.
- New, high-resolution, color graphics cards will lead to increased use of workstation-based graphics.
- Database management packages that use the relational model have the ability to handle large and diverse databases. Personal computer versions of these packages are opening the door to the development and management of local or departmental data on personal computers.
- Fourth-generation languages are making it possible for end users to produce mainframe-based applications.
- Electronic spreadsheets are leading to the rapid deployment of personal computers throughout most corporations.
- Advances in links between mainframes and personal computers are leading to the optimal partitioning of computing tasks between the two devices.
- Local area networks promise to be the major computing development during the last half of the 1980s.
- Office automation advances are fostering a new office environment that permits strong participation by mainframes, minicomputers, and the personal computer. This environment will contain data in all forms: text, coded, image, video, and voice.
- Artificial intelligence philosophies and tools are migrating from university laboratories into the corporate world. This migration is being facilitated by the "Fifth-Generation Computer Challenge" from Japan. The results will include (1) computer systems that are easier to use and (2) the acceptance of the notion that knowledge can be managed via the computer system.
- End-user computing and end-user application development are emerging as the dominant forms of computing.

These technological developments are running alongside a number of technology-based marketing trends.

- Data from UPC scanners are beginning to augment traditional market tracking data. The richness of these new data may lead to their becoming the primary means for tracking both markets and competitors.

- Scanner-panels are growing rapidly and offer a new means for tracking and understanding consumer behavior.
- These scanner-panels are being augmented with in-home devices that measure household exposure to television commercials. The result is a database that provides information on both consumer purchases and consumer exposure to advertising.
- Research firms are merging and beginning to offer an expanded view of the marketplace based on integrated databases.
- Manufacturers are starting to provide their retail sales forces with portable computers and to build computer networks throughout their field sales organizations.
- Retailers are beginning to use UPC scanner data for tactical and strategic decision making.

These technological and marketing trends are likely to change the way computers are used and marketing practices as follows:

- The data in the MMIS will be expanded to include information on marketing program events, consumer and market data, sales call report summaries, and data on wholesalers, brokers, suppliers, and competitors.
- Regional marketing will become more pronounced.
- As retail chains learn how to use their scanner data, channel power will initially shift in the direction of the retailer. The retailer will become more proactive in decisions concerning shelf-space allocations, product assortments, in-store promotions, and advertising features.
- Manufacturers of consumer goods will accelerate the computerization of their sales organizations as a means of increasing their retail oriented information base.
- Firms will begin to rethink their organizational structures (which were designed before the current technology explosion). As a result, there will be a blurring of the organizational distinction between sales and marketing, with

first-line sales managers assuming responsibility for an increasingly larger portion of tactical marketing.

- The existing computerization of the brand groups will continue, and these groups will be tied into the sales management information system.
- Knowledge management will become important as firms seek new ways to channel the marketing function into the field sales organization.
- Brand groups and sales managers will be confronted with a data overload caused by the widespread adoption of the new data sources. Thus, they will begin to search for new and innovative ways to manage their data.
- Expert systems will emerge as a way to gain control over the data overload problem and to solve the education and knowledge distribution problems caused by the change in the marketing function.
- Brand groups and marketing professionals will assume more responsibility for computerization of their own databases and the development of applications that use these databases in conjunction with the firm's corporate data.
- Networks will begin to play a large role, primarily for communications and the sharing of data and knowledge.

These activities will occur in a computer environment characterized by the following components:

- From a marketing management perspective, the data processing aspects of the mainframe will play a smaller role. The mainframe will be a data warehouse, and may even be replaced or augmented by a special purpose database computer.
- Departmental computers may become important in marketing departments, particularly for the marketing management information system.
- The workstation will be the dominant element in the marketing manager's computing environment. It will contain a workstation management program that allows the user to transparently acquire computing services from mainframes, database machines, departmental computers, and other workstations.
- Cooperative processing among the various devices, using

the concept of program-to-program communication, will be the key to producing a modular and expandable system for use by marketing managers.

- Networks will tie all of these computing devices together and provide an integrated environment known as the marketing workbench.

This book builds a case for product management to unfold in the following manner:

- The data in the marketing management information system will be expanded to include information on marketing program events, consumer and market data, sales-call report summaries, and data on wholesalers, brokers, suppliers, and competitors.
- Regional marketing will become more pronounced.
- As retail chains learn how to use their scanner data, channel power will initially shift in the direction of the retailer. The retailer will become more proactive in decisions concerning shelf space allocations, product assortments, in-store promotions, and advertising features.
- To combat this shift, manufacturers will accelerate the computerization of their sales organizations as a means of increasing their retail oriented information base.
- Firms will begin to "rethink" their organizational structure, which was designed before the current technology explosion. As a result, there will be a blurring of the organizational distinction between sales and marketing. The first-line sales managers will assume an increasing portion of the responsibility for tactical marketing.

How will the marketing managers deal with this "new world"? Must they truly abdicate tactical marketing responsibility to the field force? If not, do the marketing groups need to significantly increase in size to develop and execute regional marketing plans and programs? Or, can technology be adapted so that a small marketing group can stay in control of a brand's marketing program as the firm travels the "local-focus" path?

Perhaps technology can come to the rescue of the marketing managers. Technology would be used to increase a person's ability to comprehend the marketing and competitive situation in many markets and to design effective programs for competing in each market: it would thus expand the manager's ability.

Such a system will be called a marketing workbench (MWB) to denote the fact that it is a physical place where the marketing managers do their work. It will provide

- Computing and communications facilities.
- Access to the firm's data in all forms: numerical, text, image, video, audio.
- Analysis capabilities.
- Ties for the marketing manager to the rest of the organization and to the external world of databases, advertising agencies, and suppliers.

Such a marketing workbench would need to contain all or most of the information that a marketing manager needs to understand situations and to devise marketing strategies and programs. This database would include the following categories of information:

Media.
Markets.
Brands.
Competitors.
Marketing programs.
Marketing events.
Consumers.
Customers.
Company.
  Production.
  Finance.
  Sales force.
  Policies, objectives, constraints.
Legal.

The marketing workbench is a workstation for use by marketing managers and professionals. It builds on work in other areas, areas that are working at developing similar systems for business professionals.

The Intelligent Management System (IMS) project is part of the Factory of the Future project in the Robotics Institute of

Carnegie-Mellon University. The goals of the project have been described as follows:

> The first is concerned with creating theory and systems whose functionality will aid professionals and managers in their day-to-day decision making. These systems must integrate and communicate the knowledge and skill of the whole organization, making them available for management decisions. More importantly, they must aid professionals and managers in carrying out tasks. Management systems must become more intelligent.[1]

A related project goal is to explore the application of artificial intelligence technologies for managerial and professional problems encountered in manufacturing, particularly manufacturing in a robotics environment.

A brand group can be viewed as containing a product manager and two assistants—the associate and assistant product managers. The marketing workbench is designed to support the work of this group by providing a computing environment that increases its ability to be productive.

The MWB provides the group with another assistant. Research at MIT is aimed at building a similar assistant for a different type of group—the programming team. A programming team consists of a chief programmer surrounded by a team of assistant programmers. The assistants increase the efficiency of the chief programmer by doing the more mundane and tedious aspects of programming: debugging, documentation, writing screen interfaces, and so on. The MIT research will add another agent to the team—the programmer's apprentice. The goal is to "make it possible for the programmer to interact with the apprentice in much the same way that he interacts with another, less talented, human programmer."[2]

This book, which provides a detailed description of all of these developments, trends, forecasts, and projections, is divided into three parts. Part One discusses the computing envi-

---

[1] Mark Fox, "The Intelligent Management System: An Overview," in *Processes and Tools for Decision Support*, ed. H. G. Sol (North Holland, 1983).

[2] Charles Rich, "The Programmer's Apprentice," in *The AI Business*, eds. Patrick Winston and Karen Prendergast (Cambridge, Mass.: MIT Press, 1984), p. 123.

ronment facing today's marketing managers. This section is based on the study of computer use in marketing management conducted in 1984–85. Part Two identifies the developments and trends that are changing the computing environment and discusses their impact on both the practice of marketing and the managerial aspects of the marketing function. In addition, the concept of knowledge management is introduced as a means of improving and expanding the role of computing in marketing management. Part Three discusses the hardware and software issues involved in the evolution from today's computing environment into one that is capable of dealing with the emerging data and managerial needs.

GUIDE TO EXISTING LITERATURE

This section of the book is relatively short because of the paucity of recent articles on computers in marketing management. Perusal of marketing management textbooks reveals that most such articles were written decades ago, as evidenced by a recent marketing management text with 18 dated references to articles about computers in marketing management.[3] Fifteen of these articles were written before 1975 and eight were published before 1970.

The literature on computers in marketing management usually appears under two categories: marketing management information systems (MMIS) and marketing decision support systems (MDSS). The former focus on the storage and retrieval of marketing information from a central database, while the latter consider such data extraction and summarization as a subset of the types of activities that marketing managers and professionals can perform with computers.

In addition, there is a time dimension to this dichotomy between MMIS and MDSS. MMIS was the popular phrase in the 1960s because management information systems were being introduced into the corporate world. MDSS was a 1970s phenomenon as discussion about decision support systems began during that decade. A detailed discussion of the MMIS philosophies

---

[3] Douglas J. Dalrymple and Leonard J. Parsons, *Marketing Management: Strategy and Cases*, 3d ed. (New York: John Wiley & Sons, 1983).

and applications was provided by King in 1977.[4] The Conference Board published a report in 1973 that contains discussions of information systems in several companies and a good reference list of the articles available at that time.[5]

Two important articles were published at the time of the transition from MMIS to MDSS, both by people associated with the Sloan School at MIT. Arnold Amstutz published an article in 1969 that reported on the status of the use of management information systems in marketing.[6] Montgomery and Urban's 1970 article pointed to the future by exploring the promise of decision support systems and their application in marketing.[7]

The 1970s ended with another article from an MIT professor: John Little explored the status of MDSS and made the following projections for the next 5 to 10 years:[8]

- An order of magnitude increase in the amount of marketing data used.
- A similar tenfold increase in computer power available for marketing analysis.
- Widespread adoption of analytic computer languages.
- New methodologies for supporting strategy development.
- A shortage of marketing scientists.
- A shift from market status reporting to market response reporting.

The most recent set of articles dealing with marketing information and computers appears in a book that resulted from the Harvard Business School colloquium "Marketing and the New Information/Communication Technologies."[9] Of particular im-

---

[4] William King, *Marketing Management Information Systems* (New York: Petrocelli Charter, 1977).

[5] Stanley J. PoKempner, *Information Systems for Sales and Marketing Management* (New York: The Conference Board, 1973).

[6] Arnold E. Amstutz, "Market-Oriented Management Systems: The Current Status," *Journal of Marketing Research*, November 1969, pp. 481–96.

[7] David Montgomery and Glenn Urban, "Marketing Decision-Information Systems: An Emerging View," *Journal of Marketing Research*, May 1970, pp. 226–34.

[8] John D. C. Little, "Decision Support Systems for Marketing Management," *Journal of Marketing*, Summer 1979, pp. 9–26.

[9] Robert D. Buzzell, *Marketing in an Electronic Age* (Boston: Harvard Business School Press), 1985.

portance is an article by Rudolph Struse of the Carnation Company on the current status of MDSS.[10] In looking at the future, Struse forecasts that the MDSS area will certainly change and poses the question: Will this change be evolutionary or rapid and discontinuous? He states that discontinuous change is now possible because of the rapid pace of change in computer technology. This question was in my mind when I started the research for this book, and it is explored in considerable depth in the final chapters.

---

[10] Rudolph W. Struse III, "The Four Ps of Marketing Decision Support Systems: Promises, Payoffs, Paradoxes, and Prognostications," in *Marketing in an Electronic Age*, ed. Robert D. Buzzell (Boston: Harvard Business School Press, 1985), pp. 134–53.

Computer Use in
Marketing Management

Insight into the current use of computers in marketing management can be obtained by examining the practices of the 13 firms interviewed in the background study. By looking across these firms, it is possible to observe similarities and differences in their philosophies and practices. The similarities are described at the end of this chapter. Both this chapter and the next present an analysis of the differences.

Eleven firms are presented in case studies that provide an overview of their organizational structures and describe how computers are being used by, or in support of, marketing managers.[1] These cases, which are interspersed throughout the book, will illustrate and "put meat on the bones" of the more generalized material that summarizes and contrasts the practices in the various firms.

Three of the firms are presented in long-case format. The Pillsbury case is designed to provide an in-depth report on how one firm chose and implemented a marketing management information system that uses established technology. The General

---

[1] Two of the firms in the survey are not included in the case writeups; they were visited late in the interviewing process and sufficient time was not available to obtain the clearances necessary to publish the writeups.

Foods and Frito-Lay cases appear toward the end of the book and give the reader an opportunity to observe companies wrestling with both today's and tomorrow's technology.

With this as background, let's start our study of the current computing situation by examining two medium-sized firms—Borden and Ore-Ida—that are somewhat typical of the firms in the survey. We will build on this introduction by looking at the most important part of the marketing workbench, the marketing management information system (MMIS). We will then examine another company to learn how it adopted an MMIS and how that MMIS is being used by its marketing managers. The chapter will conclude with additional discussion of those aspects of information management and analysis that are common to most of the firms in the study.

BORDEN

The grocery products group at Borden is responsible for products such as Wyler's® drink mix, Cremora® nondairy creamer, Eagle® Brand sweetened condensed milk, Cracker Jack®, and Realemon®. Grocery products is part of the Consumer Products Division. Organizationally, it is comprised of a vice president/general manager, marketing director, product manager, and assistant product manager. Several general managers report to one of two group vice presidents who reports to the president of the Consumer Products Division. Each division in Borden has its own computer system and support group; corporate groups are used for payroll, credit, accounts payable, and benefits. Within consumer products, the grocery products department is self-contained from a systems development perspective, with the large systems running on corporate hardware.

The company went to a broker-based sales force in 1979 for its grocery products, which does not include its direct delivery dairy, bakery, and snack items. These 70 brokers perform all of the selling activities involved in the retail and wholesale grocery and nonfood trade. Each broker has two types of sales representatives: headquarter representatives and individual store representatives. The headquarter representatives call on corporate and divisional buyers in the major supermarket chains and wholesalers and sell new brands, promotions, and other programs. The store representatives call on individual stores to sell and/or implement merchandising programs that have been accepted by the buyers. The relationship between Borden and these brokers is overseen by a field sales management organization composed of 4 area managers, 22 district managers, 6 region managers, 2 division managers, a national accounts manager, and a vice president of sales.

Every time a broker sales representative sells an item to an account, the item is recorded in the Borden computer system. (An account is usually a division of a large chain or the headquarters of a small chain.) When the item is shipped, it is considered a sale and a record is created in the sales history file. This file contains over 100,000 records, with about 400 fields per record. Each record contains three years of monthly sales history, along with descriptive information to select and summarize the information in various ways:

- Product information may be summarized via marketing/ financial categories, sales categories, or customer presentation categories.
- Customer information may be summarized by customer organizational structure, Borden's broker territories (for each of several sales forces), or Borden's key account list.

The detailed sales history file, along with open-order detail, invoice detail, and a summarized sales history file, form the base of information available to marketing through inquiry- and request-reporting systems.

On-line access to this information is provided via an IBM 3083 running the Virtual Machine (VM) operating system. Queries are answered using IBM's APL Data Interface (APLDI) software. Product managers using IBM 3270 terminals interact with the system. The user specifies four items:

1. File, for example, sales history or open orders.
2. Selection criteria to indicate which records.
3. Function, for example, Sum, Sort, Subtotal.
4. Other fields to be used by the function.

An important feature of this system is that all fields are indexed, thus permitting rapid data extraction by any of the 400 items in the sales history file. A drawback of this approach is that the required flat-file (as opposed to hierarchical or relational) structure necessitates a substantial amount of redundant information.

The on-line system also contains a number of packaged routines that prompt for input and then produce key account reports, sales territory reports, brand development index, and so forth. These packaged routines are APL programs that structure complicated APLDI requests and in some cases trigger reports developed through another IBM product called A Departmental Reporting System (ADRS).

A batch sales-reporting system is also available using the same 3270 terminal. Applied Data Research's ROSCOE product leads the marketing or salesperson through a menu selection process that dynamically builds a batch-reporting job. The reports are built using Dylakor's DYL280 software. They are then submitted to the system for batch processing. Execution and delivery to the marketing area normally take four hours. Reports requested in this manner generally require a high volume of output, or formatting capabilities that are not available in the on-line inquiry system.

On-line inquiry and request reporting are available throughout the headquarters building and at regional sales office locations. The Grocery Information Systems Group has several systems project leaders who work with marketing, sales, distribution, and accounting personnel in training, day-to-day problem resolution, and special requests. They use APL, APLDI, ADRS, and DYL280 to respond to special requests, such as the evaluation of advertising-spending tests or the tracking of new product introductions.

One of the key uses of the sales data file is to identify accounts or regions that are not performing as well as was expected. The following is a typical analysis.

Step 1. Use quota reports to analyze sales in each district in percent of quota and percentage change from last year. Examine these data to identify problem districts.

Step 2. Use inquiry system to obtain comparable information

for the accounts within the district. Examine these data to identify the problem accounts.

Step 3.   Use a sales tracker report to see if the problem lies in
the distribution level or the number of items stocked by the
account. This report is a compilation of broker reports on the
distribution of brands by account.

Step 4.   Examine store audit reports to see if prices are in line
with competitive brands in the account.

Step 5.   Use the shelving information obtained from the store
audit reports to determine if the shelving matches the requirements of the planogram agreed to by the account.

Steps 1 and 2 identify problem accounts, and steps 3, 4, and 5 are
used to determine the cause of the problem. Once the cause is
identified, the product manager works with the sales force to
correct the situation.

Such detailed sales information permits the product managers to develop regional programs for their brands. One marketing director said, "In the food business, you cannot afford to
market only on a national basis." Another manager feels that
"the concept of a national brand is becoming a figment of our
imagination." The use of computer-based internal data by sales
area, customer, and product, plus the use of syndicated research
data such as SAMI and Nielsen allow for the evaluation of information to make local as well as national decisions about the
strategic implementation of plans.

Personal computers are available to the product management
groups. However, only selective use is being made of these
stand-alone computers.

The brand groups buy SAMI or Nielsen data on a regular
basis to monitor their own brands and the competition in the
various markets. At the present time, these data are not available
on computers. However, one brand group is using Nielsen's
INF*ACT package to access its data on the Nielsen mainframe.
This is an experiment to test the advantages of such on-line
access.

The INF*ACT system permits the product group to produce
reports about four attributes: product item, period, region, and
variable. The pages of the report contain matrixes with the rows

denoting one attribute and the columns another. Each page of the report corresponds to the level of a third attribute. For instance, a 16-ounce Realemon® report could have three pages, with each page having information for regions and time periods. Page 1 would contain sales data, page 2 would contain distribution levels, and page 3 would contain inventories.

ORE-IDA FOODS

The product management groups at Ore-Ida are part of a sales and marketing organization headed by a vice president. The retail sales organization consists of a general manager, 4 division managers, and 16 regional managers. The actual selling function is handled by food brokers, with the division and regional managers overseeing this system.

The brand groups have a more or less traditional structure with product managers supervising assistant product managers (APM) and marketing assistants. Typically, a person entering this organization with an M.B.A. degree spends one year as an assistant, two years as an APM, and rotates among the brands every six months or so.

The centralized computer facilities are managed by a general manager of management information systems (MIS). Reporting to this general manager are, among others, the manager of management science and the manager of systems. The company operates an IBM 3083 and a 4341. In August 1984, there were 40 personal computers, primarily IBM PCs, spread around the company. Two personal computers were located in the marketing area and used by the brand groups.

The liaison between marketing and MIS is the manager of marketing systems and planning. He coordinates all of the computer and office automation aspects of the sales and marketing operations. An example of his activities is a trade promotion-tracking system that he developed. He worked with the brand groups and the systems people in the design, programming, and implementation of the system. Its major purpose is to control and facilitate discounts to the trade for promoting Ore-Ida products. It also provides information to the brand groups about the actual spending levels and the number of cases taken on the deal. This is a batch oriented system that provides periodic reports.

In addition to the batch reports, the brand groups use three routes to access computerized data: (1) periodic batch reports, (2) direct use of interactive terminals, and (3) requests to the management science group for printed reports or tables. The company's shipment data, containing pound and dollar shipment information for items shipped both on- and off-promotion, are available through terminals. These data can be accessed by item, time period, and geography. The geographical levels (from lowest to highest) are customer, broker, region, division, and nation.

A menu-driven program is used by the brand groups to indicate the item(s), period, and geographical breaks. The system then extracts these data and reports shipment in pounds, dollars, and cases, along with promotion pounds and promotion dollars for the indicated items, periods, and geographies. This system was developed using the Model 204 database management package from Computer Corporation of America.

The second way to obtain computerized data is through requests to people in the management science group. This group uses the EXPRESS system from Management Decision Systems, which runs on an IBM 4341 under CMS. EXPRESS contains an integrated database consisting of data from various sources:

Data	Supplier
Warehouse withdrawal	SAMI
Retail distribution levels	Burgoyne
Retail advertising	MAJERS
Shipments	In-house
Promotion	In-house

This combination of data permits the calculation of various statistics and analyses, including trade inventories, market share versus distribution level, and impact of trade promotions. About 95 percent of these analyses are done at the SAMI market level, and 80 percent use data at the four-week aggregate level. One person is responsible for obtaining, loading, and overseeing the data from the outside suppliers. This is a time-consuming activity because the data formats are constantly changing due to new brands, sizes, and flavors, as well as redefinition of market areas.

Standard reports are generated and sent to the brand groups on a regular basis, for example, monthly. These reports create the need for more detailed data about certain regions or items. Thus, the brand groups ask the management science people to make additional runs.

The brand groups use these data for further analysis and decision making. The IBM PC and the Lotus 1-2-3 software package are used to support the analysis. Presently, an APM or assistant will obtain the data from the Model 204 screen or from a report, build an electronic spreadsheet with Lotus 1-2-3, and enter the data via the keyboard into the spreadsheet's cells. Primary applications have been developed for use in the annual marketing planning, the annual business review, the monthly budget analysis, and the routine and special forecast updates.

Support for such application is given by an information center, an arm of the management science group. The primary vehicle for training the PC users is a 16-hour course titled "Introduction to the PC and Lotus 1-2-3." Most people in the brand groups have taken this course.

The MIS and management science groups are evaluating new software packages that would provide easier access to the data in the two mainframe systems. Both Model 204 and EXPRESS are considered too complex for direct usage by the brand groups. However, the suppliers have developed packages that facilitate both the terminal access to the data and the downloading to personal computers. Computer Corporation of America is offering Access 204, a mainframe application that permits the end user to do ad hoc queries of the databases. Also, PC/204 turns the PC into a terminal and provides a menu-driven facility for accessing the data and downloading it to a PC file. The data on the PC file can then be read into Lotus 1-2-3 and other programs.

EASYTRAC is a companion product that is a user-friendly, menu-driven interface to the EXPRESS databases and some of its analysis capabilities. In addition, EXPRESS-link is available for extracting and downloading data to personal computers.

The management science group at Ore-Ida identifies three levels of computer and data usage: (1) data retrieval, (2) data analysis, and (3) data modeling. It views level 1, data retrieval, as playing the primary role in most companies. The group's emphasis is on levels 2 and 3, the analysis and modeling of the data, which has several implications. First, it requires the advance statistical and econometric capabilities of EXPRESS; a simple data extraction and inquiry system would not suffice. Second, the group is oriented toward solving marketing problems rather than simply providing data extraction facilities. Thus, emphasis is placed on decision support systems rather than information systems. Third, they are anxiously awaiting the widespread availability of scanner data. Such data will permit the development of models at the consumer and retailer level. However, they believe that the suppliers of scanner data must change their practices and begin to supply data at the store level rather than at the city or market level. Consumers shop in stores, and stores use different prices and promotions. Hence, models must be based upon store-level data.

Ore-Ida is evaluating a retail audit system for use by its salespeople when they visit a store. Currently under consideration is Audit One, a hardware and software package for in-store auditing from Western Systems, Inc. It is based on an interactive, notebook-sized portable computer, the Epson HX-20. The system includes custom software, the computer, a small acoustic coupler, a built-in printer, and a UPC bar code wand. The system is designed to allow the sales representative to easily input information on pricing, out-of-stocks, shelf facings and positioning, product rotation, point-of-sale activity, permanent and secondary displays, and new product introductions. The acoustic coupler can be used to transmit the information to a host computer.

MARKETING MANAGEMENT INFORMATION SYSTEMS

These two firms provide a good introduction to the practices and processes involved in computer support for marketing managers. They illustrate how a PC is used as a personal productivity tool and emphasize the importance of the mainframe computer for managing and accessing the firm's marketing data. When the practices of all of the firms were examined by the author, it was possible to observe common features, particularly in the management of marketing data via the firms' marketing management information system (MMIS).

Although the firms differ in how they support their marketing managers, the available systems have one or more of the following elements:

1. Batch reports of shipments and/or orders, issued by one of the staff organizations at regular time intervals.
2. On-line access to shipments and/or orders using the firm's mainframe computer.
3. On-line access to market and/or consumer data using
   a. The firm's mainframe computer.
   b. The data vendors' computers.
   c. A time-sharing vendor's computer.
4. Budgeting, pipeline and other analyses, database generation and management, and preparation of graphs, tables, charts, memos, and reports on personal computers.

The following is typical of the process a firm goes through in arriving at its current MMIS.

1. Marketing managers do all of their analysis and reporting on a manual basis, that is, without using computers. Batch reports on shipments and orders are provided on a daily, weekly, and monthly basis and the market information is obtained from hard-copy versions of Nielsen, SAMI, and MAJERS reports.
2. A data supplier, for example, Nielsen, introduces the idea of obtaining its data through on-line terminal access to the supplier's computer. One marketing group accepts the supplier's offer on a trial basis, thus providing the company's first exposure to on-line data and the resulting opportunity for feedback learning. The results are sufficiently positive to convince other marketing managers to use the system. On-line access spreads to similar services offered by the company's other data suppliers.
3. The need to integrate the data from the various sources leads the firm to move the data from the individual supplier's computers to a single time-sharing firm.
4. The time-sharing costs rapidly rise to the point where it is easy for the company to justify moving the data to an in-house, time-sharing computer. A selection process is initiated to choose the best software/hardware combination. Criteria such as the following (reportedly used by the Mobil Chemical Company to select a marketing decision support system for its consumer business) are used

to select the software vendor:[2]
a. Language
  (i) Ease of use.
  (ii) Overall strength.
  (iii) Flexibility.
  (iv) Integration of databases from different vendors.
  (v) Statistical capabilities.
  (vi) Flexibility and quality of outputs.
b. Firm
  (i) Experience in marketing applications.
  (ii) Level of support.
  (iii) Technical capabilities.
  (iv) Consulting capabilities.
c. Costs
  (i) Initial.
  (ii) Ongoing.
  (iii) Connect time.

5. Individual marketing managers acquire personal computers to support their personal computing needs. These computers are used on a stand-alone basis and do not interface with the MMIS.
6. As the marketing managers become proficient in using the MMIS and the personal computers, they recognize the need to download data from the MMIS into spreadsheets on the personal computers. This capability is added by the systems group.

At any point in time the firm could be using any combination of these approaches. However, the firms in the survey tended to fall into one of the following three categories.

1. Batch reports and hard-copy access to market data.
2. Batch reports, on-line access to shipments via an in-house computer, and access to either SAMI or Nielsen data from an outside computer vendor; personal computers available but used very little.
3. A formal marketing management information system is installed on either the in-house computer or an outside time-sharing system that has both the shipment and mar-

---

[2] John Quelch, "Mobil Chemical Corporation," Case Number 9-583-024, HBS Case Services (Boston: Harvard Business School, 1982).

ket data (usually Nielsen or SAMI data and the MAJERS ad feature data). Personal computers are used extensively by some marketing managers and sparingly by others.

As the firms gain experience with their current situation and as their environment changes, they will begin testing other approaches for using information and information systems in the support of marketing and sales managers. Thus, their current situation forms the base for evolution.

Approaches to MMIS

Several hardware and software approaches are available for accessing marketing data. The most common one today is mainframe computers that use dumb terminals in a time-sharing mode. Acustar, EXPRESS, FOCUS, and in-house systems provide this type of access. Marketing managers use a dumb terminal, or a personal computer acting as a dumb terminal, to interact with the software that is running on the mainframe.

A variant of this approach involves using personal computers to access mainframe applications, but those with the additional ability to download the mainframe data to the PC. EXPRESS-Link and PC FOCUS have this type of capability.

A third approach involves the use of departmental minicomputers in place of centralized mainframes. Here the same type of services are available as with a mainframe system, and the marketing people have a dedicated system.

A fourth MMIS approach is personal computers networked to a file server. One of the companies in the survey is using such a system in one of their divisions. The Metaphor system also offers such a network approach, although its workstation is not a general purpose personal computer—it is a dedicated unit that runs only the Metaphor software.

The final approach, which no firm in the survey had adopted, involves building the MMIS on a stand-alone personal computer. The currently available machines are powerful enough to facilitate an MMIS with small- to moderate-sized databases. One company reported that they had been experimenting with an eight-megabyte database on an IBM XT using the R:base database management package; the results were encouraging. Acustar is available in a package that runs on the IBM XT/370, a special version of the IBM personal computer that can run programs written for the IBM mainframes. The new IBM AT/370 could provide enough power to permit a marketing group to put its data on a stand-alone personal computer. In addition, the next round of microprocessors will probably be based on 32-bit chips and have enough power to bring the MMIS to the desktop.

DATA AND ANALYSIS

Most of the firms in the survey subscribe to either the Neilsen retail audit data or the SAMI warehouse withdrawal data. In addition, they usually purchase advertising feature data from the MAJERS Corporation. These data, along with their in-house shipment data, form the core of their information system.

The A. C. Nielsen Company's retail index service provides a syndicated database designed to measure the consumer purchase of items in retail outlets. The company employs 500 store auditors who regularly visit a large sample of grocery stores, mass merchandisers, and drugstores. These auditors record data on retail sales, prices, inventory levels, distribution levels, out-of-stock levels, and trade promotions for all the brands in a large number of product categories. The results of these surveys are reported on a bimonthly basis for both the whole country and up to 38 regions, and are broken down by store type and size. A combination of large reports, personal presentations, and data tapes containing the information in the reports is used.

Selling Areas—Marketing, Inc. (SAMI) is a division of Time, Inc. which specializes in reporting on warehouse withdrawal of products to retail outlets. SAMI offers computerized reporting and data for all brands and items in over 425 product categories sold through supermarkets and grocery stores in 42 markets. The reports and data are supplied to a manufacturer every four weeks and contain information on the firm's brands and all of its competitors.

The MAJERS Corporation tracks feature advertising by key retailers in all major markets in grocery, drug, liquor, mass merchandise, and general merchandise outlets. The feature ads in newspapers are classified using MAJERS' A, B, C weighting scheme, which takes into consideration the size and potential impact of the advertisement. Data are provided on individual advertisements and can be summarized by brand, category, region, and various time periods.

The firms also purchase data from other suppliers. However, these data are not typically used regularly for tracking purposes and are not usually computerized. They are usually managed and analyzed by specialists in marketing research departments. The marketing managers receive written reports that summarize the data. In some companies the reports also include an analysis of the strategic and tactical implications of the data analysis results.

Consumer panel data provide information on the purchase patterns of individual households. Two companies, Market Research Corporation of America (MRCA) and NPD Research, are the primary suppliers of panel data. Each of these companies recruits and manages a national consumer panel of 7,000 to 8,000 households that reports on individual purchases of a wide range of frequently bought products. These data, summarized by brand and monthly time period, provide the foundation for studying the consumer dynamics that underlie the aggregate sales data reported by Nielsen and SAMI. Reports include measures of consumer trial and repeat rates, share of household usage, degree of dual or multiple brand usage, and so on.

Scanner data are generated at those retail stores that are equipped with UPC scanners. Most of the companies in the survey had purchased scanner data from suppliers such as Nielsen, TRIM Inc., and Test Marketing Group. The data were being used for special studies, such as measuring the impact of promotions, and not as a source of tracking information. A number of companies stated that they use it to get a better idea of price dynamics than was available from traditional SAMI or Nielsen tracking data. Further, it provides data on most of the items that move through the stores, as opposed to SAMI data which does not have brands from firms that use store-door delivery.

Scanner panel data are supplied by vendors that combine the scanner and the panel data collection methodologies. A panel of consumers is recruited by firms in markets where the vendor has placed UPC scanner equipment in most of the stores. The panel members agree to shop with a plastic card (similar to a credit card) that is used by the scanner equipment to recognize the customer as a member of the panel. The scanners route the customer's purchase record to a special computer file, which is sent to the research company on a regular basis. In addition, the research company collects the aggregate scanner data on the movement and prices of all the brands in the store. This combined database provides information on individual consumers as well as the store environment in which they shop.

Store observation data, collected by firms that specialize in store audits, are used to augment the SAMI data. A team of auditors visits a sample of stores and reports on in-store conditions, that is, shelf space, shelf prices, end-aisle displays, and special promotions.

Wholesale prices are collected by several of the firms in the survey. For instance, some firms purchase data from the Leemis organization on price levels taken from a sample of large wholesalers.

Data Structure

The software that has been designed to support marketing managers in their use of data has built-in capabilities for dealing with data that are multidimensional and have a hierarchical structure on several dimensions.

From a dimensionality viewpoint, most of the data concern the performance of brands over time and in different geographical regions. These data can be considered, from a conceptual viewpoint, as arrayed in a four-dimensional space defined by (1) performance measures, for example, volume and price, (2) brand items, (3) region, and (4) time period. Most software packages are capable of extracting any two-dimensional view of the data.

Several of the dimensions have "natural" hierarchies associated with them. Brand items are arranged in an inverted tree structure, with the broadest category definition at the top of the tree, and with specific brands in specific packages with specific flavors at the bottom of the tree. Commonly, marketing managers want to display performance measures at different points in the brand hierarchy. For instance, a beer-marketing manager may want to see only canned beer, only 12-packs, or only low-calorie beer.

The geographical dimension is commonly designed around the structure of the firm's sales force. If a sales force is divided into zones, regions within zones, and districts within regions, then the data are usually organized in this manner. Similarly, monthly data have a natural structure of weeks, months, quarters, and years.

Given the large size of this database, it is advantageous to aggregate and store the data at all of its hierarchical levels. That is, data are stored at the lowest as well as the higher levels in the hierarchies. For instance, a system containing shipment data would store the data at the level of districts, regions, zone, and nation. Although such redundant storage increases storage costs, it greatly decreases access time.

The time dimension has a natural hierarchy of days, weeks, months, quarters, and years. However, some systems (for instance, the Acustar package offered by Tymshare Inc.) do not have preset aggregations along the time dimension. The designers of the system seem to have recognized that the user needs great flexibility in specifying the time aggregation of the data, and that this aggregation will vary from problem to problem because marketing events such as advertising campaigns and promotions do not fall neatly into quarterly or annual periods.

The structure of the data remains relatively fixed over time, but new items are constantly being added to the databases. Firms continually innovate by adding new brands, packages, sizes, and flavors. They undergo reorganizations that lead to redistribution of the sales territories. New brands may impact the product category to such an extent that the hierarchical structure of the market is changed. All of these changes require constant management of the databases.

This management is provided by the outside time-sharing firms when the company uses systems like Acustar or INF*ACT. When the systems run on an in-house computer, the firms must assign people to such database management. Ore-Ida, for instance, has one person assigned full time to manage their EXPRESS database. Also, consulting firms that handle this data management are beginning to emerge.

Analysis

Most of the computer applications involve the extraction, transformation, and display of brand performance measures. These summarized data are called descriptive statistics to denote the fact that they are being used to describe some underlying factor such as volume or price. Another form of statistical analysis is possible: inferential statistics. This form recognizes that the data represent a sample from one or more underlying populations and it uses the analysis to make inferences about these populations. For instance, the Nielsen store audit data are actually based on a sample of stores in each market. The adoption of the statistical inference paradigm would involve treating these data as a sample from a larger population and making inferential statements about that population. For instance, instead of reporting that sales in the Chicago market were 2.73 million cases last bimonth, one would report that "we estimate sales to be 2.73 units with a 95 percent confidence interval of .64 million cases."

No one in the survey employed the statistical inference paradigm; everyone reported descriptive statistics, inherently assuming that the data represented a census rather than a sample.

Most of the analysis being performed by the marketing managers involves the extraction of a two-dimensional view of the data from the four-dimensional data structure. The following list includes four types of reports that are available on the General Foods' MMIS.

1. Brand report (multigeography—single product).
   a. This generates an n week report with areas down the side and measures within a brand across the top of page.
   b. The report is useful in analyzing a brand within multiple geographies.
2. Topline report (multiproduct—single geography).
   a. This generates an n week report with brands down the side and measures within a geography across the top of page.
   b. The report is useful in analyzing the performance of multiple brands within specific markets.
3. Geographic time report (volume summary—multiproduct).
   a. This generates a report with brands down the side. Measures appear within the brands. Across the top, the report displays n week headings for the last four years.
   b. The report is useful in analyzing the performance of brands within a specific geography over a period of time.

4. Brand variable time report (volume summary—multigeography).
   a. This generates a report with geographies down the side. Measures appear within the geographies. Across the top, the report displays n week headings for the last four years.
   b. The report is useful in analyzing the performance of one brand within multiple geographies over a period of time.

SYNTHESIS OF COMMON PRACTICES

At this point, let's turn our attention to another company, called the Beta Company here because the actual firm wished to remain anonymous. Beta has gone farther than Borden and Ore-Ida in the integration of the MMIS into the planning, analysis, and control aspects of marketing management. Hence, the following material provides additional information about the adoption process and the uses for such a system.

BETA COMPANY

The Beta Company uses a divisional management structure and has brand management groups within its divisions. Its marketing information system is built around the Acustar software package offered by Tymshare Inc. running on that firm's time-sharing computer. Beta currently rents a fraction of a 4341 computer and pays a fixed annual fee to Tymshare. This fee includes the software, the time-sharing service, consulting, and the loading of the databases into Acustar.

Before installing the Acustar system, the brand groups went to the marketing research people with questions and requests for data. The marketing researchers would obtain the data from an in-house system or from the data supplier's computer and send it to the brand group.

Direct support to the brand groups in using the system is provided. The Information Resource Management (IRM) group provides a marketing support manager who is the liaison between IRM and the brand groups for all computer uses. His job is to interpret the needs of the brand groups and to find solutions. In addition, a Decision Support Systems (DSS) supervisor from the corporate Management Support Services Department worked closely with the brand groups in the initial installation of the system and in training and supporting the marketing groups. The particular individual in this position was invaluable because he joined Beta from Tymshare and was very familiar with Acustar. Hence, in-house support for using Acustar is quite good.

Acustar was selected over competing software packages because it was considered an application package that was developed specifically for brand groups. The other packages were positioned as high-level, user-friendly languages that could be used to tailor an application package. The evaluation and tests at Beta led to the conclusion that these competing packages might be more powerful and/or flexible than Acustar, but they lacked the user oriented interfaces. It was felt that Acustar would lead to a more rapid adoption of computerized data retrieval and analysis than the competing products. Other reasons for selecting Acustar included its question and answer interface, its ability to abbreviate commands, and its ease in creating and modifying custom reports. The primary weakness of Acustar was considered its lack of a programming language.

The company signed a contract with Tymshare in July 1983 and had the data loaded by early August. These data include retail sales information from Nielsen, warehouse withdrawal data from SAMI, and internal factory shipment figures. In addition, some brand groups purchase advertising feature data from MAJERS and add it to the database. One of the attractive features of Acustar is the existence of algorithms that intergrate data with different time intervals—its time equalization feature.

Once the data were loaded, Acustar was made available to the brand groups. Several classes were taught, and then the support people waited for requests for their help. No requests were received, and no one used the system. A meeting was held with the top marketing managers to ascertain the problem and to ask for their assistance. It was agreed that the system had to have overt support from the top. The brand groups were told that this was their last chance for computerized support in the management and analysis of their data. "If you do not use it, you will have to work with the old manual methods." To facilitate its use, the DSS project supervisor was situated in an office among the brand groups. This step seemed to greatly encourage the use of the system: people began to use it, and were praised for the timeliness and quality of their work. This created a competitive spirit, and use continued to grow.

Initially, the brand groups used the system to automate those forms of data analysis that they had been doing manually. Then they began to learn what the system could do and to develop new applications. By working with the DSS project supervisor, they developed a library of standard reports. Users can browse through these reports to find the type of information they need and then obtain the information by typing the name of the report. In addition, each standard report has an AcuExec program that facilitates the modification of the standard reports for individual needs. The individuals in the brand groups build a private library of reports that they used periodically. Although Acustar has a question and answer mode for making ad hoc queries, most people at Beta use the standard or private reports to obtain their information.

Users of this system have concluded that strong support from a knowledgeable person is absolutely necessary—particularly during the first few months.

The following observations were made by the users of the system:

- Most reports are from a single database. There has been very little combining of SAMI, Nielsen, MAJERS, and shipment data.
- Most reports cover the time period of the database, for example, SAMI reports use the SAMI four-week periods.
- SAMI and/or Nielsen data are used more than the factory shipment data.
- The system was used initially just to "cut" the data in various ways to gain a different perspective on the markets. This stage lasted for three to five months. Then the users began to create new applications or to transform the data in new and creative ways.
- There has been no downloading of data into personal computers. All work is done on terminals operating at 1200 baud (120 characters per second).

- The statistical analysis, forecasting, and graphical capabilities of Acustar have not been used.

In one of the brand groups, the major use of the system is performing various types of regional analyses. Since this group's business is very regional and there are over 350 competitive items, each person prepares his own custom decks, that is, printed reports. These reports are updated whenever the data change, and are used constantly.

An example of this regional work is the SuperMatrix report. Several measures are calculated for each market: category growth, brand growth, opportunity for share increase, and profitability. These measures are calculated for each brand item for each time period in each market. Opinions are collected to arrive at a consensus on the relative importance of each measure to the overall business. Weights are then used to produce an index for each brand item in each market for each time period. These indexes are ranked and arrayed to produce an analysis of how the brand's resources should be allocated across markets and items throughout the year. This type of analysis is typical of several data-rich procedures that were not even attempted before the arrival of Acustar.

As use of the system grows, the IRM people will investigate the feasibility of bringing it in-house. This investigation will be possible because Beta recently decided to move to IBM computers. This decision was made because IBM has a wide array of software for decision support as well as a large number of fourth-generation languages and database management systems for its computers. Acustar is considered one of a series of similar products that will be included in a new computing environment.

The brand groups also use personal computers in their work, primarily Lotus 1-2-3 on an IBM PC. The primary application involves the monthly consumption model, which uses shipment data along with Nielsen or SAMI data to do a pipeline analysis that accounts for all of the brand's shipments. It attempts to answer questions such as, "What was the status of our brand in terms of shipments, wholesale and retail inventories, and consumer sales?" The PC is also used in the preparation and projection of profit and loss statements.

These three firms, Borden, Ore-Ida, and Beta, provide the necessary background for examining a "generic" computing environment that is common to most of the firms. Study of the situation at Beta Company reveals that simply providing a computerized marketing management information system to a marketing group does not ensure its success. A number of factors influence the extent and degree of its use. The next section explores some of these issues and is followed by sections that explore the types of work and location of the computer-based analysis. The final section describes how computers are used to support the field sales force.

ADOPTION AND USE CONSIDERATIONS

The degree to which a computer system is adopted and used by marketing managers appear to be related to its ease of use, the training situation, and the system's human/machine interface. In addition, one finds a discernible evolutionary path once an MMIS has been placed in a marketing organization.

Ease of Use

Marketing managers said the systems had to be easy to use, with some saying that they would not use a system that required them to become computer knowledgeable. They believe that their job is to manage the brands, and that they do not have the time to develop their own information systems or to learn to use different systems.

At the present time, they use computers intermittently, with the heaviest use occurring during the annual planning process and the periodic brand reviews, for example, quarterly reviews. Thus, the systems must be designed for the intermittent user, and should not require him or her to remember a list of commands and codes; the time between uses will cause all of these items to be forgotten.

Systems that require the user to recall commands, that is, to use his or her recall ability, are at a distinct disadvantage. A more appropriate system would allow the user to rely on recognition, that is, his or her ability to recognize a command or code, rather than remembering the code and having to recall it at the time of use. Systems such as Acustar use recognition, that is, they ask the user a series of questions and provide a list of possible answers when needed. A third type of system would not require memory at all—it would rely on the user's interpretive ability. Systems such as MacPaint on the Apple Macintosh computer provide a rudimentary form of interpretation. The user works with the machine and accomplishes tasks by interpreting the meaning of the icons on the screen. S/he arrives at a solution by selecting different icons and observing the results.

Currently, the marketing managers have limited computer literacy. They have had a sort of "driver education" training, which enables them to start the computer and "drive" it through several packages. Typically, they can operate two packages: Lotus 1-2-3 on the PC, and a data extraction program on the mainframe.

Continual Training Requirements

The need for easy-to-use systems is amplified by the need to continually train and retrain people in the marketing groups. The world of marketing management is one of high turnover. Assistant product managers become associate product managers in a year or so, and then product managers in two to four years. During this period, they may have four to six different brand assignments, including a sales-training assignment in the sales force. These moves are usually across marketing groups, and sometimes across divisions of the company. In companies where the divisions have different systems and/or philosophies about the use of data and analysis, the people in the marketing groups require almost continual training. In addition, a new group of assistant brand managers arrives every summer from college campuses and they too require training.

Computer-User Interface Needs

All the firms in the survey have one or more employees assist the marketing managers in their systems development and use. These people have titles such as manager of marketing systems or manager, marketing information systems department. Most of these specialists have a systems background, and acquired their knowledge of marketing by interacting with the marketing managers. They provide training, assist the marketing managers in determining their systems needs, and in some companies write custom programs in high-level languages.

Evolution of Users

Users appear to go through a natural evolution when they are introduced to a flexible and programmable computer. Their first activity is to computerize the data and/or perform formulalike activities that they had been doing manually. Budgets and forecasts are put into spreadsheets on the PC, and routines that extract market-tracking data from mainframe files are prepared. The PC work is frequently done by the user, but he or she usually needs help in preparing the data extraction and reporting routines.

The marketing managers arrive at a set of reports (around 5 to 10) that they run every time the data are updated. These reports are filed and used until new data arrive. Marketing managers seem to stay at this level of usage for some time. They move to higher levels when they begin to think about new ways of using the data and technology or when a new person joins the group with fresh ideas.

At first the marketing managers learn how to use the system to accomplish known tasks. After they are comfortable with these tasks, they begin to think creatively and learn what new tasks the system can accommodate. Such "double-loop learning" occurs spontaneously in some companies, and needs to be nurtured and encouraged by marketing management in others. The difference seems to be centered around the desire of the top management to base marketing decisions on data and analysis rather than on hunches and a "feel for the market."

Assistant Product Manager as Heavy User

The newest member of a marketing group, the assistant product manager (APM), is the person assigned the responsibility of "pushing around the numbers." S/he is responsible for activities such as analyzing the performance of promotions, doing the forecasting and consumption analysis, and overseeing the budget. Since these are the very activities that require or use the computers, the assistant product manager is the heavy computer user. In most companies, use diminishes as one moves up the ladder to associate and then to product manager. Several APMs thought that this pattern might become less pronounced as they are promoted, due primarily to their familiarity with the personal computers. They felt that they would find uses for the personal computers in their new jobs.

TYPE OF WORK

This section explores the type of work the marketing managers were doing on the MMIS by looking at three dimensions: (1) standard report versus ad hoc analysis, (2) MIS versus DSS activities, and (3) status versus response reporting.

Standard Report Orientation

Most of the systems being used today for data extraction and analysis provide for either ad hoc analyses or standard reports. The first has features to extract the particular data required for the problem under study, while the second provides a series of reports that contain the same data formats every time they are run. Most of the users interviewed preferred the standard reports.

When the system is first introduced to a marketing group, the users work with a consultant or support person to develop the reports they want to run on a periodic basis. The result is usually a library of reports. The user then browses through the library to find the needed format, and generates a new report by issuing the name of the report. Most systems have been designed to make it easy for the user to make simple changes in the report. Most such changes involve the specification of brands, regions, and periods.

MIS versus DSS Orientation

One way that a management information system (MIS) differs from a decision support system (DSS) is in how each is used. If a system is used in a regular, planned, and anticipated manner, it is an MIS. If it is used in an ad hoc manner to support unstructured problem solving and decision making, then it is a DSS. The standard report orientation of the typical marketing group user places the systems in the MIS camp.

Marketing managers are responsible for certain activities that they perform on either a scheduled basis or as the need arises. For instance, a business review may be issued every bimonth, based upon the newest Nielsen data. Or a forecast may be made whenever the brand volume seems to be deviating from planned levels. To support these activities, the marketing managers prepare standard formats that they use to print the needed data. These data are then used for further analysis, by hand or in a spreadsheet, or are placed in a report.

In addition, almost all the marketing people in the survey used the personal computers for standard work. Lotus 1-2-3 templates were prepared to support those activities that would occur regularly. According to the distinction between MIS and DSS, the marketing managers are using the systems as management information systems. When the user required data in a form different from one of the standard report formats, s/he either asked a systems person to produce the data or combined data from one or more reports into a new format. Seldom was the on-line system used in an ad hoc query manner by the marketing managers.

The mainframe computer application systems were developed either by the systems people within the firm, or by the user and consultant (either an in-house or outside consultant) using application packages such as EXPRESS or Acustar. If the system had been in use for more than two years, it was usually developed by the systems group. The newer systems tend to have evolved in an end-user development environment and are likely to be based on decision support systems packages. But such end-user development had strong participation by computer knowledgeable people.

Thus, one could conclude that MIS is alive and well within marketing groups, but the concepts of DSS have not been widely adopted.

Status versus Response Reporting

In 1979, John Little published an article that described the current status of marketing decision support systems (MDSS) and provided a view of the future use of those systems. One important aspect of his argument was the emergence of market response reporting over traditional status reporting.

> Sometimes retrieval questions come up, of course, but most often the answers to important questions require nontrivial manipulation of stored data. Knowing this tells us much about the kind of

software required for an MDSS. For example, a data-based management system is not enough.[3]

The manipulation of data refers to the use of statistical modeling techniques to estimate the market's response to changes in one or more elements of the marketing mix. The resulting model is called a sales response model.

The software used by most of the marketing managers in the study contained the statistical tools for such model building, particularly the EXPRESS, Acustar, and FOCUS packages. However, none of the marketing managers made use of these facilities; all of them used the database management facilities exclusively. However, Little recognized that marketing managers would probably not use the more sophisticated aspects of the software, called for a marketing scientist to serve as an intermediary, and noted that the manager would not use the system directly for such work. His prediction was certainly true for the firms in this study. But most of them did not seem to be making use of the marketing scientist the way Little had envisioned; response models did not appear to be playing a role in the decision activities of most of the marketing managers.

PERSONAL COMPUTERS AND MAINFRAMES

The hardware in the modern corporation tends to be built around personal and mainframe computers. This section describes how these devices fit into the MMIS and the current marketing workbench.

Personal Computer Usage

Most companies provide the marketing managers with some access to personal computers. The degree of access and encouragement varies from company to company and within a company. A few marketing managers had computers in their offices; the norm was a PC in an open area near the marketing managers.

Two applications dominated the PC use: budgets and consumption analysis. The first involves spreadsheets that contain the brand's budget and/or profit and loss statement. These were used for planning and forecasting the brand's financial perfor-

---

[3] John D. C. Little, "Decision Support System for Marketing Managers," *Journal of Marketing* 43, no. 3 (Summer 1979), pp. 9–27.

mance. The consumption analysis (sometime called pipeline analysis) uses shipment, inventory, and either warehouse withdrawal or retail sales data to report the status of the flow of the brand through its channel of distribution. Almost every marketing group that used personal computers employed Lotus 1-2-3 on an IBM PC to perform these two analyses. In most instances, they were the only ways the PC was used.

Most marketing managers expressed an interest in using the personal computers for other purposes, but did not feel that they had the time to become proficient to the point of being creative in such use. They hypothesized that such use would occur with the arrival of graduates of university programs that provided in-depth computer literacy. In fact, the heaviest users of personal computers tended to be recent college students who owned a personal computer or had attended a school that emphasized their use.

Independent PC and Mainframe Uses

In most companies, the mainframe is used for certain data extraction and reporting purposes, and the personal computer is used for small-scale reporting and "what if" analyses. Mainframes and PCs usually are not integrated in any way. If a user wants to transfer data from a mainframe file to a PC, s/he obtains a printout from the mainframe file and enters the data by hand into the PC. Omega Company and General Foods are exceptions to this pattern; both provide software for extracting data from a mainframe and loading it into a spreadsheet.

This usage pattern is not unlike the one found in Pope's study of computer use at IBM's Watson Research Center.[4] This researcher found that even experienced IBM computer professionals tended to separate the PC and mainframe work. He found very little "cooperative processing," that is, computer usage that takes advantage of the strengths of the mainframe and the personal computer in an integrated manner.

The primary reason for this nonintegrated use appears to be technological: hardware and software vendors are just beginning

---

[4] Bucky Pope, "A Study of How Users of Programmable Work Stations Can Effect VM/CMS Usage," Research Paper (Yorktown Heights, N.Y.: IBM Thomas J. Watson Research Center).

to offer the necessary technology for such combined usage. However, systems such as the one being installed at Frito-Lay, which utilizes the IBM 3270-PC, will make such combined usage possible.

COMPUTERIZATION OF THE SALES FORCE

One of the recurring themes among the firms in the sample was an interest in computerizing the field sales force. In fact, this activity may be getting more attention than the introduction of computer systems into the marketing groups. This interest manifests itself in the plans, designs, and prototypes for a two-way communications network that collects, summarizes, and distributes information about customers and the selling effort.

Some of these systems are viewed as replacements for existing information systems. The hand-held computer project at Frito-Lay will replace the paper-and-pencil forms that the route sales representative uses to record the actual sales. Other systems are designed to provide new information, that is, to collect and/or disseminate data not currently available in the firm's information system. Of course, the replacement systems can also provide incremental information.

Some of the planned systems involve the use of small or hand-held computers by the sales representatives. These computers will be used to collect information about the status of the account and the activities of the sales person during the call, as well as information about any transactions. Such systems provide an information-gathering facility, that is, a system for collecting data on the trade and competition.

The sales representatives' computers can be preprogrammed to stage the user through a series of questions about the sales call. For instance, a menu could include the needed data about brands in stock, inventories, shelf space, prices, and special promotions. These data are stored in the computer during the day, and transmitted to a central computer via telephone lines during the evening.

Since the small computers can receive as well as send data, it is possible (and perhaps practical) for the host computer to send data to the sales representative's computer. This information could include

1.   Announcements

    a. Price changes.
    b. Promotion events and dates.
    c. New brands or items.
    d. Meeting and conference times.
2. Instructions
    a. Daily call route.
    b. Procedures for working a promotion.
3. Marketing research questions about
    a. Competitive activities.
    b. Store shelving plans.
4. Selling tools
    a. Facts and figures about the brand's performance in the market and/or account.

The interactive nature of the system provides the sales and marketing management people with a new and powerful marketing research tool. In a one- or two-day period, detailed data can be obtained about brands, competitors, and customers.

Hand-held computers are only one aspect of the overall systems. They are at the bottom of a hierarchical network of computers that provide the facilities for the sales information system. Most firms employ a traditional hierarchical organizational structure involving, for instance, a national sales manager, regional managers, district managers, division managers, and sales representatives. Although the number of levels and the names of the geographical breakdowns differ among firms, the overall structure is the same. Most plans call for some form of computing device at each level of the sales organization.

Differing Philosophies and Approaches

The previous chapter described the computer oriented practices common to the firms in the study. However, there were also significant differences among the firms, particularly in their philosophies about the role of data and computers in the marketing management process. This chapter highlights these differences by first presenting short descriptions of six firms and then analyzing their differences from several perspectives. In some instances, fictitious names are used for companies that did not wish to be identified. The descriptions of Pillsbury, General Foods, and Frito-Lay are short summaries of the longer cases that appear later in the book.

GAMMA COMPANY

The brand groups at Gamma are supported by two computer systems: an in-house sales-tracking system and the INF*ACT system for accessing Nielsen data. The firm's factory shipment data are available through a sales reporting system, a batch oriented system that was developed internally about 12 years ago. It provides weekly and/or monthly reports to the brand groups. The major reports are:

- Account report: aggregates and reports sales for each brand item within each account.
- Compensation report: sums the data by the various sales territories.
- Financial profit and loss: provides financial performance information about the brand.

These reports are run by the analysts in the systems and programming group, and are sent to the brand groups for further use and analysis.

The systems and programming group is currently in transition from total batch orientation to on-line access to the data. It is in the process of developing a direct-access, sales-reporting network. To assist in this effort, the group recently purchased FOCUS, a fourth-generation software product, as its initial entry into the database development area.

Plans call for the system analyst to use FOCUS as a COBOL replacement tool and to write performance reports that can be accessed by sales and marketing personnel through terminals/ personal computers. These units are to be connected to a network environment running from the mainframe to headquarters, region, district offices, and through to the sales representative's home. This process is considered the group's initial entry into the database development process for use by sales and marketing personnel. Eventually, it plans to (1) provide access to a more sophisticated database environment (ADABASE, etc.) with broader reporting capabilities, and (2) have field sales personnel use portable computers to minimize clerical responsibilities and enhance their sales-call capability.

The second system is INF*ACT, provided by CMS for on-line access to Nielsen (and other) data. The brand groups do analysis on-line via the CMS time-sharing system. They build routines in INF*ACT that provide different views of the Nielsen data. Their factory shipment data are sent to CMS, where they are combined with the Nielsen retail sales data. This combined dataset can be used for pipeline analysis, that is, to analyze the performance of the brands throughout their pipeline to the consumer.

The systems group at Gamma is considering the idea of offering a similar service on its in-house computer by either licensing INF*ACT or writing a similar system in FOCUS.

Current development efforts include an evaluation of the best approach for introducing personal computer technologies into the brand groups. Report requests will be provided primarily by the systems analyst and will be made available to sales and marketing personnel via menus on the terminals. The systems group feels this approach provides the user community with access to information available within the database without burdening these users with the task of learning a "user-friendly" language. As the user community becomes familiar with this technology, it will be given, at its request, the opportunity to develop its own reports from the database via a fourth-generation, "friendly," retrieval language.

IOTA COMPANY

The management information services (MIS) professionals at the Iota Company, an international soft drink company, recognize the need to leverage information technology and help the marketing groups. They are aware that ways must be found to provide the necessary facilities for incorporating the growing supply of information into the ongoing decision processes of the sales and marketing people.

A brand management structure is used in the marketing area. The brand groups are responsible for developing brand objectives, strategies, and programs and for working with the large number of franchised bottlers. They directly implement consumer related programs, and work with the bottlers in trade oriented programs. The sales force, with approximately 100 people in five regions, counsels and works with the franchisees.

Iota's information systems are built around an IBM 3083 running MVS and using TSO for time-sharing applications. Most systems are COBOL based and use CICS in conjunction with VSAM files. The FOCUS package was purchased two years ago for use by the MIS professionals. Its manager feels it is the "best thing since sliced bread." It is used for prototyping and developing systems that will have a short life (less than two years). End-user access to FOCUS is awaiting the MIS group's ability to provide end-user training and support.

A customer support group consisting of four people provides ad hoc data service to the marketing group, as well as to other areas of the company. However, about 90 percent of its time is spent supporting the marketing group. It has developed a set of FORTRAN programs that access internal data as well as data purchased from Nielsen and MAJERS. Most of its activity is devoted to preparing standard reports from these data. The goal is for this group to evolve into an information center.

The company has 25 personal computers, almost exclusively the IBM PC. The primary software is the Lotus 1-2-3 spreadsheet package. In fact, it is felt that the user first adopted Lotus 1-2-3, and that a hardware system (the IBM PC) was then purchased to support the software.

System W was purchased from Comshare in June 1984. A decision support system, it is currently used by the corporate planning and development group.

Almost all data access is done for the marketing groups by an intermediary. The customer support group accesses the Nielsen, MAJERS, and shipment data to write reports and make certain types of ad hoc queries. The Marketing Research Department serves as the other intermediary by using the INF*ACT system on the CMS time-sharing system to access Nielsen data, the MAJERS computer to access advertising features data, and a new MAJERS service that provides in-store display and coupon information. The marketing research people use these systems to issue standard reports and make ad hoc inquiries.

The marketing research group has established "ownership" of the consumer and market data. It controls access to the data, and operates in a problem rather than a data mode. A brand person goes to the group with a problem or question. The marketing researcher determines the appropriate data and analysis procedure, accesses the data, and provides the brand manager with an analysis that answers the questions or solves the problem.

The marketing research group has been purchasing scanner data from TRIM Inc. in three markets for the last four years. The group uses these data for evaluative work, that is, to evaluate pricing levels, deal activities, and new brand introductions. It is working with TRIM and several noncompeting manufacturers to develop SALES SCAN. The primary purpose of this system, which runs on an IBM PC, is to use the scanner and sales data to evaluate promotion activities.

The marketing research group believes that the scanner data contain errors and ambiguities, and that the data are too massive to be useful. The group feels that the current data supplier practice of trying to sell raw data tapes is not adequate. The data must be cleaned and aggregated so that they are actionable. Further, it feels that the suppliers should provide these services *plus* the data processing facilities for preparing customized reports.

The brand groups use Lotus 1-2-3 on an IBM PC. They combine sales and Nielsen information to establish quotas, do pipeline analysis, and prepare profit and loss (P&L) statements. The spreadsheets are used to develop extensive "what if" scenarios. The graphics capabilities of Lotus have been a real aid. However, a lot of time is spent extracting numbers from reports and putting them into Lotus.

One brand manager believes that his work would be greatly facilitated by on-line access to market data on shipments and retail sales. He has been experimenting with a small "lap" portable computer that he took to a recent meeting in which he used Lotus 1-2-3 to graphically display some sales figures. The ability to display and change graphs on-line facilitated a major decision and permitted the group to move on to other issues.

ZETA COMPANY

The Zeta Company currently has a marketing information systems department (MISD) within the company's marketing division. This group's three primary roles are (1) to coordinate requests for mainframe applications and systems, (2) to oversee requests for personal computers, and (3) to provide indirect access to computerized data.

Standard reports, which report and analyze marketing and sales data, are issued on a regular basis by MISD. When the brand groups need additional information from the computer databases, they submit a request to an analyst in the MISD. S/he writes a program to access the data and sends a report to the marketing people.

If a brand group (or any other group in the company) wants to purchase a personal computer, it must base its request on an efficiency argument in that the use of the personal computer must lead to a net savings as measured by the expected rate of return on the investment. If a manager bases the request on the notion that the PC will allow his or her group to perform new and different types of analysis, this does not qualify as an efficiency argument.

Zeta plans to provide on-line access to market data to the managers in its Field Sales Department, which calls on the large retail chains. The MASTERTRACK service offered by MAJERS will be made available to the sales managers via personal computers in their offices.

MASTERTRACK provides data at the retail chain level on ad features, shelf prices, and displays of all the brands in the product category. These data can be used on the MAJERS computer or downloaded to the personal computers.

PILLSBURY[1]

The Acustar system in the pizza group contains internal data on shipments, SAMI data on warehouse withdrawals, and MAJERS data on advertising features. Marketing managers are able to quickly understand what has happened to the business by using the system for tracking the performance of different brand items and identifying problems. The efficiency gained here allows them to devote more time to strategic thinking. Two key uses: tracking the performance of the different brand items and identifying problems. Since the pizza business is primarily a sales "push" business, the brand groups are able to spot problems by focusing on the shipment data.

The introduction of the system corresponded to the annual planning period, so the brand groups spent a lot of time with the system preparing the plan.

---

[1] This description is a short, condensed version of the Pillsbury case that appears in Chapter Five.

As the pizza group was gaining experience with Acustar, the marketing group in the Dry Grocery Products Division formed an MIS task force to study the group's marketing information needs. The task force recommended that the dry grocery information management system be computerized to address the needs of the marketing groups today and in the future.

Hal Ransom, a group marketing manager of the Consumer Foods Group in the Dry Grocery Products Division, is a strong proponent of the task force's views and recommendations. The use of spreadsheets for model building, "what if" conjecturing, and hypothesis testing has changed the decision-making process within his group. Everyone in his group has a PC and is proficient in Acustar. They have also standardized on the Symphony integrated software package and the IBM PC.

The real advantage of Acustar is the availability of data. According to Ransom,

> We had to rely on systems people for our data and the quality depended upon our ability to tell them what we wanted, and we were not very good at telling them. The process took months, and when we got the reports, our needs had changed. So the process started again. It was very frustrating.
>
> We are making real progress; Acustar will replace the status reports and provide a real-time, dynamic environment. Its only limitation will be our limitation and imagination. We will be able to make better decisions and to track their impact on the business.

GENERAL FOODS[2]

The marketing information systems (MIS) group had come a long way in the last 18 months; the divisional approach to computing had resulted in over 3,000 hours of computer use each month by the brand groups. The MIS group has become part of a new organization, the Information Management Department (IMD), formed to closely link two existing departments, Information

---

[2] This section contains material extracted from the longer General Foods case in Chapter Twelve.

Services (ISD) and Marketing Research (MRD). By jointly applying marketing research methodologies and information technologies, management believes that GF will be better able to anticipate and respond to consumer and customer trends.

The philosophy underlying the MIS's approach to supporting marketing managers is built on the idea that a product manager is also a manager of marketing information. Thus, the person in the product manager position was going to insist on being in control of that information. The implication for MIS was clear: put information and information technology in the hands of the marketing groups. This idea became the cornerstone of the emerging philosophy for the management of marketing information. Two objectives were set for management information systems: (1) make data available to whoever wanted it, and (2) make decision aids available to the data users.

Based on discussions with the marketing managers, MIS recommended a program that involved placing minicomputers in each division that wanted one. This program was approved in December 1982. It involved selecting one brand of computer, buying software packages, and using "hired guns" to work with the managers on the computers.

Computer usage by product groups involves a combination of personal computers and minicomputers. Data oriented work is done on the minicomputer, and user-developed applications tend to be done on personal computers. In terms of statistics like usage level or number of users, the minicomputer program is a big success. The marketing groups are using the systems and becoming self-sufficient.

FRITO-LAY[3]

A new group, market analysis, was formed in July 1984 to give support to the brand groups by providing data, systems, and analytical tools to study the markets for Frito-Lay's products. A key function of this group is the translation of information and

---

[3] This section contains material extracted from the longer Frito-Lay case presented in Chapter Eleven.

analysis needs of the brand groups into system needs and strategies for meeting these needs. One reason for forming this group was the realization that developments within and outside the company could have strong impacts on marketing and product management at Frito-Lay.

The Management Services Department was implementing a new systems strategy that would provide a state-of-the-art computer system throughout the company. The Sales Department was implementing a hand-held computer program that was a major component of the systems strategy. This program would dramatically change the information base with which the brand groups work.

A new philosophy for providing computer-based management services has emerged that is based on four related ideas.

- Integration is key for economics.
- Control is key for integration.
- Leadership is key for control.
- Vision and execution are the keys to leadership.

To achieve integration, the Management Services Department must be in control. But Frito-Lay recognized that the old totally centralized approach does not fit the current world of technology and systems. Management recognized that they could not get the information and reports needed by the people in the company with an army of programmers, so they began to "unravel a strong central government into a strong federation."

The Central Department will design the technical architecture, operate the mainframes and the network, build and maintain the transaction systems, specify the types of distributed hardware and software that will be networked, determine the appropriate data structures, and provide access to the data via end-user languages and packages. The functional departments (marketing, manufacturing, finance, and so on) will be responsible for employing end-user languages to access, analyze, and report the information. The departments will use management service's "information and computing utility" to do their end-user application development.

The primary system for accessing the marketing data is the marketing management information system (MMIS). Its development started about six years ago when a systems analyst went and "lived" in the marketing area for one year to study the information needs of the brand groups. The result was an architecture for supporting ad hoc queries to produce rapid retrieval of data. It is used by the brand groups and the professionals in market analysis.

The MMIS provides the following functions:

- Graphics.
- Flexible report writing in which the user's inquiry produces a dataset of rows and columns for a given topic; that is, the three-dimensional dataset is "cut" along one dimension to produce a two-dimensional matrix of data.
- Language, similar to BASIC, that runs in the IMS environment and permits analysis of the datasets obtained by the query.
- Predefined analytical routines, for example, a pipeline analysis routine.
- Statistical forecasting routines.

This system was first implemented in 1980 and continues to evolve. The initial data included weekly shipment information and the Nielsen bimonthly retail sales data. The MAJERS ad feature data are being added, along with retail display data.

The marketing managers have access to personal computers and to terminals for accessing MMIS. This equipment was in special rooms near the brand groups. The personal computers were the most heavily used, except at the close of each four-week period, at which time the brand groups used the MMIS to determine what had happened during that period and to forecast performance during the next few periods. Whereas the MMIS was used to access data, the analysis of the data was done on the IBM PCs and XTs, which were used to

- Integrate data from different sources.
- Display, graph, and analyze the data.
- Perform calculations that were not possible with the MMIS.
- Perform simple simulations.

The market analysis group has recommended that the personal computers and dumb terminals be replaced with IBM 3270 PCs. In addition, it has recommended that the equipment rooms be augmented by placing individual 3270 PCs on the desks of the heavy users in the brand groups, and that the long-run goal be one 3270 PC on each desk.

Several approaches are used to examine the significant differences among the companies in the survey. First, the firms are examined using Nolan's stage model. Next, the notions of intellectual and industrial technologies are introduced, followed by the concept of end-user computing and application development.

NOLAN'S STAGES

This section discusses the firm's practices from the viewpoint of Nolan's stage model, which was developed by Richard Nolan, a well-known consultant and originator of the concept of stages of EDP growth.[4]

Nolan's model provides a structured scheme for explaining the growth of data processing in an organization. He defines the various dimensions of data processing (e.g., people, hardware technology, control processes) and proposes that a company can be in one of the following six stages on these dimensions:

1. Initiation: adoption and beginning of growth.
2. Contagion: rapid and uncontrolled growth in use/cost terms.
3. Control: computing expansion greatly restricted; missed opportunities.
4. Integration: combination of improved management technique and planning results in "fine tuning" of controls.
5. Data administration: DP role changes to management of organizational data resources.
6. Maturity: application portfolio complete and mirrors organization and data flows.[5]

Firms in the survey tend to be at one of two stages in the Nolan model: control or integration.

The control stage (Stage 3) is characterized by tight controls

[4] C. F. Gibson and R. L. Nolan, "Managing the Four Stages of EDP Growth," *Harvard Business Review*, January/February 1974, pp. 76–88.

[5] John Leslie King and Kenneth L. Kraemer, "Evolution and Organizational Information Systems: An Assessment of Nolan's Stage Model," *Communications of the ACM*, May 1984, pp. 466–75.

and difficult interactions between data processing management and the firm's managers and computer users. Users give up on getting what they want, and top management eventually rethinks computing in data resources rather than computer resources terms.

Stage 4, the integration stage, is one of rapid increase in computer usage and the move to database systems and data resource management.

Firms in Stage 3 view computing as a cost that must be controlled. Computing is assigned to the individual responsible for controlling costs, usually the chief financial officer. Those firms in Stage 4 see computing as a resource and try to find ways to turn it into a competitive weapon. Since they compete in terms of their products, services, and supporting programs, they tend to assign the computing responsibilities to those individuals who are leading the competitive efforts—the line vice presidents and general managers.

Those companies in Stage 3 are characterized by tightly controlled central processing and little use of personal computers. Those in Stage 4 have gone to distributed processing or have an information systems management that reaches out to the operating groups and responds to their needs by pushing computing out into the hands of the users. They practice a form of distributed computing by devising an organizational structure that puts the professional data processing personnel in close contact with the line managers and their staff. Further, they encourage the active participation of the marketing managers in the use and extension of the computing tools.

LEVELS OF COMPUTER USAGE IN MARKETING

With this stage model as background, it is possible to develop a new three-level or stage model that fits the circumstances in marketing management. This model identifies three levels of computer usage and examines the philosophies and practices of firms at each level.

Level 1 firms tend to isolate the marketing managers from direct computer access to data. When the marketing managers need information, they contact an analyst in the marketing research department or a MIS specialist. These MIS people are either in the MIS department or in a special unit in the marketing department. These "intermediaries" access the data, prepare a printed output, and send a report to the requesting manager. This process typically takes a day or so. When marketing managers do get direct access, it tends to be via the INF*ACT system provided by CMS Inc. for access to Nielsen store audit data stored on the CMS computers.

The firms in this group tend to assign tight control of computing to a central data processing organization. Requests for systems and personal computers are evaluated against financial standards and procedures that ascertain the expected return on the investment. Emphasis tends to be placed on efficiency justification; that is, the new system must make it possible to save money in doing an existing operation. The result is a low level of personal computer usage and almost no direct use of computers by marketing managers. In some firms, marketing management computing is actively discouraged.

Level 2 firms also employ a central data processing philosophy but strongly encourage end-user computing. They organize the data processing department so that adequate support is available for marketing managers. An information center usually exists to advise and educate end users. High-level languages such as FOCUS and application packages such as Acustar are available for use by marketing managers. The business or line managers tend to play a stronger role in investment and expenditure decisions concerning new systems and personal computers. The result is direct access to the data and the use of personal computers. Data processing and marketing managers encourage end-user computing because it provides "feedback learning" in which the user gets some information, studies it for new insights, recognizes the need for additional information, immediately gets the new information, and continues in this manner until conclusions can be reached. These managers seem to believe that the immediacy of the information provides a rich environment for additional learning and analysis.

Level 3 firms have distributed the management and control of computing throughout the organization as opposed to keeping it in one central department. Two models are available for this decentralization. The General Foods model places hardware, that is, physical computers, in each division of the company for use by the marketing managers. A central Marketing Information Systems Department coordinates the divisional work. Each division has a systems administrator who keeps the computer running, maintains the databases, and assists the marketing managers.

The Omega Company model employs centralized mainframes but distributes the data processing professionals throughout the business units. Each division has its own systems group that works closely with the marketing managers to design and implement systems. Further, each division may have its own programs and purchase its own data.

Personal computing is strongly supported in Level 3 firms, and projects are underway for developing workstations that integrate the data oriented work on the host machine with the modeling, graphics, and simulation work done on the personal computer.

Since the marketing groups assume the responsibility for competing in the consumer and retail markets, they are beginning to view computing as a means of achieving a competitive edge. Their emphasis is on using the computer for data resource management and analysis, as a way of accomplishing their "detective work"; that is, investigating the forces that drive and motivate the consumers and the wholesale/retail trade. Once the marketing managers are exposed to a friendly and interactive information system, they quickly recognize the advantage of "feedback learning"; one data query or analysis raises questions that can only be answered with another series of queries and analyses. This experience leads some brand people to want to explore the additional possibilities of using the computer for other tasks.

Once marketing managers gain a timely and detailed understanding of the markets, they develop strategies and design programs for impacting those markets. They then turn to their personal computers to assess the potential impact of these programs on the market and the subsequent impact on the profitability of the brands. These experiences with computer systems result in the managers recognizing that they cannot accurately foresee the impact of new technology on their work.

INTELLECTUAL TECHNOLOGY

Managers and accountants always justify the purchase of a new machine on an economic basis. Yet the real test of a new technology like computers is not that it performs the same task faster or cheaper than before; it must do something that one could not even conceive of doing before.[6]

One of the most dominant differences among the firms in the three levels was in their implicit conceptualization of the computer as either an "industrial" or an "intellectual" technology.

The difference between these two concepts can be understood by examining the work of Curley and Pyburn in their study of the adoption of office automation (OA) technology in 46 firms.[7] They found that a large gap existed in most firms between the technology's potential and actual use, and they explained the gap by introducing the intellectual and industrial technology concepts. One explanation they give for the difference between the two is that the purchaser of an industrial technology can accurately project the return on investment because s/he knows in advance how it will be used. If s/he does not know what the purchase will do for the firm, it is an intellectual technology.

An intellectual technology's "function is not clearly prescribed by its physical design" because the user can "prescribe the function of the machine; in other words, they are programmable." Their usefulness to the firm is only limited by the "vision of the management . . . and the user's imagination." Intellectual technologies are dedicated to "expanding the intellectual power of the human brain."[8]

Curley and Pyburn also propose that the two different technologies require two different types of learning: Type A and Type B learning. An industrial technology, such as a steam engine, requires Type A learning, which is defined as

> the specific training required to operate the technology—the acquisition of a predetermined set of skills that can be specified a priori and standardized. Ongoing feedback between the learner and the technology is unnecessary, since there is little uncertainty about what must be learned. It is essentially "single-loop" learning.[9]

---

[6] Jacques Vallee, *The Network Revolution: Confessions of a Computer Scientist* (Berkeley, Calif.: AND/OR Press, 1982).

[7] Kathleen Foley Curley and Philip J. Pyburn, " 'Intellectual' Technologies: The Key to Improving White-Collar Productivity," *Sloan Management Review* 24, no. 1 (Fall 1982).

[8] Ibid., pp. 31–39.

[9] Ibid.

Intellectual technology requires Type B learning:

> an adaptive process which is ongoing and iterative; the dimensions and direction of Type B learning cannot be easily specified in advance. The tasks require assessment of the technology's potential, rather than an effort to make the technology "work" properly. It is a process of "double-loop learning" in which the learner significantly influences the decision about what is to be learned.[10]

Double-loop learning seems to be characterized by an iterative sequence of training, learning, training, learning, and so on. The user is trained to use the technology for a specific purpose. Once s/he conquers the task, s/he begins to explore its use for other purposes—to learn. Once a new application is identified, training is usually required so that the person can develop the new application, that is, extend the use of the technology.

In the background study for this book, firms were encountered that approached computers from both perspectives. The most dominant view was to regard the computer as an industrial technology. In particular, most users seem to regard it as a tool for extracting numbers from a database. This was especially true for mainframe or large computers that had been programmed by someone else. The purchase of the technology was predicated on a financial justification that it be treated as an industrial technology.

However, some firms are beginning to treat computers as strategic resources: they assign the management of the information resources to line managers and expect them to become creative in devising uses for computing that will increase the firm's competitive position. They realize that an investment is being made in resources with an uncertain return. Their vision tells them that creative managers and professionals will find ways to exploit the new technologies. They speak of changing the way we do business, of constantly improving our business processes, of reinventing or reconstituting the company.

These findings agree with those of the Curley and Pyburn 46-firm study. "Some companies were willing to experiment and to learn from their experiences, while others were unwilling to experiment without a clear up front notion of the costs and benefits involved."[11] Curley and Pyburn recommend that firms be

---

[10] Ibid.
[11] Ibid., p. 35.

willing to experiment and to realize that uncertainty about how the equipment will be used should be anticipated.

END-USER APPLICATION DEVELOPMENT

There is an uncertainty principle with data processing. The act of implementing a user-driven system changes the requirements of that system. The solution to a problem changes the problem.[12]

End-user computing is growing very rapidly in U.S. corporations. One observer reports the end users control about 40 percent of the world's computing power, and they, rather than the data processing professionals, will control the majority of computing power in the next few years.[13] The greater use of personal computers is perhaps the driving force behind this increase in the control of computing resources, and the trend toward personal computer usage is expected to continue. One observer believes that "within five years, 80 percent of all computer program applications will be running at the micro level."[14]

The personal computer came onto the scene at a time when traditional data processing groups and methods were not able to provide managers with the type of support they needed. Most information systems groups have a known backlog of two to three years, and an "invisible backlog" that may be five times the known backlog.[15] The invisible backlog represents systems and applications that users need but for which they have not issued a request to the information systems group. This reluctance to issue such a request can be traced to several causes, including the existing backlog and a history of unsuccessful applications.

Part of the reason for this situation is the inability of a user to state exactly what s/he wants from a system.

End users have a long learning curve to climb in assessing how they should use today's data processing. They cannot climb far on this curve as long as it remains at the talking stage. It is only when

---

[12] James Martin, *An Information System Manifesto* (Englewood Cliffs, N.J.: Prentice-Hall, 1984), p. 43.

[13] James R. Porter, quoted in *Datamation*, August 1, 1984, p. 141.

[14] Bryan Wilkins, "Micro-CPU Links Ushering in 'Police' Function for Minis," *Computer World*, October 15, 1984, p. 16.

[15] Robert M. Alloway and Judith A. Quillard, "User Managers' Systems Needs," *MIS Quarterly*, June 1983, pp. 27–41.

they have a terminal and use it on their work that they can begin to understand the reality of the computer's challenge and limitations. . . . It is often the case that the end user does not know what he wants until he gets it. When he gets it, he wants something different.[16]

Traditional application development processes require the user to state what s/he wants from the system. Since this is difficult or impossible, the development process is doomed before it starts.

The personal computer and software such as the electronic spreadsheets have given the user the chance to go down the learning curve in an evolutionary manner. S/he can start by developing a small application and learn the real needs by using this application. The system is then redone and learning continues.

The new members of the marketing group are recent graduates from the leading business schools. In fact, the people in most marketing groups have a four to six year "life cycle" in that it takes about that length of time to be promoted through the brand organization and into other positions. The graduates who are being trained on personal computers are more open to active involvement in computing and will take more responsibility for the use of computers in the management of marketing information.

This end-user computing is being encouraged by management because of rapidly changing cost factors. The costs of computing and people time are changing. In the 1970s, computer time became cheaper than people time. "Before long the cost of a person for an hour will be 10 times greater than the cost of a computer for an hour."[17] These costs are causing management to realize that they can and should work to increase worker productivity by providing the resources for end-user computing.

The firms in the survey exhibited rather drastic differences in attitude toward the concept of application development by the marketing managers. Some firms actively encouraged their marketing managers to learn high-level languages and packages such as Lotus 1-2-3 so that they can develop their own applications.

---

[16] Martin, *System Manifesto*, p. 45.

[17] James Martin, *Application Development without Programmers* (Englewood Cliffs, N.J.: Prentice-Hall, 1982), p. 3.

Other firms were opposed to such practices and reserved application development for the professionals in the data processing departments. Such practices were reflected in a statement such as, "We do not want our brand managers to become programmers." But this philosophy is conflicting with the firms' recognition that the best place for information management and application development may very well be in the marketing group.

> I believe we'll see a trend to move information out of the central DP/MIS department and back into the user departments. Before computers, information was kept by the people who understood and used the data themselves. These same people were responsible for the accuracy of the information. Today, a gap has grown between the people responsible for the accuracy and use of the data and the computers which actually keep it. A desktop computer with adequate storage and appropriate links to the central MIS facility could live on the desk of the very clerk who understands and needs the information.[18]

Most installed computer systems are transaction-based systems that generate the firm's accounting information. Emphasis on these systems led firms to place their data processing function in the finance/accounting organization; that is, data processing is usually an arm of finance or accounting. Since the computerized data were accounting data, the firm was, in effect, complying with Fastie's idea of giving control of the data to the people who understand and use it. Since computers were difficult to use, requiring highly trained professionals, specialists were created for managing the firm's information—the systems analysts and programmers.

But we are entering a new era in which information management can be and is being assigned to the people most able to exploit it for strategic and tactical purposes. Decentralized decision making has been with us for decades. The current trend is toward the creation of *intrepreneurs*—individuals who work in large organizations but operate in a manner similar to entrepreneurs in small firms. They are given control over the resources needed to bring innovative products and services to the market-

---

[18] Will Fastie, "What's Next from IBM?" *PC Magazine* 3, no 4 (March 6, 1984), p. 267.

place. As information becomes recognized as a resource, its management is being diffused throughout the organization.

As operating managers turn more to computers for information, they are finding that the existing systems do not meet their needs. These systems either do not have the needed information or the data are so tightly coupled with the firm's transaction systems that they cannot be made available in the required form and/or in a timely manner.

Studies by Alloway and Quillard reveal that the existing systems were built to serve the needs of the firm's operational personnel.[19] Most of the systems have computerized the basic business aspects of the company: order entry, inventory control, and so on. However, most managers and professionals work on tactical and strategic issues, not operational issues. Hence, new and/or different information sources are required. This is particularly true in marketing, where the focus is on the consumer, competitors, and the marketplace. The firm's transaction systems provide little, if any, information of real value in marketing.

The inability of managers to get their information out of the existing systems and the long backlog for developing new systems have made top executives receptive to new approaches to the management of information; they are beginning to adopt a new attitude toward computing. In particular, they are beginning to move from the belief that "we hire Fred Jones to run our data processing shop; information management is his responsibility" to the notion that "we are drowning in data; let's get it into the hands of the people who know how to exploit it" to the recognition that "we no longer have to run the data through a very narrow pipeline—the data processing operation."

To exploit the data, it must flow around the organization and into the hands of the people who are involved in planning and decision making. It must flow through a very wide pipeline—the communications channel must have high bandwidth. People who have information, who collect, store, and disseminate it as part of their jobs, must be given the tools to increase the bandwidth of the pipeline through which the information flows into the decision-making process. These knowledge workers must

---

[19] Alloway and Quillard, "Systems Needs," pp. 27–41.

become more involved with the computerization and management of information in their area of expertise.

The information pipeline consists of three entities: electronics, people, and organizational structures. Its width depends on the degree to which these entities facilitate, rather than impede, the flow of information. Installing a local area network that moves data at 10 million bits per second will not produce rapid flow if the individuals on the network do not send or make the data available.

One barrier to such information flow is an organizational structure and policy that prevents information sharing. When firms establish policies that preclude direct dialogue between marketing managers and sales managers, they are decreasing the size of the information pipeline. Another constraining factor is the notion of "data ownership" in which a group holds the belief that they own a database and will permit other groups to see only the result of their analysis, not the underlying data. Information must then flow through the minds of the data owners, which can severely reduce the bandwidth of the transmission, as well as introduce considerable "noise" into the data.

If all data and data access must flow through a central mainframe, then its flow is limited by the ability of the people in the organization to make the mainframe "do their bidding." Historically, most managers and business analysts have not been very successful in this area, so the notion that the mainframe is *the* computer will have this limiting effect.

Finally, information access and flow are limited by organizational philosophies that place *all* systems and applications development in a single department and exercise tight control over the creation of *information* systems and applications. Since most companies are backlogged by several years in such development, the pipeline may be effectively "turned off" while the business departments wait for programs to be designed, written, debugged, documented, tested, and released.

The experience of some firms in the survey indicate that it is possible to distribute systems and applications throughout the organization based on the relative degree to which the problem under study requires professional computer skills versus business skills and knowledge. When computer expertise dominates, a central department should be responsible. When business knowledge dominates, a distributed, business/computer partnership can evolve and be directed by the responsible department. For example, the Omega Company places most of its data processing professionals in the business and staff divisions, perhaps because the company feels that business knowledge is very important in systems development. A central staff works on highly technical problems such as database management systems and procedures.

The search for new ways to increase the size of the information pipeline is being facilitated by emerging technology that makes it possible to spread information and its management throughout the organization. Rapid gains in the performance-to-cost ratio of desktop computers, small departmental-level computers, and local area networks permit an entirely different approach to computing. Individuals or small groups of knowledge workers can use this technology to build information systems that permit rapid access to their information, and perhaps even their knowledge.

The innovative computer applications identified during the company interviews tended to be developed by groups operating outside the traditional, centralized, data processing structure. These groups seem able to assume a more entrepreneural approach, one unencumbered by the techniques and procedures used in the development of standard data processing systems. They can and do take advantage of the strengths of the PC or the mainframe where appropriate.

Most of these innovative applications were started by individuals who did not have a clear view of the form or substance of the end result. Rather, they had a vague idea of the solution and tended to evolve toward it. Perhaps when one knows exactly what s/he wants from a system, the traditional organization and approach offer an efficient solution. But when one does not know what to do or how to do it, one tends to abandon the strictures of organizational structure and look instead for innovative solutions. This analogy applies to information systems. If a project is easily structured, then traditional data processing techniques yield innovative solutions. But, if the user has trouble articulating his or her needs, the data processing techniques for producing transaction oriented systems or for providing menu-based information systems may yield such a narrow "solution set" that the problem remains unsolved.

The now-famous process that produced VisiCalc, the first

electronic spreadsheet, is a good example of the combination of skills that produces innovative systems. This process seems to involve either a person with the full range of business and computing knowledge and skills or a small team with management by the business interest rather than by the computer interest.

The major problem involves developing management oriented systems as opposed to the currently available transaction systems used to support the people in the lower levels of the organization. Firms have developed efficient methods and management structures for producing these transaction-based systems. People have been trained in these methods and have applied them for the last 15 to 20 years. Program generators and other tools have evolved for optimizing this development process. The common characteristic of these systems is the "computerization" of procedures previously performed manually. Since the system's user is the same person who has been applying the manual procedures, it is relatively easy to build systems by studying or interviewing that person. The resulting system makes the user more efficient.

But management systems attack the effectiveness aspect of the work instead of, or in addition to, the efficiency of the work. Well-thought-out and/or documented procedures do not exist for doing managerial work. The problem here involves an intricate relationship between learning what to do and how to do it, that is, double-loop learning. The manager or the knowledge workers who assist the manager must be intimately involved in the development of the systems that support managers.

In summary, the firm must decide how it is going to deal with the emerging issues involving end-user computing and application development. Some see this issue as a revolution, not an evolutionary change.

> We're managing a *revolution*, not an evolution. Changes will occur very rapidly. Among other things, the languages for making computers do your bidding will change dramatically in the next few years. Application development without programmers is the most important revolution since the transistor was invented. . . . Management must first recognize that computer responsibility will certainly be decentralized and diffused. Personnel outside of DP departments will have to be willing to transport nonprocedural languages to their specific areas of responsibility. They will need to

be able to use those new tools to create custom applications on the spot.[20]

Martin presents several justifications for his prognosis, the primary one being that the demand for computing services is simply outstripping the ability of the data processing departments to develop the needed applications. He estimates that today there is one professional programmer for every 300 employees, and that in the near future there will be one computer for every 10 employees. Rather than the data processing department growing to one programmer for every 10 people, Martin concludes that the users of the computers must take responsibility for the development of the applications.

If James Martin is correct, the next generation of marketing managers and professionals is going to have to be proficient at the art and science of application development without programmers. Hence, there needs to be a new level of computer literacy among the marketing managers and professionals, perhaps as described by Alan Kay.

> What then is computer literacy? It is not learning to manipulate a word processor, a spreadsheet or a modern user interface; those are paper-and-pencil skills. Computer literacy is not even learning to program. That can always be learned, in ways no more uplifting than learning grammar instead of writing. Computer literacy is a contact with the activity of computing deep enough to make the computational equivalent of reading and writing fluent and enjoyable.[21]

This feeling about computing was expressed by one product manager who said "God help the next manager I am assigned to who does not like computers . . . I cannot do without mine."

EMERGING ORGANIZATIONS

There is a "quiet revolution" underway in some of the firms who are trying to deal with these issues. These firms are discovering

---

[20] James Martin, "We're Managing a Revolution. . .," *Business Computer Systems* 2, no. 1 (January 1985), p. 24.

[21] Martin, "Managing a Revolution," p. 24.

that they must create new organizational structures to deal with the technological developments and the pending data explosion. For instance, Frito-Lay and General Foods have recently added new organizational units that specialize in the development of modeling approaches and information systems for use in marketing. Frito-Lay has formed marketing systems and General Foods has created the Marketing Information Systems Department. These groups are usually separate and distinct from marketing research and data processing, the two departments that have traditionally dealt with marketing information and marketing systems, respectively.

The new departments specialize in the use of marketing research for ongoing marketing problems. They provide the concepts, models, and tools that are useful in building information and knowledge systems for answering a series of related questions that occur over time. The *traditional* marketing research department performs studies that answer one-time questions (e.g., a market segmentation analysis or an experiment for measuring the relative strengths of two advertising copy approaches). The *new* department builds systems and techniques for use in answering a series of ongoing and related questions. The president of one of the survey firms told the manager of the new department: "You people must learn how to manage information."

The managers of these new groups have recognized the need for people trained in the relevant aspects of marketing, data collection and management, model building, statistical analysis, and systems development. People who work in these new departments need to know how to

- Recognize an ongoing marketing information problem.
- Design a data collection mechanism.
- Build an information system for managing the data.
- Build a model that provides a framework for understanding the problem and the data.
- Use statistical inference to estimate the parameters of the model.
- Build a simulator for applying the model.
- Develop new knowledge based on the model.
- Develop a knowledge base for managing the firm's marketing research knowledge.

These people need education and training in the following areas:

- Quasi-experimental design.
- Experimental designs for measuring change.
- Survey designs for tracking trends and changes.
- Collection of market data.
- Database management systems.
- Information systems.
- Model building.
- Statistical inference.
- Econometrics.
- Simulation.
- Expert systems.
- Library retrieval systems.
- Knowledge support environments.
- Meta-analysis.

Whereas the traditional marketing research department conducts studies and then reports the results to the marketing managers, the new group builds systems and tools for their own and the marketing groups use. Therefore, the people in these emerging groups need good interpersonal skills and the ability to teach others how to use their tools and systems.

CHAPTER FOUR

A Design for Today

This chapter discusses information systems that can be installed *today* to support the current activities of marketing managers. These information systems can support a broad range of managerial activities—not just the data oriented aspect of marketing management. Therefore, before discussing the specification and design of a marketing support system, it is essential that we take a broader view of information systems and managerial activities.

First, the need for such an expanded view is illustrated with the Omega Company case. Using this case as a springboard, we will then explore the activities of managers in general and marketing groups in particular. Next, we will present a general design for an information system, after which we will discuss specific hardware and software combinations that could constitute such a system.

OMEGA COMPANY

Omega Company is organized around product oriented divisions, such as a food division or a soap division. Each division is relatively self-contained in that it has most of the people and resources required to run the business—a controller, and managers of manufacturing, sales, product development, and advertising. The advertising manager has a staff hierarchy that includes associate advertising managers, brand managers, assistant brand managers, and brand assistants. The last three categories of managers comprise a brand group.

These operating divisions are supported by staff divisions that correspond to the departments within the operating divisions. For instance, there are staff organizations for advertising, sales, manufacturing, and product development. The staff people perform functions that cut across the divisions, and have career responsibility for the divisional people in their areas of expertise. For example, the vice president of advertising has career responsibility for the people who report to the advertising managers in the divisions. Each of these operating divisions has its own computer systems group.

Systems people are also located in the staff divisions. They provide occupation-specific support to the divisions for problems that cut across the divisions and/or are unique to the occupations. If, for instance, a division were implementing a program for placing computers in all field sales offices, the systems people in the staff sales division would become involved, as would the systems people in the business.

A central Management Systems Division supports all divisions, operates the large IBM and IBM-compatible mainframes, provides telecommunications services, and identifies and explores the usefulness of new technology. This central group also provides career management for the systems people in the divisions.

An integrated workstation (IWS), a prototypical set of hardware and software, has been designed to support the brand groups. The IWS consists of an IBM XT, a black and white monitor capable of displaying graphics, modem, and mouse and equipped with a dot-matrix printer. Software includes Lotus 1-2-3, Multimate (a word processing package), and Datatrev. The last item is a program that facilitates the downloading of data from the large databases on the mainframe. The user interacts with Datatrev via the mouse to select items from menus. These menus lead the user through the process of building an "extract" datafile, a portion of larger files stored on the mainframe. This extract file arrives at the IWS in a form that can be input into Lotus 1-2-3 for analysis and graphing. The entire system is menu driven, provides interaction via the mouse or the keyboard, and is designed to make it easy to move data among the various software packages. Hence, the IWS is an integrated system that includes a PC, PC-based software, mainframe resident data and Datatrev for retrieval, computer-based training, and a computer-based conferencing capacity.

The integrated workstation includes the software for attaching the IWS to Omega's electronic communication system. This system, developed internally and run on a dedicated IBM 4300 computer, has five features.

1. Electronic document distribution. Documents and messages can be sent anywhere in Omega's worldwide operation.
2. Document translation. Facilities are provided for transferring and translating documents across equipment from five different manufacturers.
3. Electronic conferencing. Messages and questions can be sent to other people in the company who are registered in a conference.
4. Messaging from one individual to another.
5. Archiving, filing, and retrieving.

The company is also experimenting with a local area network (LAN) as an alternative to the IWS and its reliance on mainframe data. The approach Omega is taking is to use existing hardware and software in the workstation and the LAN. A prototype has been developed that consists of an IBM PC configured similar to the IWS. However, instead of being tied to the mainframe computer via the Datatrev system, the user accesses data stored on a hard disk and accessible via the network. A file server manages the shared disk and provides users with private and shared files on the common disk. In addition, the software programs are stored on the shared disk and downloaded to the workstation when needed. This file server can address disks that contain up to 500 megabytes of data.

The user interacts with the network by selecting items from an on-screen menu. The large data files are stored on the mainframe and downloaded to the file server in extract form. The designers of the network elected to download data rectangles, that is, two-dimensional arrays of data.

Omega has historically relied on Nielsen data to analyze the performance in the market of their brands and competitors. In addition, brand groups in several of Omega's product categories purchased SAMI data, primarily because it increased their ability to "read" the results of their test programs. SAMI's short time interval (4 weeks) and large number of regional markets (51) permit finer test markets. Scanner data are also purchased from Nielsen. These data, based on a sample of 130 stores, are at the weekly level, thus providing increased diagnostic information on the effectiveness of promotional programs.

Omega relies quite heavily on analysis and testing before making business decisions. Hence, its need for information systems is strong. This reliance on data and analysis explains some of the company's progress. Other reasons include the involvement of top management with computers, including the chairman of the board.

MARKETING MANAGERS' ACTIVITIES

The description of computer oriented activities at Omega indicates the existence of a philosophy that a marketing workbench can support a wide range of marketing activities. To expand on this point, this section presents an analysis of the activities of managers in general, and marketing managers in particular. Existing and future systems should be designed to support these activities.

Several researchers have studied how managers spent their time. One of the original studies was by Mintzberg, who found that top executives spend most of their time communicating with other people.[1] A replication and extension of this study by Kurke and Aldrich yielded the same result.[2] The following table lists the key findings of these studies in percentage of time the managers spent in each of five activities.

---

[1] Henry Mintzberg, *The Nature of Managerial Work* (New York: Harper & Row, 1973).

[2] Lance B. Kurke and Howard E. Aldrich, "Mintzberg was Right: A Replication and Extension of the Nature of Managerial Work," *Management Science*, August 1983, pp. 975–84.

Work Activity	Mintzberg Study	Kurke and Aldrich Study
Scheduled meetings	59%	50%
Desk work	22	26
Unscheduled meetings	10	12
Telephone	6	8
Other	3	4

Additional studies by Christie support this general pattern.[3] These studies indicate that most managers spend their time communicating with others in scheduled and unscheduled activities. Only about one fourth of their time is spent doing desk work.

A recent study by AT&T provides new insight into the activities of white-collar workers. This study, which found that white-collar workers spend 80 percent to 95 percent of their time communicating and managing information, provides a breakdown of the average time spent at all levels of white-collar positions in face-to-face, voice, and document communications.

Percent of Time Spent by Media

	Executive	Manager	Professional	Secretary
Face-to-face	53%	47%	23%	negligible
Document	25	29	42	55
Voice	16	9	17	20
Other activity	6	15	18	25

SOURCE: S. L. Teger, "Factors Impacting the Evolution of Office Automation," *Proceedings IEEE* 71, no. 4 (April 1983), pp. 503–11. Reported in Hoo-Min D. Tong and Amar Gupta, "A New Direction in Personal Computer Software," *Proceeding IEEE* 72, no. 3 (March 1984), p. 379.

The major purposes of a product manager have been stated by Luck:

1. "Creation and conceptualization of strategies for improving and marketing the assigned product line or brands.
2. Projection and determination of financial and operating plans for such products.
3. Monitoring execution and results of plans, with possible adaptation of tactics to evolving conditions.

---

[3] Bruce Christie, *Face to File Communication: A Psychological Approach to Information Systems* (New York: John Wiley & Sons, 1981).

4. Serving as the information center on the assigned products."[4]

The marketing group's work can be broken into the following steps:

1. Analysis of historical data to detect abnormal conditions.
2. Identification of problems and opportunities.
3. Design of possible solutions.
4. Analysis and/or testing of solutions.
5. Selection of a preferred solution.
6. Championing the solution.
7. Implementation.
8. Evaluation of program's effectiveness.

The current uses of computing—extracting numbers and spreadsheet calculations—relate to only a few of the activities of marketing managers. These activities usually involve acquiring the proper numbers, transforming and summarizing them, building a story that identifies the key numbers and their interrelationships, building a simple simulation model that depicts the impact of changing one of the numbers, and writing a short report that summarizes the numbers and discusses their implications. Most of the interfaces involve discussions with individuals in other groups about the numbers—their source, meaning, and interpretation.

THE FOUR Ds OF MARKETING MANAGEMENT

The current MMIS is used to support marketing managers in the performance of their activities. The work of marketing management involves the combination of four talents because the marketing managers must play four distinct but related roles: detective, designer, decision influencer, and diplomat. These can be called the four-D roles of brand management.

1. Detective. The firm should constantly search for ways to improve the sales and profits of its brands, which means search-

---

[4] David J. Luck, "Interfaces of a Product Manager," *Journal of Marketing*, October 1969, pp. 32–36.

ing for clues in the market and in consumer data. This search involves the identification of problems and opportunities facing the brand. Thus, marketing managers must be good detectives in that they must be able to analyze brand performance measures and trends by examining the evidence in the consumer and market data. This detective work is the first step in the creative aspect of brand management.

2. Designer. Once an opportunity has been identified, a strategy must be devised and programs designed for capturing that opportunity. Alternative solutions are formulated and tested until an optimal solution is found.

3. Decision influencer. The marketing and general managers usually make the final decision concerning brand related programs. Brand managers must be able to influence these managers' decisions by convincing them that the brand group has in fact identified a significant opportunity and that its design has been optimized.

4. Diplomat. The actual implementation of the program is done by other people in the company. The essence of marketing implementation in such an environment is the location and removal of bottlenecks obstructing the transformation of a planned activity into an actual product, service, or program. Finding and removing the obstacles is a communication-intensive activity in which the brand groups apply their detective abilities throughout the firm. They must locate the departments or individuals who are slowing or impeding the progress of their program implementation. Diplomacy is then needed to remove the obstacle and keep the program on schedule.

The Appendix at the end of this chapter elaborates on these roles by listing typical activities of marketing managers in each of these four roles.

The use of computers in each of these managerial roles can be identified. Each role requires a somewhat different combination of the system components, which are the marketing management information system (MMIS), office automation (OA), and personal computing (PC).

The detective work involved in the identification of opportunities makes heavy use of the MMIS because it is primarily a data-intensive activity. Assistant product managers are constantly coming up with different views of the data. George Williams at General Foods views this as a growing desire to "roam freely through the database." An MMIS should enable a relatively untrained marketing manager to easily observe any aspect of the business that is available in the databases.

Another source of "clues" about brand problems and opportunities is provided by the field sales force. They are in a position to observe and report about abnormal conditions or situations in their local markets. The OA aspect of the system would offer a communications pipeline between sales representatives and marketing managers. Messages could be left in electronic mailboxes, thus precluding the need for phone conversations and letters.

Personal computers are used today primarily in the design role of the marketing managers, who build spreadsheets containing models of the brand's performance in the various markets. These models are used to simulate the effect of a program in sales and profits.

Also, personal computers have been a good tool for use in the managers' decision-influencing role because PCs make it possible to quickly prepare graphical presentations that capture the essence of the brand group's arguments. A number of marketing managers reported that the graphics generated by Lotus 1-2-3 and Chartmaster had enhanced their ability to sell their ideas to top management.

The office automation facilities would improve the implementation phase of the brand group's work. Since most programs involve the work of different departments, marketing managers are in constant communication with people throughout the organization. The messaging, scheduling, and calendaring aspects of a modern OA environment would facilitate the implementation work by permitting brand people to remain in their offices, and thus be available for communication with others, rather than going around the company in search of people involved in the implementation.

GENERAL SPECIFICATION

One of the results of the survey of companies was the recognition that almost every firm had a unique approach to the use of computers in the support of marketing. Every company seems to have unique needs, perhaps because each company has its own "corporate culture," which has been defined by Marvin Bower of McKinsey & Co. to mean "the way we do things around here."[5]

Because each company does things differently, the managers have different styles and information needs. Some of these needs are common to all marketing managers because they all tend to have similar training and backgrounds. But it has been pointed out that "human culture is a result of learned behavior; it is not an intrinsic human characteristic. Therefore, the culture of an organization is a result of 'programming' people how to behave in the organization's environment."[6] These differences tend to result in different information system needs.

An example of such cultures and their impact on computer use by marketing managers is the differences between companies with a broad range of products versus those that are basically single-product firms. In a single product firm, the chief executive officer (or a small group of senior executives) tends to do most of the strategic thinking about the brands and to make almost all of the decisions. This is an effective form of management because one individual can have sufficient knowledge about the firm's products, processes, customers, and competitors to make the important decisions.

In companies with multiple products, managerial decision making tends to be diffused, mainly because one person cannot effectively make all the decisions. In this kind of organization, the marketing managers have more responsibility for strategic decision making than they do in a single-product firm. Since information is important for strategic analysis, the marketing managers in the multiproduct firms use the computer for more than those in the single-product firms. However, in those multiproduct firms where the marketing managers are not actively involved in data analysis, staff groups do the data analysis, and report the results to the marketing managers and senior executives.

Although different corporate cultures require different information, there are enough common needs to make it possible to

---

[5] David Vincent, "Corporate Culture," *Computer World*, November 5, 1984, p. ID/21.

[6] Ibid.

design a generic workstation around both functionality and a procedure for achieving that functionality.

The following is a general specification of the functionality of a workstation and supporting systems that is based on our interviews with the firms.

- Data retrieval: the ability to extract data from large databases and move it to the workstation for analysis, review, and reporting.
- Data analysis: the ability to analyze data in ways that fit the needs and management styles of the organization, including simple listing and ranking, graphics display and manipulation, and sophisticated statistical analysis.
- Reporting: tools for preparing management reports, including the use of text, graphics, and sophisticated formatting and printing capabilities.
- Document handling: the ability to send and receive documents through a network and to edit and/or revise the received document.
- Communications: the ability to send and receive messages and to hold computer-based conferences.
- Data processing service: the ability to use the workstation as a window to in-house and outside computing services for access to data or for processing tasks not available on the workstation.
- Training: computer-based training on how to use the systems, as well as training in various business subjects.

RECOMMENDED CONFIGURATION FOR TODAY[7]

Given the state of today's technology and the current role of computers and data in product management, it is possible to identify several hardware and software configurations that would provide adequate support to the marketing managers and other marketing professionals. This section describes one config-

---

[7] The author has not conducted a detailed, hands-on evaluation of all the available hardware and software. Rather, this recommendation is based on reported use and evaluation by the companies in the survey and some hands-on use by the author.

uration that can be implemented today and that seems to correspond with the computing skill and interest of the people currently in product management teams. This configuration assumes that there exists a need for three types of computing services.

1. Data retrieval and analysis via an MMIS.
2. Office automation services such as document filing and retrieving, electronic mail, and messaging.
3. Personal computing.

Further, it is assumed that the firm is interested in acquiring off-the-shelf components and systems that have been proven useful and reliable in meeting most of today's marketing managers' computing needs.

Marketing Management Information System

Before discussing specific products and systems the firm can use to build its MMIS, let's examine some of the issues uncovered by the Alpha Company as it moved toward an information environment using a combination of traditional languages, fourth generation languages, and specialized packages.

ALPHA COMPANY

Alpha's computer operation is headed by a vice president of information systems (IS) who reports to the president. Reporting to the vice president are two managers who are directly involved with information systems for marketing managers. A systems development group develops MIS applications and a decision support system (DSS) group develops systems that support marketing decisions. The systems group develops applications using COBOL and the IBM IMS file system to run on an IBM 3083 under MVS. The DSS group primarily uses the EXPRESS system from Management Decision Systems, Inc. (MDS), and the FOCUS system from Information Builders, Inc. (IBI) to run on an IBM 4341 under VM.

When the DSS group was formed around four years ago, the decision about which group would develop an application was based almost entirely on which language was being used. Presently, the same decision is strongly influenced by the nature of the application. If the system is primarily a standard one that will be run on a regular basis, it is programmed in COBOL by the systems development group to run under MVS. If the system is primarily one for ad hoc inquiry and analysis, it is developed in a high-level package such as EXPRESS or FOCUS.

The IS philosophy is that systems that run on a regular basis are production systems that should be written in a language such as COBOL because of COBOL's superior data security, data integrity, file backup, and system recovery capabilities.

An example of the operationalization of this philosophy is the sales forecasting system that was under development in the fall of 1984. Alpha purchased a system called Sales Forecasting from American Software. This system, which is written in COBOL, interfaces with the company's sales data stored in IMS files and produces forecasts for each brand in each region using a variant of the exponential-smoothing forecasting model. However, an additional feature of the system is its capacity for managerial override of the automated forecast; that is, the brand groups can insert their own forecasts, which "override" the system's forecast. The system stores both forecasts (the automated and the managerial override) for subsequent comparison with actual values.

The FOCUS system is being used to develop a user front end for this forecasting package. The historical data and automated forecast will be sent from the transactional applications on the MVS computer to the FOCUS application on the VM computer. The user will review the data and make overrides in the FOCUS application. The modified data file will be sent back to the MVS computer for updating the Sales Forecasting system. This combination of packages and systems was selected for the superior file management capabilities of the COBOL-based Sales Forecasting system and the superior interactive user interfaces of FOCUS running in the VM environment.

After working with several languages and packages, the DSS people have recognized that there are important tradeoffs to be considered when selecting a package or language, and that each application should be carefully matched with the available resources. For instance, one programmer believed that EXPRESS is more "programmer friendly" than FOCUS because of the breadth and depth of its programming language, but he felt that FOCUS is more "user friendly" for the nonprogrammer. Further, Alpha has observed that packages with extensive analytic capability tend to be inefficient at maintaining large volumes of data and at providing easy access to the data by marketing people. Thus, the company believes that languages for maintaining and accessing data should be different from analysis languages. It is felt that technology will evolve in a manner that will permit the analysis to be done at the individual workstation, with data maintenance and access remaining on the mainframe.

Most of the marketing applications are done with EXPRESS. Alpha started using EXPRESS to access SAMI data on the Tymshare time-sharing system. After incurring an annual time-sharing cost of more than $1 million, the company brought the system in-house by purchasing EXPRESS and leasing an IBM 4341; Alpha believes that considerable cost savings have been achieved. The 4341 has 16 megabytes of memory and will support about 20 simultaneous EXPRESS users. The EXPRESS system contains SAMI data on warehouse withdrawals, company shipment data, and retailing advertising data purchased from MAJERS.

The marketing managers are supported in their EXPRESS use by the DSS group and by a staff of seven people in the marketing services area. These support people work with the marketing users to develop EXPRESS programs that provide different cuts or views of the data. The users can then choose among these preformatted EXPRESS reports for most of their data access needs.

The FOCUS package is being used to manage and access shipment data at the customer level. FOCUS was selected because of its ability to manage and interface with such large databases. However, the sheer size of the database has made it necessary to run the system in batch mode for overnight turnaround.

This description of marketing applications at Alpha Company focuses on the software for the marketing management information system and highlights the differences between "programmer-friendly" and "user-friendly" software. In general, the differences seem most apparent across mainframe software packages, although there are strong differences in user friendliness of software designed for personal computers.

Software packages that seem to be gaining rapid acceptance by marketing people are those that give the user a lot of support. Specifically, they are the ones that present the user with clear options or guides in performing data extraction and analysis. With such systems, the marketing managers can do most of their own computer-based analysis rather than having to rely on the services of a "computer expert." These packages should be contrasted with command oriented systems that present the user with a "blinking cursor" and require him or her to first think through the type and form of data needed to solve a problem and then compose a command that tells the computer how to do the data extraction and manipulation.

The computer/human dialogue at the end of the Pillsbury case in Chapter Five is an example of the type of system design that seems to result in rapid adoption of the system by marketing managers because it leads the user through the analysis. In other words, it seems to know what question to ask to extract the appropriate data and do a particular type of analysis. In contrast, the command oriented software does not seem amenable to use by marketing managers and often requires an intermediary.

The Acustar system is a workable solution for the firm's current MMIS.[8] Those firms in the study that have adopted Acustar have had little problem getting the marketing managers to use it in a feedback-learning mode of inquiry and analysis. The question-and-answer interface seems amenable to the interest and experience level of the marketing managers. Because it is an application package that was specifically designed for use by marketing managers, Acustar contains most of the features needed to report and analyze the time-series oriented data in current use.

In addition, Acustar provides several features that increase its functionality when combined with a personal computer.

- It can transmit data to personal computers in various formats. For example, it can download (and upload) data in DIF format, which is used in most PC applications.

---

[8] Acustar may be purchased from Decision Support Services, 1100 West 78th Street, Eadon Prairie, Minn. 55344.

- It facilitates the preparation of graphics at the workstation. For instance, it will ask the user a series of questions concerning his or her graphics needs, retrieve the necessary data, generate the necessary commands to produce the graph on Chartmaster (a popular PC graphics package), and download the graphics commands to the PC.

Another viable product is EXPRESS and its associated software.[9] EXPRESS is a large marketing decision-support system that runs on IBM and Prime computers. It is primarily a command oriented system that contains sophisticated analytical and graphical capabilities. To make the system more amenable to the casual or intermittent user, IRI offers EASYTRAC, a menu-driven front-end software package designed for the marketing manager's day-to-day analysis and reporting needs.

EASYTRAC offers three types of user interfaces: a full menu system that lists *and* describes each possible user action, an abbreviated menu system that only presents the command names, and a brief menu system that prompts for a command. The last feature is important because it allows the system to adapt to the user as s/he learns EASYTRAC's capabilities and language.

A similar product, EASYCAST, opens the more analytical tools of EXPRESS to the manager who is interested in forecasting. It is an integrated package that uses prompted menus for data entry, statistical analysis, reporting, graphics, and consolidation.

To bring EXPRESS' power to the desktop, IRI has written a version in the C programming language to run on IBM personal computers called pcEXPRESS. This product contains data communication facilities that provide a window into the mainframe environment, allowing data to be easily exchanged between the desktop and the mainframe. It has full capabilities for local data management, graphing, reporting, and simple analysis. It uses "pop-up" menus and takes advantage of the PC's color capabilities.

---

[9] EXPRESS may be purchased from Information Resources, Inc., 200 Fifth Avenue, Waltham, Mass. 02254.

Dialogue, Inc. offers ANALECT, a software product designed for marketing managers.[10] Actually, three levels of systems are available: (1) ANALECT/ACCESS is designed with the marketing manager as the target user and provides HELP prompts so that infrequent users can get the reports they need without having to memorize commands, product names, and so on; (2) more analytically oriented users can use the ANALECT/MDA system to develop new reporting formats and analyses; and (3) ANALECT DSS provides a powerful package for analyzing nonrecurring problems.

In addition, Dialogue offers both a sophisticated graphics package that can be integrated into the analysis and reporting software and a relational database management system. These packages run on IBM, Prime, and DEC/VAX computers. In addition, there are versions available for the IBM PC and for computers that run UNIX System V.

Another package, ADDATA, provides a system for interactive information retrieval, data manipulation, and ad hoc reporting on Burroughs, DEC, Prime, and IBM PC computers.[11] One of ADDATA's unique features is fast data retrieval, which is achieved by the use of random access files rather than the more traditional indexed sequential files.

Since ADDATA can also run on desktop computers, it provides a means of distributing the data management and analysis activities throughout the organization. An important feature is the PC/REFRESH package, which allows PC/ADDATA databases to be automatically updated from a host ADDATA database.

Personal Computing

The firms who have made personal computing part of the work of their marketing managers have adopted the IBM PC and the Lotus 1-2-3 spreadsheet package. In addition, the Multimate word processing package is popular with marketing managers and secretaries for document preparation. However, the need

---

[10] This product may be purchased from Dialogue, Inc., 19 Rector Street, New York, N.Y. 10006.

[11] ADDATA may be purchased from Applied Decision Systems, a division of Temple, Barker & Sloane, Inc., 33 Hayden Avenue, Lexington, Mass. 02173.

to integrate the personal computer into a communications net-work calls for the adoption of a text-editing package that lends itself to the interchange of documents among different compu-ters. The IBM Display Write package offers the best word processing system for those firms that anticipate needing to in-terchange documents in an IBM oriented, office automation en-vironment.

The Lotus 1-2-3 package offers easy-to-use features for gener-ating graphics. Some marketing managers report using 1-2-3 for all their graphics needs, while other users feel that they need an additional package to prepare the graphics that are used in re-ports and presentations to senior managers. The ChartMaster graphics package seems to be preferred by these users.

The PC must be enhanced with communications adapters so that it can communicate with the MMIS and participate in the office automation aspects of the system. The exact adapter de-pends on the type of mainframe (and its location), as well as the office automation equipment. Some firms access their in-house and external time-sharing vendors via asynchronous commu-nications adapters on the PC; others use bisynchronous com-munications adapters to connect to IBM mainframes through communications controllers. The advantage of using the communications controller is speed, with the asynchronous con-nection usually limited to a speed of 1200 baud (120 characters per second).

Another PC package deserves consideration by marketing managers, particularly those who are more oriented toward "words" than "numbers." Framework is a system designed to integrate the writing or text-preparation activities into the numerical, spreadsheet activities. A word processor is an in-tegral part of Framework's spreadsheet, graphics, and telecom-munications package. More importantly, Framework has an outlining feature that allows the manager to quickly prepare and revise an outline of a marketing plan, sales presentation, or any textual material. By switching from the outline to the word processor, the manager can easily add textual material to the outline. This feature makes Framework an attractive personal productivity tool for use with the firm's MMIS (which can be accessed from within Framework via its telecommunications facility).

Office Automation

The incorporation of office automation (OA) capabilities into the system must be based on the entire company's OA strategy and implementation process. Since the brand group is the communication center for people throughout the company around issues that relate to their brand, this group does most of its communicating with people outside the marketing department. Thus, its OA facility must be an integral part of the company's OA facility.

It the firm does not have an existing OA strategy and implementation process, then the marketing area can build around the same hardware system that runs the MMIS. Most of these products (e.g., Acustar, EXPRESS, and ANALECT) run under the IBM VM operating system. IBM offers the Professional Office System (PROFS) package, which can be used to provide the OA services. PROFS offers the following "services" from its main menu:

- Processes schedules: works with daily and monthly schedules, schedules for other people, and schedules for conference rooms and equipment.
- Opens the mail: works with notes and memos, letters, and other documents sent by people who also use PROFS.
- Searches for documents: finds documents that have been filed in mail logs.
- Processes notes and messages: writes, edits, and sends documents such as memos, reports, and letters.
- Processes documents from other sources: adds information about documents (both paper and electronic) that were not created using PROFS to the PROFS files.
- Processes the mail log: organizes and works with key information about documents.

These services would allow marketing managers to begin to communicate in an electronic fashion. Further, people outside the marketing area could be given access to the PROFS system so that communications could be extended throughout the company.

APPENDIX: SPECIFIC BRAND GROUP ACTIVITIES

The following list is a *sample* of the activities of marketing managers. The activities are organized according to the "Four-Ds" aspect of marketing management: detective, designer, decision influencer, and diplomat.

Detective

- Analyze the results of the brand's marketing strategy over the past five years, giving attention to the nature, effectiveness, and profitability of sales promotions.
- Prepare charts of trade promotions of brands by size of product packages over five-year period.
- Examine the extent of "inventory loading" during periods of heavy trade promotion.
- Study levels of merchandising support the brand received at retail level during trade promotion periods.
- Examine amount of cross-line promotions among brand sizes.
- Commission study of consumer and trade promotions.
- Evaluate market surveys: draw conclusions from data.
- Estimate product distribution in various markets.
- Understand consumer responses to product in markets.
- Estimate cost of shipping and cost of product's promotional materials.
- Understand the "trade's" resistance to various new ideas.
- Understand impact of various media types for advertising and promotional purposes.
- Estimate incremental impact of promotional activities.
- Evaluate possible entry into new market.
- Visit large discount stores and drug chains to evaluate product positionings.
- Study television advertising of competitive brands.
- Hire outside consultants to study the markets; hold meetings with them to discuss findings.
- Analyze and attack problems of declining brand sales.
- Evaluate price changes on the brand's bottom line.
- Monitor/analyze test-market results.
- Analyze the results/data derived from test advertisements.

- Evaluate effectiveness of consumer promotions in magazine ads, direct mailings, cash refunds, and point of purchase materials.

Designer

- Prepare annual budget for brand's projected sales and profits.
- Develop a marketing plan specifying expenditure levels for advertising, consumer, and trade promotions.
- Determine type, planning, and timing of consumer promotions.
- Define objectives for future consumer promotions.
- Make decision to reduce advertising expenditures as a result of studies conducted.
- Establish a complete promotion plan including pricing, allowances and terms, brand package sizes, and a calendar of events.
- Make decision on supplemental advertising and promotion activities.
- Evaluate packaging designs.
- Select TV commercials for brand from those suggested by the ad agency.
- Authorize increase in promotional expenditures.
- Approve new copy (creative work plan) from ad agency.
- Select "ideas" for testing in TV commercials.
- Complete a product-positioning plan.
- Recommend name for new product.
- Develop and evaluate new-product introduction tests.
- Select test-market cities for new-product testing.
- Use test results to determine new product's positioning within the market.
- Determine strategic opportunities for new product to exploit weaknesses of competing products.
- Determine levels of trade promotions for national expansion.

Decision Influencer

- Negotiate for resources with division general manager.
- Receive profit target from general manager that was to be included in budget plan.

- Meet with corporate executives in planning sessions.
- Make decisions on brand and present for approval of business unit manager.
- Request approval of plans from business unit managers.
- Meet with other marketing managers to examine various elements of the new product's marketing plan.
- Prepare and present a recommendation to top management concerning national expansion/distribution of the new product.
- Prepare financial statements highlighting profit and loss estimates of new product and new product's manageable risks.
- Meet with division president to discuss strategies and tactics for entering new markets.

Diplomat

- Hold meetings with sales force management to negotiate quarterly volume quotas and promotion schedules.
- Work with functional managers to develop plans for entering new businesses.
- Work with advertising agency to develop new approaches to improve brand sales.
- Meet regularly with ad agency account executive.
- Propose strategy for sales force management of new product introduction; work closely with sales management executives.

CHAPTER FIVE

Pillsbury

In the early 1980s, Pillsbury management realized that computer systems at Pillsbury had not kept up with the growth of the businesses. Pillsbury had been acquiring companies, and found that they needed outstanding computer support services to run them, combine them into an integrated company, and deal with an increasingly sophisticated wholesale and retail trade. Their studies led them to conclude that they needed a new and expanded effort to support businesses with the right kind of data and analysis. This need was becoming more important due to the extreme competitive and local nature of their businesses, so they put top priority on computer systems and made marketing systems an area of strategic focus.

Dr. Les Wanninger was appointed director of management systems at Pillsbury Foods, the arm of Pillsbury that contains the consumer and agriculture businesses. Les had worked in computing since his student days at Northwestern University in 1960. He was heavily involved with computing through his doctoral degree in chemical engineering (which centered around computing and model building). He worked for General Mills, Inc. in various areas: process control, marketing, and management of computing in the R&D organization. Les joined Pillsbury to run the technical support group. From there he moved into line product development; his job at that point was the development of new products. Les agreed to take his current position when it became clear that systems development was a top company priority.

One of Les's early activities was to develop the following, four-component strategic plan for management systems development at Pillsbury:

1. Ensure that end-user computing constitutes 70 percent of Pillsbury's total computing. Only the transaction-based systems should be centrally managed by a professional data processing group.
2. Update the 15-year-old systems. Pillsbury had historically been a batch, COBOL oriented company. They must modernize their systems and be constantly aware that new systems may change the way they do business. Les believes that business computing is becoming similar to R&D computing, which emphasizes data analysis. The users of the systems must have access to their data and the appropriate tools for doing analysis.
3. Develop the capability to get on top of new technology. The primary approach is to pilot test those new technologies that seem promising.
4. Look for areas where computing can be used in a competitive manner.

Within the marketing areas of the divisions, considerable progress had been made in giving the brand groups access to their data and in getting them to assume some of the responsibility for applying computing to their businesses.

THE MANAGEMENT SYSTEMS DEPARTMENT

Les realized that he needed a new organizational structure and operating philosophy for the management systems department. He saw that R&D was well run at Pillsbury and thus decided to use it as the role model for computing. R&D had a decentralized philosophy and structure that mirrored the company's divisional organization. Groups within the R&D organization were devoted to working with each division; they had a direct reporting relationship with the R&D management and an indirect relationship with the divisions; the management systems group was organized in the same way.

There were two key ingredients to this organizational approach: technologies and projects that used the technologies. Les created directors who have organizations that correspond to the divisions. For example, there is a director of the dry foods group within MSD who "belongs" to the dry foods people; in fact, the dry foods division pays for this group. To provide the technologies and technical support to these project oriented groups, Les created a technical core—the "emerging technologies" group—composed of an information center, the PC and office systems group, the development center, and a data management group. All of these groups support the division oriented project groups, who build systems for the divisions and provide support for end-user computing.

MARKETING RESEARCH

One of the key departments involved in the design and implementation of marketing databases and analysis systems is marketing research (MRD). Joel Levine, MRD's vice president, has been involved with the emerging computer systems since their inception. In the early 1980s, Joel attended an annual meeting of "The Workshop Group," a group of marketing research directors from large firms and a few research suppliers: the topic of the meeting was decision support systems. One of the important points made at that meeting was that "the products manager of the 1990s is entering high school today." These people will be joining Pillsbury with an entirely different set of computer skills than the people who joined the company in 1980. Thus, Pillsbury had better get ready to use the skills and knowledge of its future employees.

To this end, Joel joined with Les Wanninger and others in looking at what the company could (and should) be doing with computers. They looked at available decision support systems and talked to marketing people. The management of the pizza business was interested in taking the leadership in applying data oriented decision support systems in brand management. So a team from MSD, MRD, and the pizza group assessed the available decision support packages. After narrowing the choice to two packages, they sent each vendor a problem and a set of data, along with an invitation to make a presentation on the use of their system in solving the problem. One vendor gave a highly technical presentation about how to use his system that no one understood; the vendor had completely misread the audience. The other vendor, Tymshare, Inc., gave a presentation of Acustar that convinced both the technical people and the users that it was the appropriate system. Therefore, Pillsbury signed a contract with Tymshare to use Acustar on Tymshare computers.

A task force has been created within MRD to investigate the feasibility and desirability of acquiring the capability to analyze consumer and market research data on in-house computers. Currently, all such work is done by the research supplier. The task force is looking into downloading the data from the suppliers into personal computers for further analysis and reworking.

EXPERIENCE IN THE PIZZA GROUP

The Acustar system in the pizza group contains internal data on shipments, SAMI data on warehouse withdrawals, and MAJERS data on advertising features. The system has enabled the brand groups to quickly understand what has happened to the business. The resulting efficiency allows the groups to devote more time to thinking about the business rather than analyzing it. Two key uses of the system are tracking performance of the different brand items and identifying problems. Since the pizza business is primarily a sales "push" business, the brand groups are able to spot problems by focusing on the shipment data.

The primary users of Acustar are the assistant brand managers. Since the introduction of the system corresponded with Pillsbury's annual planning period, the brand groups spent a lot of time using the system to prepare the plan. They used it to replace reports and tables previously prepared by hand. The system is being used as a data retrieval and organization tool, not as an analysis tool. The assistant brand managers worked with the MSD people to create and then name a set of reports that are run regularly. These reports appear on a menu, thus eliminating the need to remember the names of the report-generation routines. Appendix A contains sample interactions between Acustar and a user.

DRY GROCERY MARKETING MIS STUDY

As the pizza group was gaining experience with Acustar, the marketing group in the dry grocery products division formed an MIS task force to study its own marketing information needs. This group completed its work in May 1984.

The task force concluded that the various brand groups were "data rich and information poor." Most of the needed data existed in some form, but the group's ability to transform these data into actionable information was inadequate. The practice of hand manipulation was labor intensive and time consuming, and it limited the group's exploration of alternatives. The task force felt that the group's information system was not capable of addressing marketing needs because it was designed for reporting, not analysis; formats and slow turnaround limited the analysis, and the needed data were on different computers and systems.

This study resulted in the identification of two categories of information needs: reporting and analysis.

Reporting

- Goal management required timely and actionable information to monitor and respond to changing business conditions.
- Crisis management required timely and actionable information to understand and respond to national and regional business issues.

Analysis

Computer capabilities to support the following activities were needed:

- Evaluate business problems and opportunities.
- Determine marketing programs on a regional basis.
- Measure program performance.
- Determine spending efficiencies.

Based on this evaluation, the task force recommended that the dry grocery information management system be computerized to address the needs of present and future marketing groups. Its recommendations included database and system needs.

Database Needs

1. Revise current information systems to provide actionable data.
   a. Revise current reports.
   b. Delete unnecessary reports.
   c. Improve access to "hidden" data, that is, data that are computerized but not available for tracking.
2. Generate additional data.
   a. Keep data at the lowest possible level of aggregation.
   b. Provide the following new data:
      (i) Daily and weekly deliveries by deal area/region/account.
      (ii) Deal tracking.
      (iii) Advertising and promotion spending by region.
      (iv) Financial reports by brand/area/region/deal area.
      (v) Display tracking.
3. Centralize all the data in one database.

System Needs

The key need was a system with analytical as well as reporting capabilities. Data and user oriented factors were considered important.

1. Data oriented factors.
   a. Accessibility: ease of data retrieval and expansion of the database.
   b. Flexibility to analyze data within various time parameters (days, weeks, months).
   c. Integration of data from different sources (shipments, SAMI, MAJERS, Leemis).
2. User oriented factors.
   a. Allow "think time" with interactive analytical capabilities. This need involves the iterative procedure of downloading some data, charting and graphing it, thinking about the data, doing more data extraction and analysis, thinking, and so on.
   b. Fast turnaround.

    c. Communications between the workstation and the mainframe should provide for local display and printing, graphics, state-of-the-art tools, and ergonomics.

    d. System must be user friendly.

    e. Adequate training must be provided to users.

    f. Management must be educated about issues and the value of the system.

    g. The workstations must fit into the current office arrangement.

To implement these recommendations, the task force suggested that Acustar be installed and that an IBM PC be provided to every member of the brand groups who desired one. The task force also designed the following training program:

1. Introduction to PC: 0.5 day.
2. Lotus 1-2-3: 2.0 days.
3. Acustar: 2.5 days.
4. PC and marketing reports: 0.5 day.

The task force organized and led an ongoing users group to support the individual users.

INTERVIEW WITH A GROUP MARKETING MANAGER

Hal Ransom, a group marketing manager of the consumer foods group in the dry grocery products division, is a strong proponent of the task force's views and recommendations. The use of spreadsheets for model building, "what-if" conjecturing, and hypothesis testing has changed his group's decision-making process. Everyone in Hal's group has a PC and had become proficient in Acustar by March 1, 1985. The group has standardized on the Symphony integrated software package and the IBM PC.

The real advantage of Acustar is the availability of data.

> We had to rely on systems people for our data and the quality depended upon our ability to tell them what we wanted, and we were not very good at telling them. The process took months, and when we got the reports, our needs had changed. So the process started again. It was very frustrating.

> Since we were limited to national numbers in static report form, we "big-pictured" it. But we need to view "little pictures," that is, to base our analysis and decision on 60 local markets.

The workstation should give us the capability to prepare reports and presentations with graphs integrated into text. We will soon have one secretary working for 10 to 15 people versus 4 or 5 today. I foresee the day when we will speak to the PC rather than type on it.

Personal computers tied to Acustar will free us from the financial orientation of the old systems in which everything was reported in calendar months. Since marketing programs do not begin and end on calendar months, we need the capability of delivering the data in periods that correspond to the problem under study.

We are making real progress; Acustar will replace the status reports and provide a real-time, dynamic environment. Its only limitation will be our limitation and imagination. We will be able to make better decisions and to track their impact on the business.

One of our current projects is the development of a system for regional profit and loss statements. Data are being pulled from the financial systems and input into SAS for on-line analysis and downloading into personal computers.

One of my assignments is to demonstrate to my boss, the marketing director, and his boss, the general manager, how personal computers can be useful to them. They are word oriented people; we must find ways to make the PC amenable to them.

We are at the bottom of a mountain that we cannot see the top of.

APPENDIX: ACUSTAR DIALOGUE[1]

The user interacts with Acustar by answering questions that appear on the screen. If the user does not know the answer, s/he types a question mark and the system responds with a list of legal answers.

The following dialogue was used to integrate databases with different time periods and to deseasonalize the data. (Note: User responses are underlined.)

---

[1] The material in this Appendix was taken from "Acustar—Your Marketing Information Assistant," a marketing brochure distributed by Tymshare.

```
EQUALIZE DATABASE(S) TO ONE OF THE STANDARD TIME FRAMES
(Y/N)?  Y
EQUALIZE DATABASE(S) TO WHICH TIME FRAME?  MONTHS

ADJUST PERIOD ENDING DATES OF ANY DATABASE(S) (Y/N)  Y
ENTER THE # OF DAYS TO ADJUST THE PERIOD ENDING DATES OF
EACH DATABASE (E.G. ''15 EARLIER'', ''20 LATER'', OR
''0'' FOR NO ADJUSTMENT):
        # OF DAYS TO ADJUST DATABASE: FACTORY?  0
        # OF DAYS TO ADJUST DATABASE: SAMI?  28 EARLIER
        # OF DAYS TO ADJUST DATABASE: NIELSEN?  56 EARLIER

ADD ANY DESEASONALIZED MEASURE (''Y'', ''N'', OR ''LIST'')?  Y
ENTER NAME OF MEASURE TO DESEASONALIZE?  ?

LEGAL ANSWERS TO THIS QUESTION INCLUDE:
            FACTORY DOLLARS
            FACTORY POUNDS
            SAMI DOLLARS
            SAMI EQUIVALENT UNITS
            NIELSEN DOLLARS
            NIELSEN EQUIVALENT UNITS
            NIELSEN DISTRIBUTION
            NIELSEN OUT OF STOCK

ENTER NAME OF MEASURE TO DESEASONALIZE?  DOLLAR
**THE FOLLOWING LEGAL ANSWERS MATCH YOUR ANSWER:  DOLLAR
            FACTORY DOLLARS
            SAMI DOLLARS
            NIELSEN DOLLARS

ENTER NAME OF MEASURE TO DESEASONALIZE?  SAMI DOL
```

Acustar allows the user to print reports in a standard format
or to customize reports using various options. The following
dialogue produced a report showing regional trends in market
share and price for competitive brands. The report format had
been prespecified, but facilities were provided for changing two
parameters.

```
ENTER REPORT TYPE?  BRAND TREND

USE ''STANDARD'', ''SEQUENTIAL'', OR ''VARIABLE'' TREND
FORMAT?  VARIABLE

PRINT EACH CALCULATION IN SEPARATE ''ROW'', ''COLUMN'', OR
''PAGE''?  ROW
```

The following dialogue produced a regression equation with sales as the dependent variable and price and advertising share as the predictor variables.

ENTER ANALYZE COMMAND? <u>DISPLAY COLUMNS</u>

WHICH COLUMNS (C##-## ''ALL'', OR ''SAME'')? <u>ALL</u>
            COL1-   CASE SALES
            COL2-   SHARE OF VOICE
            COL3-   RETAIL PRICE/OUNCE
            COL4-   PROMOTIONAL SPENDING
            COL5-   NET DISTRIBUTION

ENTER ANALYZE COMMAND? <u>COMPUTE</u>

WHICH TEST OR CALCULATION? <u>MULTIPLE REGRESSION</u>

USE WHICH COLUMN AS DEPENDENT VARIABLE (C##)? <u>C1</u>

USE WHICH COLUMNS AS INDEPENDENT VARIABLES (C##-##)? <u>C2-3</u>

PART TWO

The Changing Environment

This part of the book takes the reader on a journey through the author's vision of the future marketing and computing environment. Chapter Six describes a multitude of trends and developments that are or will be occurring in the marketing world. Chapter Seven analyzes these developments and discusses their impact on the practice of marketing and the conduct of marketing management. One implication of the new data and technology is the need and the facilities for the management of the firm's knowledge as well as its information. Chapter Eight explores knowledge management and shows how it can be used to support sales and marketing.

Marketing Trends

This chapter discusses the dynamics of marketing; it focuses on the forces and developments that are or will be impacting both the practice of marketing and the use of computers in support of marketing activities. The major forces, developments, and trends involve the collection of marketing data and the use of computer technology.

DATA COLLECTION

The many recent developments in the methods of collecting marketing data will significantly alter the type of data available to marketing management. Two of these developments are the emergence of new firms, such as Information Resources, Inc., and the merger of older companies. Dun & Bradstreet, a major publisher, data supplier, and computer services company, purchased the A. C. Nielsen Company; the MAJERS Corporation purchased TRIM, Inc., a major vendor of scanner data and analysis; and Burke Marketing has merged with Time, Inc. (which owns SAMI). These developments seem to be pointing toward the use of electronics and telecommunications in the collection and dissemination of marketing information.

The following sections examine data collection trends in scanners, scanner panels, in-home monitoring of TV viewing, the use of computers by sales representatives, and integrated databases such as the MAJERS' MASTERTRACK.

Scanners

> Data point explosion! It's the researcher's dream come true. Data on thousands of UPCs from thousands of stores 52 times a year. Heaven![1]

A growing number of supermarket chains are installing UPC scanners in their stores, primarily to increase the efficiency of their check-out counters and their ordering and inventory control systems. Estimates by A. C. Nielsen Company indicate that as of December 1983, 8,150 stores were equipped with scanners, and that these stores accounted for over one third of total food-store sales. According to these estimates, there will be scanners in about 15,000 stores by 1988, accounting for 56 percent of total food-store sales.[2] Some companies in the survey thought this estimate was too low and anticipated a more rapid spread of the scanning technology.

A number of research data suppliers are signing contracts with the chains that permit them to purchase the data for resale to grocery manufacturers. The major suppliers of scanner data include Nielsen, TRIM, and NabScan. The last firm receives data from 700 stores representing over 30 chains in over 100 SMSAs. The data can be reported at the store, chain, or region level.

In addition, most scanner data suppliers offer a store observation service in which auditors visit the store on a weekly basis. With this service, data are available on volume, price, share, distribution, and in-store promotions. The data are usually collected weekly, and reported at either one- two- or four-week intervals.

The suppliers operate in one of two ways: collect and distribute data from all stores willing to supply data, or draw a scientific sample of stores in a chain or a market. Suppliers who use

---

[1] T. A. Clemens, "Scanning Store-by-Store Research—Management for Action." Presentation to the Advertising Research Foundation's 30th Annual Conference, Working Paper, A. C. Nielsen Co., March 6, 1984.

[2] "The Realization of Scanner-Based Research," *The Nielsen Researcher*, no. 1, 1985.

the second approach present the results at the chain and/or market levels but do not present the data at the store level.

Scanner data are currently being used primarily for testing and analysis. The weekly reporting frequency makes these data much better for reading the effects of promotions and price/product package changes than SAMI or Nielsen data. One manufacturer in the survey reported buying scanner data as a source of information on competitive brands that use store-door delivery and thus bypass the warehouses monitored by SAMI. Another manufacturer bought scanner data because it provides better retail price information than SAMI data.

The widespread use of scanner data as the primary source of volume tracking awaits several developments:

- Increase in the number of participating stores to the point where the results are projectable to numerous geographical regions.
- Research showing that the scanner data are congruent with the currently used tracking data (e.g., Nielsen or SAMI).
- Proof that the scanner data are "clean," that is, that they are relatively error free and capture almost all of the movement through the scanner stores.

However, the advantages of scanner data are so great that such data will almost surely supplant other data sources as the primary tracking and analysis system. Brand managers complain that data from bimonthly store audits arrive too late to be "actionable"—the data only explain what happened but do not provide the opportunity for corrective action. Weekly data at the store and/or chain level provide a base for observing problems as they arise. The existence of scanner data at the individual market and chain level will accelerate the growing interest in regional marketing. A detailed description of the efforts of one data supplier provides a view of the scanner oriented software being developed by all the suppliers.

TRIM, Inc., recently purchased by the MAJERS Corporation from Harte-Hanks Communications, is a pioneer in supplying scanner data to manufacturers and their advertising agencies. TRIM purchases scanner data from retail chains and sells these data on a syndicated basis to the manufacturers. To facilitate this process, TRIM has developed the SalesScan system.

SalesScan does three things. First, it provides TRIM's clients with a source of combined TRIM scanner data and data supplied by the client about coupon drops, in-store displays, and advertising features. Second, it is a linking facility for establishing communication between a client PC and the databases on the TRIM computer. The client uses a menu-based system on a local PC to indicate the parts or structure of the database s/he wants to use. When the user is finished making the database selection, the software dials the TRIM computer, logs the user onto the software, transfers the desired database information to the TRIM mainframe, extracts the data from the files, and transfers the data to a file on the PC disk drive. This data-extraction software is menu driven; the user moves the cursor with the arrow keys and indicates the desired data by pressing the ENTER key.

The third component of SalesScan is PC-based software for doing promotion and price analysis. The analysis system is written specifically for the PC and the database; it knows the variables and the structure of the data. Its capabilities include graphics, a special spreadsheet-type environment, and tools for forecasting and analysis. Output can be routed to PC printers and plotters.

The promotion/pricing analysis component develops a baseline sales curve that shows the levels of sales the brands would have achieved in the absence of seasonal factors and promotions. A standard deviation is placed around this baseline. Each promotional event is then displayed in relation to the baseline. Thus, one can use the difference between actual sales and baseline sales to ascertain the impact of the event.

The software on the PC does not provide a general-purpose system for reporting and analysis; it is specifically written for the analysis of promotions and promotion related price changes. However, the client can contract with TRIM to tailor the system for specific needs of the managers in the client firm. The actual software is written and maintained by Mathematica, Inc. on a contract basis with TRIM. At the present time, the data that have been downloaded to the PC are in a format that matches the needs of the application package running on the PC. These data are not easily accessed by other PC programs.

TRIM has adopted an interesting pricing strategy for SalesScan: the system is free to firms that purchase the scanner data. TRIM is in the business of selling data; it is not a systems or time-sharing company. It views SalesScan as a value-added component of its basic product—the scanner data. In addition, SalesScan lowers TRIM's business costs by reducing the mailing and communication expense associated with distributing data.

TRIM sees that products such as SalesScan call for a different type of computer than those generally available, specifically, computers with large disk space and very fast input/output capabilities. Such a computer needs maximal data management capabilities and minimal computational capabilities. It will do only storage and input/output, and very little processing of the data.

Scanner Panels

Scanner panels involve samples of people in different markets who shop in scanner-equipped stores that record and store data on every item purchased by the household. The panels in each market include about 2,000 to 2,500 households. The major suppliers of scanner panel data are Information Resources, Inc. (IRI), with its Behavior Scan service and Burke Marketing's Test Marketing Group. In addition, the A. C. Nielsen Company offers a service called Electronic Research for Insights into Marketing (ERIM). The new versions of the scanner panel services provide (in addition to the panel data) store-level data from the scanners and in-store audits. Hence, they supply data on individual consumer purchases and data on the environment the consumer faces when making a purchase. In addition, most of these services have split-cable television facilities that permit the manufacturer to send different or additional advertising messages to a portion of the panel.

Before the advent of scanners, the primary source of data on consumer purchase behavior was national diary panels. Such data come from a sample of 8,000 to 10,000 people who keep diaries of their households' purchases in many product categories. The data are subject to recording error and suffer from perceived projectability problems.

In general, scanner panels are currently being used as test-marketing vehicles, and not for tracking and diagnostic purposes. Such usage awaits the expansion of the services to more and larger markets. Whereas the scanner data provide performance data at the store, chain, and market level, the scanner-panel data provide insight into the brand's performance at the individual consumer level. These panel data can be aggregated to consumer segments defined by demographic, psychographic, or buying behavior characteristics. They permit the determination of trends in trial, repeat, brand switching, coupon usage, and other consumer related behaviors.

Scanner data will allow firms to develop response functions at the store, chain, or market level. These response functions will relate volume to causal factors, such as price, displays, promotions, and so on. Given these response functions, the brand manager can optimize the placement of his or her marketing resources.

Scanner panel data will permit the development of similar response functions for different demographic segments. These models will play a role in the selection of target markets and media selection.

The trend toward using scanner panel data was accelerated with the formation of Information Resources, Inc., (IRI), which offers a data collection service called Behavior Scan that collects data from UPC scanners, household scanner panels, monitoring devices on household TV sets, and in-store audits. In early 1984, IRI offered Behavior Scan information in 8 markets, with about 80 scanner-equipped stores and 20,000 scanner-panel households.

IRI equips almost every grocery store in its markets with scanner equipment. These devices collect and send data on the total store movement to the IRI computers. A panel composed of 2,500 households uses an identification card when shopping, and the scanner collects and stores the panel's purchases for later transmittal to IRI. Each panel household has microcomputers on the rear of its television sets that monitor the status of the TV (on/off and channel selection) every five seconds. The IRI computer telephones each household computer nightly and downloads the TV status data to the central computer. In addition, IRI has a team of auditors who are in each store in the eight markets three to five times per week monitoring prices and display and promotional activities, collecting coupons the consumers redeemed in the store, and gathering data on the advertising features being run by the stores in local newspapers. By mid-1984, this system had generated 16 billion characters of data that IRI stores on-line and offers to its clients.

An additional feature of the household panels is that each member is a cable-TV subscriber. IRI has arrangements with the cable companies that allow them to split the households into two or more matched groups and send different TV commercials to each group, thus permitting testing of advertising variables such as content, level, or time of day.

While most of its current markets are relatively small, IRI is beginning to provide similar services in major markets. Its goal is to have 12 to 15 such markets; the first three are Los Angeles, Chicago, and New York. The approach is to use sampling techniques to identify several demographically defined neighborhoods. IRI will then equip the neighborhood stores with scanners, use auditors to monitor the in-store activities, and recruit a scanner panel in each market. IRI plans to have a national database generated by 35,000 households.

Recently, IRI began developing a modeling service in which IRI analysts will work with clients to develop models that link a brand's volume to the price and promotion activities of the brand and its competitors. The models relate volume to price, ad features, displays, and coupons. They are configured to measure the impact of each factor either alone or in combination.

IRI has received enthusiastic response to this new service. However, it became clear that the brand managers needed a way to integrate the model into their ongoing planning and evaluation activities. To this end, IRI is offering a marketing planning simulator that runs on an IBM PC in Lotus 1-2-3. This simulator takes the response function developed in the modeling activity and integrates it into the brand's business plan. The result is a diskette containing a Lotus 1-2-3 spreadsheet that permits the brand manager to simulate the volume and profit impact of various marketing strategies.

IRI is currently taking this modeling and simulation approach to local markets. The company combines its response function with market information to provide a market-level simulator.

Also under development is a simulator for the retailer. IRI will analyze the retailer's scanner data and provide a simulator to the retailer for use on a PC. Retailers are requesting analyses of each of their categories to determine its sensitivity to price, display, shelf space, and ad featuring. These models are combined with volume and margin information to provide each store with the ability to optimize its product selection, as well as its advertising and merchandising activities.

In-Home Measurement of TV Viewing

An additional feature being added to the scanner panel system is the placement of a small microcomputer in each television set in the panelists' households. This computer reads and records the status of the TV at regular intervals, for example, every five seconds. These data are stored in the microcomputer, and transmitted via telephone lines to a host computer once a day.

Such augmented scanner panel systems provide data on

- Purchases.
- TV viewing patterns.
- Coupon usage.
- Store environment while the purchase is being made.

Also, the systems are technically capable of collecting data from household members by an interactive, on-screen questionnaire.

Burke Marketing Services and Arbitron Ratings Company are testing the ScanAmerica meter, which measures TV viewing by individuals and tracks product purchases at the household level. Consumers record their TV viewing choices by pushing buttons on the meter's remote control keypad. These same consumers will use a hand-held scanning wand to record their purchases; the wand will read the UPC stripes on products. The TV viewing and purchase data will be stored in the meter and periodically uploaded to large computers.

Retail Audits by Computers

The declining price of small computers is making it economically practical to equip a firm's field sales force with small computers. These computers can be used by the salespeople to audit their product categories in the retail stores. They make it easy to collect and store information such as pricing, out-of-stocks, number of shelf facings, shelf positioning, product rotation, point-of-sale usage, display activities, new brands, and so on. These small computers can transmit their data files to larger machines at the end of the day.

MAJERS MASTERTRACK

The MAJERS Corporation has initiated a new service called MASTERTRACK that uses modern information-processing technology to measure, analyze, and report promotion activity of retailers and manufacturers. Software is provided for gaining instant access to the data stored on the MAJERS computer in Omaha, Nebraska. The user interacts with the computer via a series of menus that lead to a specification of the desired data in time period, brands, manufacturers, retail accounts, geographical region, and measure. Future developments call for downloading data to a promotion management workstation built around an IBM PC.

MAJERS offers three separate databases that can be accessed in an integrated manner. The data are available on a weekly and account-level basis.

- Feature Ad database contains data on advertising features (advertisements placed by retailers in local newspapers) in all major markets.
- Consumer Promotion database contains couponing, refund, and special event activity. It contains data on all consumer promotion activity delivered in newspapers, freestanding inserts, magazines, and direct mail vehicles.
- Display and Shelf Management database is a tracking of in-store retail conditions in each market.

These three databases are integrated because measures are made in common markets and in the same stores in the markets. The result is a database that contains "causal" information, that is, information on the factors that cause or influence consumer purchases. To obtain the other piece of the consumer picture, the purchase data, MAJERS recently purchased TRIM, Inc., which collects and markets retail scanner data. The result will be a truly integrated database that will permit the analysis and reporting of promotion activity and its sales impact on a weekly and account-specific basis. The data will permit brand groups to obtain precise and specific information on the impact of their own or competing promotions. For instance, a manufacturer will be able to measure the impact of an end-aisle display on the sales of the displayed brand and all other brands in Safeway stores in San Francisco.

TRADE PRACTICES

Computer technology is also impacting the retail and wholesale trade. Retailers are beginning to use their scanner data for strategic and tactical decision making. Also, manufacturers, wholesalers, and retailers are adopting a uniform communications standard that permits their computers to "talk" to each other.

Retail Use of Scanner Data

Retail stores have been installing UPC scanners to improve their ordering and inventory control systems and to increase the efficiency of their customer check-out lanes. Recently, they have been able to develop the tools and systems that allow store managers to use the data for merchandising decisions. An example of such a system is ScanLab, developed by General Foods and available through the Food Marketing Institute (FMI).[3]

General Foods undertook the development of the system to learn how scanner data could be used as a resource for their 2,400 salespeople. They have given the system's rights to FMI, who sells the system to retailers for $1,500 to run on IBM computers. The software running on a small IBM System 34 or 36 provides a highly economical means of building a store-level information system.

ScanLab provides seven weekly averages for each item in the store: unit sales, dollar sales, gross profit, gross profit per cubic foot, estimated shelf inventory, return on inventory invested (ROII), and an ROII index. These data can be used to reallocate the shelf space and make decisions about which products to carry. Analysts can use them to track and test merchandising, pricing, advertising, and promotion alternatives.

With the retailer having this type of information system, the "channel control" will shift from the manufacturers to the retailers and manufacturers will be required to collect and/or purchase a comparable database. Manufacturers will have to know as much about their brands as do their customers. The brand groups will use these data to prepare microlevel marketing pro-

---

[3] Robert E. O'Neill, "A Competitive Weapon with a Future," *Progressive Grocer*, June 1984, pp. 53–59.

grams that enhance or build on each brand's performance in a chain, a division of a chain, or even a single retail store.

Uniform Communications Standards

Companies such as General Foods and Pillsbury sell their products to wholesalers and large chains. This selling and buying process generates a lot of paper and telephone calls. To improve the efficiency of this process, the industry has adopted Uniform Communications Standards (UCS) that make it possible for manufacturers, wholesalers, brokers, and retailers to exchange information electronically.

The purpose of the standards is to facilitate the development of communications systems that will lead to lower costs of doing business. Buyers issue 15 million purchase orders each year, which in turn trigger 15 million bills of lading and 15 million invoices. The overall transactions result in about 100 million messages flowing among the 2,000 distributors, 5,000 manufacturers, and 2,000 brokers. The goal is to reduce the overall number of messages by half.[4]

The implementation of such computer-to-computer ordering could impact the practice of brand management by increasing the amount of available data and reducing the time lags involved in getting the data to the brand groups. Most brand managers monitor their brand's shipment data very closely. However, it is not unusual for the firms to use relatively old systems for tracking their shipments. These systems tend to operate on a batch basis, and only provide information at regular intervals. The new communications standards may cause the firms to rewrite their systems using new software technologies. Hence, the data may be in a form that permits easy extraction and transmittal to the marketing information databases. The result would be accurate and timely data on orders and shipments of brand items to individual customers.

---

[4] Robert E. O'Neill, "A Better Way to Do Business," *Progressive Grocer*, August 1984, pp. 71–74.

Impact on Marketing and Management

The practice of marketing will be altered by computing and information technology. This chapter contains a group of scenarios that provide a "window" into the future.

EXPANDED VIEW OF MARKETING DATA

The data in the typical marketing information system are one part of a relatively vast information base available to marketing managers. A considerable portion of the data are not in the computer systems. Thus, marketing and data processing managers are beginning to consider the computerization of additional marketing data.

A considerable amount of the brand group's time is spent locating additional data and combining it with the data in the MMIS. For example, a common activity of an assistant product manager is to assess the effectiveness of a promotional program. One typical approach is to calculate the change in sales or market share before, during, and after the promotion, broken down by on- and off-promotion geographical areas. Before the MMIS can be used to extract and summarize the data, the assistant product manager must determine the actual dates of the promotion and the regions where the product was promoted. Depending on the manual filing and information system, this process can require several phone calls and considerable time. The time spent in this single activity must be multiplied many times because brand groups that have direct access to a good MMIS are constantly using it to design and evaluate their various marketing programs.

Traditional databases contain data that vary along two dichotomous dimensions. First, they are either time oriented or cross sectional. Time oriented data measure a phenomenon for which the time of occurrence is of primary importance. The time of a sale is important for tracking purposes, as is the date of the airing of a television commercial or the date a member of a consumer panel made a purchase. Cross-sectional data tend to have a common data associated with all the observations in the database. A consumer survey is an example of cross-sectional data; all the respondents were surveyed during the same time period, for example, August 1984.

The second dimension is whether the data are collected and stored on an individual or an aggregate level. Consumer panel and survey data are collected and stored at the level of the individual respondent; Nielsen retail audit and scanner data are aggregated to the chain or market level.

The following chart shows a breakdown of traditional data along these two dimensions.

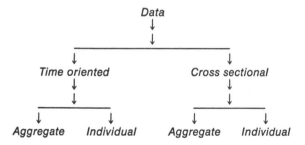

Time oriented/aggregate data are what constitute today's MMIS; it contains shipments, warehouse withdrawals, retail sales, market share, price, distribution, inventory, advertising features, and promotional expenditure data at the national and regional level. These data are organized or aggregated around regularly occurring intervals such as weeks, months, or bimonths.

Another type of time-oriented/aggregate data exists that is heavily used but not generally computerized: the marketing program events. These data cannot be included in the MMIS because they occur at irregular intervals and, as stated above, the MMIS is organized around regularly occurring time periods. As was shown in the example above, the brand groups are repeatedly extracting and summarizing the MMIS data so that these data correspond to the timing and location of marketing programs. If the MMIS had the appropriate software and event oriented data, the user could issue commands such as

GET SALES WHEN BRAND X WAS ON DEAL AND OFF DEAL.

As the systems are currently constructed, the user must manually locate the dates of each deal and then use the MMIS commands to partition the sales data into the two time periods (on deal and off deal). The marriage of time and event oriented data awaits a future MMIS.

Time oriented/individual data include consumer panel data, transactions, sales orders, and sales calls. These items are similar to the program events as they do not occur at regular time periods—they occur irregularly. The firms tends to computerize their transactions and summarize them for inclusion in the MMIS. The sales calls data also tend to be computerized, but are not included in today's MMIS. And consumer panel data are computerized, but usually not accessible to the brand groups. However, as scanner panels spread throughout the country, there will be increased demand for the inclusion of scanner-panel data in the MMIS databases.

Scanner and/or scanner-panel data will allow the firm to trace the impact of marketing events, such as an end-aisle display or an ad feature, on sales or brand switching. However, the file management facilities in the MMIS must evolve to deal with the combination of data that occur at regular *and* irregular intervals.

Cross-sectional/individual data include information on individual consumers (from surveys), retail and wholesale customers, brokers, suppliers, and competitors. Some of the data are computerized; the marketing research group may have computer tapes from the surveys, and a trade relations group may have a database about the firm's retailers, wholesalers, and brokers.

However, these data are not a part of today's MMIS. Data on the trade would be useful for answering a question like: What is our share in large chains versus small chains versus independents? A brand group could answer this question if the MMIS contained data at the chain level. However, the user would have to manually determine which chains belonged to which category, and then devise a method of extracting and summarizing the data by the three categories. But, if the MMIS contained data on each chain (such as location, size, number of stores, and total annual sales), and if the MMIS had the appropriate software, then this question could be answered without resort to manual methods and recoding of the data. The new databases emerging from scanner data will make it possible to ask such a question.

Cross-sectional/aggregate data are used for media analysis and regional segmentation, and have been computerized by some firms. In addition, several outside, time-sharing companies offer access to these types of data. A number of these companies was using systems like the ClusterPlus Zip Code system offered by Donnelly Marketing Information Services and Simmons Market Research Bureau. ClusterPlus was developed from an analysis of the 1980 U.S. census data, using more than 1,500 demographic variables to develop 47 distinctive lifestyle clusters and product consumption profiles. This system has been adapted to the Area of Dominant Influence (ADI) geographical breakdowns and married with television-viewing and radio-listening data from Arbitron Ratings to produce a database on media exposure, product purchase, and demographic characteristics, broken down by regions of the country. If these data were part of the MMIS, a manager could easily ask questions of the following type:

- What is our share trend in regions where the average age is greater than 30?
- What is the propensity for buying our brand when it is on deal in those regions where the typical consumer has above-average income, is in a blue-collar family, and lives in a rural area?
- How do our sales break down by regions in which TV situation comedies have below average, average, and above average ratings?

This breakdown of data into time oriented versus cross-sectional/aggregate versus individual/regular versus irregular has uncovered the need to combine tracking and event data that are dynamic with relatively static information on customers and regions. Therefore, the MMIS must evolve to handle the marriage of data that have different attributes and structures. Perhaps the future MMIS will have to be built around flexible database management systems rather than the file management systems that are at the core of today's MMIS.

The trend away from the analysis of national data and toward sales region analysis to market analysis to chain analysis and perhaps to store-level analysis will require the marriage of the time oriented performance data with the more static entity data on regions, chains, markets, and stores. These small datasets will usually involve (1) the status of a market participant (competitors, chains, stores), (2) the status of the consumers in geographical regions (age, income, housing type), and (3) marketing events (new product introduction, promotion). While today's firm has most of the needed data, these data are in the hands of many individuals throughout the organization. In an end-user and distributed-processing environment, those individuals would be the best people to computerize and maintain the datafiles containing information in their area of expertise. The software and hardware should accommodate such companywide distribution of responsibility. In addition, some of these data files currently reside at the firm's advertising agencies. The telecommunications facilities should exist for tying these data into the system.

REGIONAL MARKETING

Almost all of the firms interviewed in this survey indicated an increased or new emphasis on regional marketing. These firms have recognized that consumers exhibit different types of behaviors in different areas of the country, and that these differences offer an opportunity to the brand groups. Moreover, the brands face a different competitive structure in the various geographical regions. One brand manager defined regions according to which brands lead the market in a given area. He has his information system tuned to this regional definition, and aggregates his SAMI and shipment data to correspond to these regions rather than the SAMI markets or the firm's sales territories. Finally, wholesale and retail practices vary throughout the United States.

This emphasis on regional marketing is relatively new in most of the firms. It is replacing the notion that "we have national brands and market them the same way across the country." There seem to be several reasons behind this shift.

1. Books such as *The Nine Nations of North America* and magazines such as *The American Demographer* have served to increase the general awareness of regional differences in the United States.[1] The first depicts the North American continent as being composed of nine separate nations rather than the three nations (United States, Canada, and Mexico).

2. Data are becoming available for analyzing regional and local markets. For instance, Ogilvy & Mather, the New York ad agency, offers a computerized database of consumer profiles segmented by the "nine nations." Also, National Decision Systems offers six national, demographic, databases on a single optical disk for access via an IBM PC.

3. Executive development seminars run by consulting firms and universities have highlighted the differences and introduced the notion of taking strategic advantage of these differences.

4. The firms have recognized that on a national basis their product categories are growing slowly, if at all. However, growth rates vary by region, thus providing opportunities for growth not available when viewed from a national perspective.

5. The firms are facing a more sophisticated trade, one with better information about the desires of the consumers in their location. To deal with this situation, the firms must recognize the regional differences and offer marketing programs to their customers accordingly.

The following statements by marketing managers interviewed during the background study indicate the extent and type of interest in regional marketing.

- "It used to be if you mentioned regional, the response was 'too inefficient, we are a national brand.' Now, emphasis on regional is much greater. Big impact of *Nine Nations*."
- "The world is very different from the way we have defined it in the past; we need to develop spending principles that recognize regional differences."

---

[1] Joel Garreau, *The Nine Nations of North America* (Boston: Houghton Mifflin, 1981).

- "The concept of a national brand is becoming a figment of our imagination."
- "For this company to achieve its objectives, it must go to local focus and learn how to better manage marketing data."
- "We 'big-pictured" it because we were limited to national numbers in static report form; we need to view 'little pictures' in 60 markets."
- "We will bite the bullet and do everything regionally."
- "We built a 'megadatabase' in Lotus 1-2-3 that contained a lot of data from many sources. We did this because we were frustrated with not being able to understand local markets."
- "Regional marketing has become so important that we have put zone managers into the field; they analyze local markets and prepare regional marketing programs."

This shift in emphasis is forcing the brand groups to do more thorough analyses of the regions and to deal with much more data. Some of them speak of "data overload" when referring to the stacks of reports from SAMI (on warehouse withdrawals by brand in each of 51 regions), and from MAJERS (on advertising features by each chain in the same 51 markets.

The firms are searching for ways to implement the regional marketing concepts. One company has instituted a new organizational structure that has 10 zone managers in the marketing organization. These managers have brand experience and oversee the activities of all the brands in their zone. They will be able to design marketing programs and events that take advantage of the unique aspects of the consumers and market in their zone. This scheme provides a matrixed product management organization as well as a regional sales force.

CHANNEL POWER SHIFT

The spread of UPC scanners in supermarkets is causing a shift in "channel power" toward the retailer. Whereas scanners were originally installed as devices for improving the efficiency of store operations, they are now beginning to provide data for use in tactical and strategic decision making at the retail store level.

Since scanner data have value to manufacturers, the retailers began to save it for resale. Technological developments are now making it possible to provide computer access to the data at the store level in a form that facilitates merchandising decision making. The price of small minicomputers has fallen to the point where it is economically feasible to consider placing computers in the individual stores. An entry-level IBM System 36 costs under $25,000 and runs the ScanLab software being distributed to retailers by the Ford Marketing Institute. This software allows the retailer to measure the volume, profit, and return on inventory of all the items in the store.

Moreover, consulting firms such as McKinsey & Company and Information Resources, Inc., as well as the Food Marketing Institute, are providing consulting and data analysis services that make it easier for retailers to take advantage of their scanner data in making merchandising decisions. The result will be an increase in the retailer's knowledge about the products and merchandising programs that increase the profits in each individual store.

Having gained this knowledge and analysis capability, the retailer will play an increased role, that is, become more proactive, in decisions concerning products, prices, promotions, shelf placement and space, and advertising features. This proactive decision making will result in the retailer assuming even more control over the way products are marketed and merchandised in the store. Hence, a shift in channel power toward the retailer.

SALES FORCE COMPUTERIZATION

Increased usage of computerized information by the retailers will cause the firm to provide similar facilities to the field sales force. And falling computer prices will facilitate sales force computerization.

Small, hand-held computers will be used by the sales representatives to enter data on sales call activities and the store's status. Such devices can even be used to assist in a sales presentation. The regional offices of the hierarchical sales organization can be economically equipped with personal computers or small multiuser machines. These computers can be connected to the firm's main network, thus providing direct communication between the field representatives and the home-marketing managers.

MERGER OF SALES AND MARKETING

The new technological developments may lead to a blurring of the distinction between marketing and sales, or even to a merger of the two functions. Most packaged goods firms now separate marketing activities from selling activities. Most of the marketing planning, analysis, and decision making is assigned to the brand groups and the higher-level marketing managers. The implementation of the marketing programs and the actual selling function is assigned to the sales organization. However, this separation may be short-lived.

The root cause of the anticipated blurring/merger can be traced to scanner data and other associated technological developments that will make it possible to distribute some of the marketing functions throughout the sales organization. And the shift in channel power to the retailer may dictate that this redistribution occur.

As the use of scanners spreads and the data suppliers learn to handle the data, scanner data will begin to replace store audit data (e.g., traditional Nielsen data) as the primary data source for tracking consumer sales. Nielsen, for example, has begun to "bundle" their scanner data with their store audit data. In addition, new services will provide highly detailed views of the in-store environment faced by the consumer. An example is the MAJERS MASTERTRACK service, which provides information on ad feature and display activity in over 100 markets by product category, brand, and individual account. Finally, the use of hand-held computers by a firm's sales force will provide data on store conditions in most of the country's stores.

These new data will provide much more detail: more markets, weekly reporting, and even store-level data. The result will be a data explosion that will lead to an increased ability to "read" and understand local markets, and to measure the impact of promotional events in these markets.

The natural move toward local marketing will be accentuated by the new ability to understand the markets and to base plans and programs on analysis rather than intuitive feelings. The result will be increased emphasis on local marketing.

But how can a three-person brand group plan, direct, implement, and evaluate local marketing activities in 100 markets? The concept of product management seems to be based on the idea of national programs for national brands, programs that make heavy use of mass media and national promotional events. These marketing programs can be managed by a brand group, provided that advertising agencies do most of the advertising work and other marketing professionals assist with the details of the promotional planning and direct the implementation (which is now handled by the field sales organization). Going from a strategy of national marketing with some regional promotions to a local marketing philosophy calls for major organizational changes.

One approach to local marketing is to assign some of the marketing responsibility to the people in the local markets—the local sales managers. The future will probably see these managers assuming more formal responsibility for the tactical marketing programs in their markets. This in turn will result in a blurring of the split between sales and marketing because the field people will be "adding local value" to a national brand via advertising and sales promotion vehicles.

The hierarchical organizational structures and the division between the sales and marketing organizations were designed decades ago—before the arrival of current information technologies. Gorry and Scott Morton believe that firms will restructure their decision processes to take advantage of new technologies.[2] The spread of information technologies may indeed cause the firms to undertake a restructuring that permits them to increase their competitive position by leveraging the use of information and knowledge for both marketing and sales.

This restructuring may lead to more marketing responsibility for the managers in the field, particularly for tactical marketing or marketing aimed at the trade rather than the consumer. This situation is similar to that faced by soft drink companies who have an independent bottler network. The bottlers are usually responsible for all local marketing activities, with the brand manager providing advice and assistance.

---

[2] G. A. Gorry and M. Scott Morton, "A Framework for Management Information Systems," *Sloan Management Review*, Fall 1971, pp. 55–70.

What is the role of a brand group if this scenerio proves to be correct? Clearly, brand groups will continue to be responsible for national marketing programs, for example, network advertising. The importance of a unified brand strategy will require that these groups be the primary brand strategists. Study of the consumer will remain their province. They can conduct research that looks across the sales regions and districts to learn the effectiveness of the tactical elements being employed in the various regions; they can devise tactical plans and programs for the field force.

Perhaps the brand manager will become more of an educator and researcher. S/he studies the broader markets and issues, devises general strategies and tactics, and then educates the field force on the issues and approaches. These future managers may evolve to become a combination of today's brand manager and brand research manager, with a touch of the educator thrown in.

NEW WAYS TO EXPLOIT INFORMATION

The following story was told to the author by a vice president in a large package goods firm:

> We have had an extended debate for one of our major brands. Its sales have steadily increased, but it has been losing market share for the past few years. I was only able to understand the reasons for this situation by inputting several different data series into my personal computer and viewing the market from different perspectives. A graph containing three different data items produced an insightful view of the situation, and allowed me to conclude that the brand was inherently strong, and that we needed an additional brand, one with attributes that match the way a new set of consumers are now approaching the product category.

This quote provides an illustration of the role of graphics in marketing analysis and decision making. The firms in the survey that had adopted personal computers beyond those capable of simple budget analysis had begun to use graphics in their daily work. Most reported that their company was oriented to numerical display of data before the arrival of the personal computers. The ease of producing graphs and charts in packages such as Lotus 1-2-3 and Chartmaster has greatly facilitated their use.

Further, firms that are planning for the "data overload" problem when scanner and scanner-panel data become widely available are beginning to think about the use of graphics as a means of "wading through all of that data." And, hardware and software vendors are beginning to develop software for use with such data. Intelligent Software Systems in Amherst, Massachusetts, is working on an intelligent, trainable, graphic display package designed to assist decision makers in analyzing large amounts of data.

> It has three features: it is personalizable, it has facilities for the graphical presentation of data in a wide variety of formats, and it contains a user-programmable event monitor that automatically searches the data for user-defined patterns and triggers corresponding actions.[3]

BRAND GROUP COMPUTERIZATION

Several developments are occurring that will increase the trend toward computerization of the brand groups and other marketing organizations.

The data management languages and packages (the Fourth Generation Languages) are becoming more powerful and easier to use, and firms are adopting them for developing end-user applications. These packages will make it possible for vendors and the firms' data processing personnel to develop powerful packages that take advantage of the unique strengths of the personal computer and the mainframe. And the personal computer continues to acquire capabilities. We are not far from seeing the "meg-cubed" personal computer—a computer with 1 million bytes of RAM, operating at 1 million instructions per second, and having 1 million pixels on the screen, that is, a screen resolution of 1,000 by 1,000 pixels. Further, business schools are beginning to make extensive use of personal computers in the training and education of future brand managers and other marketing professionals. This newly trained individual will be able to develop personal applications and databases. S/he will have the tools and knowledge for building small systems for use by individuals in the brand groups.

Firms are introducing broadband networks for linking personal and mainframe computers. These networks permit the si-

---

[3] Alan C. Morse, "The Development of an Intelligent, Trainable Graphic Display Assistant for the Decisionmaker." Paper presented at the ORSA/TIMS Conference (Orlando, Florida, November 1983).

multaneous transmission of text, numbers, voice, video, and images among the various computers. This is important for marketing management because brand groups are the communication hub for their brands, and the firm's information base goes beyond numerical data. Television commercials use video, radio commercials use voice, and print advertisements and consumer promotions can be captured as digitized images for storage, retrieval, and transmission. These networks will lead to the adoption of an integrated office automation philosophy in which the firm uses computer technology as a major element in its communication process. The transmittal of all forms of marketing information over the network will become commonplace. Brand groups and marketing professionals will become accustomed to sharing their information bases with others within the firm.

The network will make it possible for individuals to share or syndicate their personal information systems. For instance, a promotion specialist will be able to develop an application that can track the status of all the firm's promotions. Any person authorized by the promotion specialist will be able to access that information system via the network and query it for the status of a particular promotion.

KNOWLEDGE MANAGEMENT

The developments that are bringing artificial intelligence out of the lab and into the business arena will have an impact on the practice of marketing management. One somewhat intangible impact will be the awareness that knowledge is a reusable resource and, as such, something that can be computerized and used along with other information.

An examination of the work of brand groups and other marketing specialists leads to the realization that these are knowledge workers. In fact, they are links in a chain of knowledge workers in that marketing management functions in a knowledge- and information-rich environment and most marketing positions involve knowledge workers. Brand groups specialize in their brand; they are the experts on the brand; they use their knowledge about all aspects of the brand to develop strategies and programs that sustain the life of the brand. Similarly, marketing specialists are experts in their area of responsibility. The promotion manager is a specialist in promotions; s/he builds a knowledge base around the strengths and weaknesses of the various promotion vehicles; s/he uses this base to advise the brand groups on the design and execution of promotions.

The computerization of the sales force and the adoption of computers by the brand groups and specialists will lay the foundation for the use of computers for knowledge management. Similarly, the sharing of information and information systems in the office automation environment will make it easy to accept the idea of building and sharing knowledge systems. The data explosion will cause the brand groups and the field sales organization to seek assistance from knowledgeable consultants in the analysis and interpretation of the data. A computer can be taught such analysis and interpretation using AI tools and concepts. Since marketing managers and professionals will become comfortable with networked computers for information management, the use of networks for knowledge management will seem a natural extension of current practice.

The move to local marketing will cause the field organization to assume more tactical brand responsibilities, which will give the front-line "soldiers and commanders" the tools for doing their job. But these workers will also need a new knowledge base to effectively apply their new marketing tools. This base currently resides with the brand groups and the marketing specialists. When the firm realizes the magnitude of the problem of providing such knowledge to hundreds, even thousands, of salespeople they will be receptive to the use of computers in the management of the firm's knowledge.

Hence, these technology driven developments will lead to a new philosophy and practice concerning the management of knowledge. We will see brand groups and marketing specialists—domain experts in the AI terminology—working with "knowledge engineers" and/or using advanced computer tools to build personal knowledge bases and personal expert systems that they will manage and share with others in the networked organization.

CHAPTER EIGHT

Knowledge Management: The Missing Element

The discussion to this point has revealed a need for, and an interest in, expanding the role currently played by computers in marketing management. Computers are now being used to store large numerical data files, to extract subsets of the data from these files for analysis and display, and to do financial calculations and simulations. The brand groups are barely able to do the required analyses with today's databases and computer tools. Further, several trends point to an increased need for analysis and an environment characterized by data overload. In addition, there is a trend toward regional or local-focus marketing that will probably result in increased sales force involvement in tactical marketing decisions.

These trends have caused the leading firms to look for ways to make the computers "smarter"; that is, the computer would play a more active role in assisting the user in the analysis and interpretation of the data, and in the design of tactical marketing programs. This search for ways to add intelligence to marketing computer systems is being facilitated by the emergence of technologies for capturing, using, and managing knowledge as well as information.

This chapter discusses some of the issues and approaches involved in providing such machine intelligence and knowledge management. The first section discusses the political and technological forces that underlie the emergence of the knowledge management concepts. The notion of a knowledge support environment is then introduced, followed by a description of an information, knowledge, reasoning, and conclusion paradigm. The next-to-last section discusses the form of a knowledge support environment for marketing (KSEM). In that section, expert systems are explored and a description of how such an environment could be developed and used by a promotion specialist is discussed.

THE KNOWLEDGE MANAGEMENT "EXPLOSION"

The Japanese government has launched a "Fifth Generation" computer project that it hopes will propel Japan into a leadership position in information technology. This project has stirred considerable interest in the United States, as witnessed by the best-selling book *The Fifth Generation* and dedication of the 1984 annual conference of the Association of Computing Machinery to "The Fifth Generation Challenge."[1]

The Japanese project has several research and development goals: problem solving and inference systems, knowledge-based systems, intelligent human-machine interface systems, development support systems, and basic application systems.[2] The main idea is to develop computer systems that process nonnumeric information. The Japanese government recently doubled the annual funding of the Institute of New Generation Computer Technology, which will now get about $40 million a year to develop the software and hardware for its new fifth-generation computer systems.[3]

One of the key components in this computer system will be knowledge information processing systems with knowledge ba-

[1] Edward A. Feigenbaum and Pamela McCorduck, *The Fifth Generation* (Reading, Mass.: Addison-Wesley Publishing, 1983).

[2] George E. Lindamood, "The Structure of the Japanese Fifth Generation Computer Project—Then and Now," *Future Generation Computer Systems 1*, no. 1 (July 1984).

[3] Paul E. Schindler Jr., *Information Systems News*, November 26, 1984, p. 34.

ses and the ability to infer from knowledge and solve problems in a manner similar to that of humans.[4]

America is devoting much activity to meeting what it perceives as the Japanese challenge. Michael Dertouzos, director of the MIT Laboratory for Computer Science, states that the challenge has severe implications: "Whoever controls the knowledge of the fifth generation information technology will hold supremacy in the geopolitical arena."[5] In this country, the National Science Foundation (NSF) and the Defence Advance Research Project Agency (DARPA) have increased their research and development budgets for information technology, particularly for projects involving knowledge-based systems and supercomputers. The European countries have formed ESPRIT, the European Strategic Programme for Research and Development in Information Technology. Companies are joining forces to pool their resources through projects such as the Microelectronics and Computer Technology Corporation and the Semiconductor Research Corporation.

The end result of all these competitive and cooperative efforts is likely to be a new wave of information technologies that extend the capabilities of computers to support people in their professional and personal lives. In particular, we should see systems that assist managers by making knowledge more accessible and perhaps even assume some of the routine "knowledge work" of these managers.

One worker in this area, Frederick Hayes-Roth, expresses the potential of such systems quite eloquently.

> For nearly 500 years, books have been the primary means of retaining knowledge and transmitting it to humans. To achieve excellence in a profession, humans have studied, interpreted, and memorized these books; apprenticed and trained with someone who could clarify and illustrate the books' principles; then practiced for years and learned practical rules from experience. The development of printing made an enormous impact on human culture by providing a means to distribute records of human expertise to larger numbers of potential practitioners. However, because it

---

[4] L. O. Hertzberger, "The Architecture of Fifth Generation Inference Computers," *Future Generation Computer Systems* 1, no. 1 (July 1984).

[5] Michael L. Dertouzos, A Talk at ACM '84, San Francisco, Calif., October 8, 1984.

could not explain or apply its knowledge directly, the passive book left much of the work to the reader.

As technology progressed and economics advanced, knowledge transfer became a bottleneck in cultural development. In highly advanced fields, such as medicine and electronics, knowledge creation outpaced knowledge dissemination and use. In information-processing fields, such as military intelligence and earth resources, data was acquired faster than it could be analyzed and interpreted. In highly capitalized fields, such as automotive and electronics manufacturing, global competition based on price and quality has highlighted the need to integrate and coordinate knowledge about all phases of product development. This challenge is exacerbated by the significant acceleration of new technologies and rapid shortening of product lifetimes. In all of these areas, the same point is evident: the computer has created both the need and the opportunity to enhance knowledge distribution. Knowledge systems address that need.[6]

Work is actively underway in computer science departments and research labs to develop the methodologies and tools for building these types of knowledge systems.

Marketing oriented companies are beginning to recognize the need for knowledge management. The following quote is from an article by a Procter & Gamble manager:

> We are currently in a period of time when managers are becoming computer literate and focusing their attention on acquiring personal computers and powerful terminals. It is not hard to imagine that the next stage we will experience is the expectation of managers to be able to easily get high-quality, well-defined, and timely data delivered to their terminals. (I choose to lump personal computers and terminals together.) The stage following this data-focused era will center on the analytical technologies needed by managers to gain insight and synthesize the masses of data available to them by this time. These analytical technologies will include artificial intelligence applications such as expert systems, as well as the more classic management science and statistical techniques.[7]

---

[6] Frederick Hayes-Roth, "Knowledge-Based Expert Systems," *Computer*, October 1984, p. 272. © 1984 IEEE.

[7] Laurence J. Laning, "Corporate Data Architecture: The Key to Supporting Management," *DATA BASE*, Summer 1983, p. 14.

THE KNOWLEDGE SUPPORT ENVIRONMENT

Tools that are used by individuals and organizations involved in creating, learning, and using a body of knowledge constitute a knowledge support environment.[8] Wegner believes that "the computer revolution will fundamentally amplify man's ability to manage knowledge, just as the industrial revolution fundamentally amplified man's ability to manage physical phenomena."[9] One mechanism by which this revolution will come about is with the creation of "dynamic documents" that would be read from the computer screen and would contain traditional text as well as dynamically changing tables, graphs, and user-interface facilities. The computer could even interpret the tables and graphs in order to make the text dynamic, that is, *to change the text in response to changes in the data.*

This is a powerful idea and one that can be applied to the support of marketing managers when they are using a body of knowledge to solve business problems. The knowledge support environment would contain data and knowledge about using these data to solve problems. It would thus serve to amplify human intelligence.

The dynamic document notion could be used in writing standard memos that specialists prepare on a regular basis. For instance, it is common for the firm to assign one person to analyze the bimonthly Nielsen data and to prepare a "Top Line Retail Sales Report" that contains summary tables (in standard format) of all the firm's brands and a short narrative that highlights the significant numbers in the report and identifies the causal factors underlying the trends and changes from the last period. This report, which is circulated to the higher levels of the marketing organization and to senior management, augments the product-specific reports prepared by the individual brand groups. As weekly scanner-based data replace bimonthly Nielsen retail audit data, the need will arise to "automate" this process as much as possible.

Today's technology permits the development of programs that read data and prepare an interpretive memo composed of

---

[8] Peter Wegner, "Capital-Intensive Software Technology," *IEEE Software*, July 1984, p. 35.

[9] Ibid., p. 33.

standard phrases and words selected from a database. Tomorrow's technology might permit such a system to go beyond this simple, "brute-force" level and actually write a document based on *machine* reasoning.[10]

The knowledge support environment concept builds on and broadens the notion of knowledge engineering originally defined by Edward Feigenbaum as the art of representing knowledge so that it can be used by computers to perform intelligent tasks.[11] This definition refers to the expert systems that contain both knowledge and a way to reason with the knowledge, the so-called inference engine. With the broader definition, the inference engine can be the human, the computer, or both.

Wherever the reasoning or inferencing occurs, it should be recognized that managerial and professional work can be characterized as combining information with knowledge to produce a conclusion, a decision, more information, or more knowledge. Perhaps we can consider thinking just such an activity.

Information requires knowledge and knowledge requires information. Information to one person is data to another; the difference lies in the person's knowledge. If s/he has the appropriate knowledge, the data have meaning—they are information. If s/he does not have the appropriate knowledge, the data are just data in that they are just more facts or figures that pass into and perhaps through the receiver's intellect.

Most, if not all, of today's computer systems store numbers and have the ability to retrieve and display these numbers in various forms and aggregations. The usefulness of such systems depends on the user's ability to handle the numbers in his or her professional role. Do the numbers have meaning? Are they actionable? These questions can only be answered yes or no. The answer is yes when the recipient of the numbers has a knowledge base that can incorporate and interpret the numbers; in this instance, the numbers are information. The answer is no when the recipient does not have the appropriate knowledge base.

Thus, the management process involves the marriage of knowledge and information; each requires the other. A knowl-

---

[10] Roger C. Schank, *The Cognitive Computer: On Language, Learning, and Artificial Intelligence* (Reading, Mass.: Addison-Wesley Publishing, 1984).

[11] Feigenbaum and McCorduck, *The Fifth Generation.* p. 64.

edge support environment would:

- Contain data in many forms: numerical, graphical, and textual.
- Contain knowledge as well as data.
- Provide a facility for bringing together the appropriate knowledge and data.

Such an environment brings together knowledge and information; it provides a knowledge management system as well as a database management system; it recognizes that knowledge resides in both the computer and the user's intellect. In a knowledge support environment's early stages, the inference or reasoning processes will remain with the user. One goal is to provide an environment that will join knowledge with information.

INFORMATION/KNOWLEDGE/REASONING/ CONCLUSION PARADIGM

Firms can be seen as composed of three types of people: decision makers, knowledge workers, and laborers. Most of the existing information systems were built to serve the lower-level supervisors and certain knowledge workers, particularly those concerned with the operational aspects of the firm: ordering supplies, issuing invoices, controlling inventory, paying bills, and so on. The new challenge is to develop information systems that will support the decision makers and knowledge workers who deal with the firm's strategic and tactical decision-making and implementation processes.

Our model of knowledge workers and decision makers involves four components: information, knowledge, reasoning, and conclusions. Information refers to traditional data and facts (e.g., last week's sales, the value of the inventory, the competitors' most recent bids, and so on). Knowledge encompasses heuristics, rules of thumb, and relationships among facts. For example, a manager may know or believe that advertising is best used in situations where the consumers have low brand awareness and high trial rates (among those who are aware of the brand). S/he may also know that consumer promotions (e.g., coupons) are best used when awareness is high but trial is low. These relationships or beliefs exist in a "knowledge base" in the brand manager's mind. To decide whether to use advertising or sales promotions, the manager needs two pieces of information: awareness levels and trial rates.

The third component is the reasoning process used to choose the information, select the appropriate knowledge from the knowledge base, and use or process both information and knowledge to reach a conclusion. For instance, the manager or knowledge worker can use an inferential process or a deductive process. If an inferential process is used, that process could mean going from goal to information or from information to goal.

The first process can be termed *backward processing* and the second *forward processing* or *reasoning*. The manager can start with the notion that s/he needs to decide between advertising and promotion (backward processing), search his/her knowledge base for knowledge that is appropriate to the question, then search the information system for data needed by the retrieved knowledge to reach a conclusion. For instance, the manager would locate the knowledge that advertising is needed when brand awareness is low and promotion is needed when brand awareness is high but trial is low. Then s/he would need information about brand awareness and trial before deciding to allocate resources to advertising or promotion.

Or the manager can scan the information (forward processing) in search of interesting patterns or situations. When something abnormal is found or detected, s/he can then search his or her knowledge base to see if anything is known about the implications of this situation. After knowledge is selected, it is applied to the data and conclusions are reached. For instance, in scanning the database the manager could observe that brand awareness is low. Then s/he would search his or her knowledge base for knowledge that deals with low brand awareness. This search might result in the retrieval of the knowledge that advertising is needed when awareness is low. Given these pieces of information and knowledge, the manager would conclude that advertising is needed.

Sometimes the manager uses a two-stage (or multistage) reasoning process. In a situation where a manager's goal is to find abnormalities in the data, s/he uses knowledge about how to scan data; that is, a data-scanning schema is the knowledge structure being applied. The conclusion is the set of data that are abnormal. This conclusion then becomes the information in the second stage in which the user searches her or his knowledge base to find knowledge that uses the new information.

Conclusions are simply that—conclusions. Sometimes a conclusion is a decision in that the person has decided to do something. Most often, it does not have an action component. We can portray this process with a four-block model:

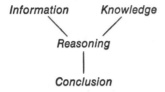

In addition, the links among the four components are important. The link from information to reasoning denotes the information retrieval process; the link from knowledge to reasoning denotes the knowledge retrieval process; and the link from reasoning to conclusion denotes various processes (e.g., decision making, problem solving, and environmental scanning).

We can identify four different approaches to using computers to support executives and knowledge workers.

- Management information systems (MIS).
- Expert systems (ES).
- Decision support systems (DSS).
- Library retrieval systems (LRS).

One key difference among these systems is the location of the information, knowledge, and reasoning in either the human mind or the computer. Consider the following table:

	MIS	ES	DSS	LRS
Information	C[a]	H[b]	C	C
Knowledge	H	C	C/H	C
Reasoning	H	C	H	H

[a] C = Computer
[b] H = Human

In an MIS, the computer contains the information and the human has the knowledge and does the reasoning. Most successful expert systems reverse this situation: the human has the information and the computer has the knowledge, queries the user for information, and arrives at a conclusion through an "inference engine" (the phrase used by the artificial intelligence community to denote the reasoning component of an expert system).

A DSS usually contains a database of information and knowledge in the form of mathematical models. However, most DSSs require the user to provide part of the knowledge (the part that cannot be put into math models) and to do the reasoning. An LRS usually contains knowledge in the form of articles and speeches. The human retrieves the knowledge and provides whatever information is required for him or her to arrive at a conclusion. The on-line information retrieval systems (such as Dialog) provide such a facility.

It is possible to generalize the expert system view or approach so that the reasoning is either performed by a human or by the computer and information is in the machine. This system is called a knowledge support system (KSS). In this conceptualization, an expert system is one type of KSS. However, we can put knowledge and information into a computer system and provide facilities for their retrieval and use in the reasoning process, whether that process is done by the computer, the human, or both.

Our view of the future computing environment calls for knowledge workers to develop personal information systems, denoted IS(P) and personal knowledge bases, denoted KB(P) that run on personal or departmental machines that may contain reasoning processes. We also believe that these computers will be tied together into a network so that each knowledge worker can access other workers' IS(P) or KB(P). We, of course, recognize that these personal information systems interact with the user's mind, which also contains information, knowledge, and reasoning processes.

Knowledge workers or executives can reach a conclusion by using internal information, knowledge, and reasoning processes, that is, they use what is in their minds. In addition, they can use their personal information systems IS(P), knowledge bases KB(P), and reasoning systems RS(P), which may be in their hardcopy filing system or in computer applications created by or for them. We call this collection of applications and files a personal support environment (PSE). Finally, they may resort to the firm's organizational information systems and knowledge bases in the organizational support environment.

The computer-based entities in this organizational support environment are of two types: centrally controlled and developed DP or MIS applications, and the collected personal support environments of the other knowledge workers. Today, most entities are of the first type; however, we forecast that the second type (the personal support environment) will begin to emerge as the key aspect of managerial (as opposed to operational) computing.

These PSEs will be linked by high-speed networks that will make it possible for individual knowledge workers to share their information systems and knowledge bases with other knowledge workers. In addition, some of these PSEs will contain expert systems. That is, the knowledge worker will develop an expert system that makes her or his expertise available throughout the organization.

We envision these PSEs being used in a manner that enables the conclusion from one PSE to become either the information or the knowledge for another PSE. There will be a flow of information, knowledge, conclusions, and reasoning processes throughout the organization. In that way, firms will be making their knowledge workers "resusable." They will begin to think of a knowledge worker's PSE as a capital good. They will want to make that capital available throughout the organization 24-hours a day, 7-days a week.

Today, knowledge workers must acquire and retain sufficient knowledge so they can process information and reach accurate, timely, and insightful conclusions. Whenever such a conclusion must be reached, the appropriate knowledge worker must use his or her mind to reach the appropriate conclusion. If the volume of such work becomes too great, the firm hires an assistant for the knowledge worker. Once the assistant has been trained, s/he starts reaching conclusions for the less important and more routine problems. This process can continue until a large department of knowledge workers exists who are essentially using a common knowledge base to draw conclusions about a common set of problems and situations.

Technology is evolving to the point where we can adopt a new model. Knowledge workers will continue to be asked to use their knowledge and reasoning processes to reach conclusions in their areas of expertise. However, they will be given another task; instead of having to train an army of assistants, knowledge workers will be given the responsibility of training computers to reach conclusions. Or they will make their information systems and knowledge bases available to other knowledge workers and executives who can then use their own reasoning processes to reach conclusions.

A key concept is the notion of knowledge sharing in which one person's knowledge is needed to "actionalize" the information held by others. Each specialist or knowledge worker is responsible for building a personal support environment (PSE). Each PSE would contain two files with the titles: "What do I know?" "What information do I have?"

A person who is searching for information or knowledge can read each PSE's files to determine whether that specialist has the appropriate knowledge or information. These files refer to what has been computerized, not what is in the specialist's mind. A specialist can be a company employee or an outside consultant who provides a knowledge or information base. For instance, a marketing research firm could build a knowledge base from its studies of scanner data and make it available to firms for a fee.

This interconnected, networked collection of knowledge workers and personal support environments comprise the organizational support environment.

A KNOWLEDGE SUPPORT ENVIRONMENT FOR MARKETING MANAGEMENT

One of the essential features of the information/knowledge/reasoning/conclusion paradigm is the idea that functional experts will be managing information *and* knowledge. Since the computer field has many facilities for managing information, the information aspects of this work will be minimal. However, knowledge management is just now becoming an area of discussion, and there are few available systems and packages for the management of knowledge in electronic form. Thus, a major part of our work will be the development of concepts and tools for knowledge management.

The Knowledge Tree

We have begun to design a knowledge architecture, that is, to specify a set of concepts and their interrelationships for the management of knowledge. The essential elements of this knowledge management system include the:

- KnChunk: a piece or chunk of knowledge.
- KnBase: the collection of KnChunks.
- KnManager: the software for managing the KnBase.
- KnTree: the KnBase organized into a hierarchical tree structure.
- KnStation: a workstation for using the KnBase.
- KnWorker: a person who uses a KnStation.
- KnNet: an electronic network that ties together the KnStations.
- KnConference: a computer-based conference about one or more KnChunks.

The KnTree is a knowledge perusal system in which knowledge is arranged in a hierarchy or network. The user can begin at the top or at any point by entering the appropriate key word. The elements at the bottom of the KnTree are called KnChunks; they contain pieces or chunks of knowledge. Each KnChunk is attached to one branch of a tree. Branches can have knowledge or simply be nodes for further branching; those with knowledge are termed *terminal nodes.*

The following figure is a sample of such a KnTree. Marketing knowledge is first organized into the four-P categories (price, promotion, product, and place). Then promotion knowledge is classified into public relations, advertising, sales promotion, and selling. Sales promotion knowledge is further classified in various categories: tutorial, literature, strategies, types, studies, and so on. Finally, promotion strategies include increase trial, increase repeat, image reinforcement, store inventory build, and so on.

In this sample KnTree, increase trial, increase repeat, image reinforcement, and store inventory are terminal nodes. Each such node contains one or more KnChunks. For example, the increase repeat node could contain the following KnChunks:

- Sampling is not a good device for increasing repeat.
- Refund coupons are outstanding ways of increasing repeat purchases.
- Bonus packs tend to generate 22 percent more business from repeat purchasers.

The Marketing KnTree

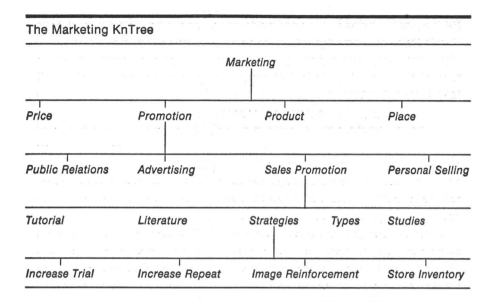

The KnTree system has a program that can write a form to display the names of the KnChunks on the screen and ask the user to select one for viewing. The KnChunks should be able to hold text, charts, graphs, spreadsheets, and models, that is, knowledge in any form. Ideally the charts, graphs, and tables would be dynamic in that they would contain the most recent data available to the system. For instance, if a KnChunk refers to the costs of different advertising media, it should be able to select the most recent prices from a media cost table and insert it at the appropriate place in the KnChunk. This facility requires the KnTree and KnBase to be intimately tied to traditional databases.

The KnChunks should be data independent; they should exist independent of the program(s) that uses them. If the system were implemented in IBM PC DOS or UNIX, the KnChunks could be organized into file directories. A separate program must be provided for managing these KnChunks—the KnManager.

The KnTree provides a structure for bringing knowledge to bear on a problem. It is an "action education' vehicle—a system for delivering education and information when the user is preparing to take action or reach a conclusion.

The KnSystem should permit conferencing. Users who read a section of the tree can start and/or participate in a conference on the subject. Consider a KnChunk on the use of a particular model or strategy. A user should be able to comment on the subject and have the comment stored in a file for later review by other KnWorkers. Ideally, this conferencing would occur in a window above the KnTree screen. The conference would "follow" the KnTree and appear when appropriate.

This arrangement is similar to the annotation system called Annoland developed at the Xerox Corporation's Palo Alto Research Center.[12] Annoland provides a facility for annotating a piece of text. These annotations appear in a window and travel with the text in the file system; that is, they are saved with the text. Since an annotation is itself a piece of text, it too can be annotated. Each KnChunk that has a conference would show a conferencing symbol on the screen. The program would have a pointer to the file containing the conference. The file would be displayed when desired, and the user would be able to enter additional comments.

This type of system produces a dynamic, user-controlled KnTree. Brown has recognized that this dynamic environment facilitates "activity-based learning" on the part of the user. It creates a

> community information space, browsed through the tools, or "eyes," residing on one's personal computer. Important to the success of such a communication device is the notion of adding context, or writing mechanisms, to enable readers not only to view a public document but also to add their own ideas, criticisms, and observations.[13]

The reader becomes "active" by adding his or her own comments, views, experiences, and knowledge. The comment files could contain knowledge in many forms: text, graphics, numbers, or any combination. Or they could contain instructions for starting another program or process that would illustrate a point.

A system that offers some of the features of the KnTree and

---

[12] John Seely Brown, "Process versus Product: A Perspective on Tools for Communal and Informal Electronic Learning," in *Education in the Electronic Age: Report from the Learning Lab* ed. Susan Newman and Edith Poor (New York: WNET, 1983), p. 52.

[13] Brown, "Informal Electronic Learning," p. 51.

related components has been developed at Carnegie Mellon University. ZOG provides an environment for accessing information and knowledge in a manner similar to the KnTree system.[14,15]

Expert Systems

Alan Kay provides a description of a computer "agent":

> a system that, when given a goal, could carry out the details of the appropriate computer operations and could ask for and receive advice, offered in human terms, when it was stuck. An agent would be a "soft robot" living and doing its business within the computer's world. . . . A persistent "go-fer" that for 24-hours a day looks for things it knows a user is interested in and presents them as a personal magazine would be most welcome.[16]

An agent is an example of an expert system. Kay's view of an agent could be used to analyze marketing data, build a story from its findings, identify an appropriate marketing mix for dealing with the situation, and devise a tactical marketing plan. It would be programmed to act as an intelligent analyst. It would go through the large databases and search for problems and opportunities. Such an analyst could even be programmed to write English-language summaries of its findings. Lesk reports on the development of such a program that reads stock exchange data and prepares written summaries of the data.[17]

One marketing manager has issued a call for such agents in the analysis of marketing data. Rudolph Struse at Carnation states that the marketing decision support system (MDSS) should become more proactive.

> At present, the technology sits mute unless instructed to do something. In effect, the manager is to be the scout or problem

---

[14] G. Robertson, D. McCracken, and A. Newell, "The ZOG Approach to Man-Machine Communications," *International Journal of Man-Machine Studies* 14 (1981), pp. 461–88.

[15] Donald L. McCracken and Robert M. Akscyn, "Experience with the ZOG Human-Computer Interface System," *International Journal of Man-Machine Studies* 21 (1984), pp. 293–310.

[16] Alan Kay, "Computer Software," *Scientific American* 251, no. 3 (September 1984), pp. 52–59.

[17] Michael Lesk, "Computer Software for Information Management," *Scientific American* 251, no. 3 (September 1984), pp. 163–72.

spotter who calls in the MDSS. Some managers have exception reports run on regular cycles in order to identify areas where a business is not performing as expected. This is a step forward, but one of low generality and power. This division of labor between the manager and the MDSS may not be optimal: The computer, while very poor at "thinking associatively," can handle vast amounts of data quickly. A possible approach would be to give the MDSS some basic rules for recognizing relationships within a data set that it could then use to search a database on its "own" initiative. These rules might even be modified in light of experience.[18]

Rather than the manager being the scout or problem spotter, the computerized agent could assume some part of this role if it contained the appropriate knowledge base.

The potential usefulness of such agents can be illustrated by examining a series of steps that brand groups at Borden execute on a regular basis. The goal of this analysis is the generation of a memo to the appropriate sales manager that alerts him or her to problem accounts and suggests appropriate corrective action.

Step 1. Use the *sales file* to obtain sales in each district for each UPC code in percentage of quota and percentage change from last year. Examine these data to identify problem districts.

Step 2. Use the *accounts sales file* to obtain comparable information for the accounts within the problem districts. Examine these data to identify the problem accounts.

Step 3. Use the *sales tracker report* to see if the problem lies in the distribution level or with the number of items stocked by each problem account.

Step 4. Examine the *store audit reports* to see if prices are in line with competitive brands in the accounts.

Step 5. Use the same reports to determine if the shelving matches the requirements of the planogram agreed to by the accounts.

---

[18] Rudolph W. Struse III, "The Four Ps of Marketing Decision Support Systems: Promises, Payoffs, Paradoxes, and Prognostications," in *Marketing in an Electronic Age,* ed. Robert D. Buzzell (Boston: Harvard Business School Press, 1985), p. 152.

Step 6. Write memos to the appropriate sales managers that detail the findings of this analysis and suggest corrective actions.

These steps could be easily programmed for execution on a personal computer. They are well defined and seem to be applied in a relatively uniform manner. What is lacking is a set of processing and decision rules that the product manager can use to perform the analysis and prepare the memo.

The generation of the list of decision and processing rules involves the practice of "knowledge engineering," which is the necessary first step in building an expert system. These rules are then converted into computer form and a program is created that executes the rules in the necessary sequence. The aspect of the program that differentiates an expert system from a normal program is the separation of the knowledge base (i.e., the decision rules) from the logical flow of the program. In a conventional program, one program or system is built that contains both the problem-solving logic and the knowledge about the problem under study. It reads data, and uses the rules and knowledge embedded in the program to process the data. This type of program must be modified every time new knowledge needs to be applied to the problem. And the code that controls the program flow is unique to that program.

An expert system treats the knowledge rules as data and applies a standard and reusable processing procedure, a so-called inference engine, to process the rules. This arrangement permits the building of one "program" (the inference engine) that can be applied to many different areas of expertise. Recent advances in program design are resulting in systems that allow a relatively inexperienced computer user to build a knowledge base and use a standard inference procedure to turn the knowledge base into an agent.

Expert Systems and Marketing Activities

Marketing managers tend to undertake the following activities:

- Recognition: realize the need for action.
- Diagnosis: identify the appropriate situation or context.
- Generate alternatives.
- Evaluate the alternatives.
- Select the preferred alternative.

- Implementation.
- Monitoring.

Expert systems are potentially useful in the recognition, diagnosis, and alternative generation activities.

1. *Recognition* involves the analysis of large databases about consumers, competitors, trade relationships, marketing events, and market conditions. Managers need support in such analysis because they have limited data analysis training, finite capacities to process multidimensional and dynamic data, short time periods for doing the analysis, and short attention spans because they are involved in many diverse and ongoing activities.

2. *Diagnosis* involves selecting the appropriate information from all the available data, combining the data with their personal knowledge system, and making the appropriate decision. However, evidence indicates that certain information is over- or underused because people perceive what they expect, understand based on what they have experienced, and remember only the information that is congruent with their existing knowledge.[19]

3. *Generating alternatives* is a process that people seem to stop early, which results in incomplete lists.

Expert systems have been praised because they overcome some of these human limitations. One expert who supplied the knowledge base for an expert system reported that "The knowledge system works every day as I do on my best days. It never forgets, never fails to consider relevant facts, never jumps prematurely to an incorrect conclusion."[20]

Personal Support Environment for Promotion Specialist

Most firms have one or more people who are promotion specialists; they monitor all of the brands' promotions and work with

---

[19] Robert Zmud, "DSS Support for Informal Organizational Information Systems," in *DSS-82 Transactions*, ed. Gary W. Dickson (San Francisco, 1982), pp. 160–69.

[20] Frederick Hayes-Roth, "The Machine as Partner of the New Professional," *IEEE Spectrum*, June 1984, p. 29.

brand groups in devising promotions and test programs. Such specialists would play a major role in the knowledge support environment by building and maintaining (1) the promotion branch of the KnTree, and (2) a system of promotion advisers and/or agents.

The promotion specialists collect, generate, and make available the firm's store of knowledge about promotions. Hence, it would be appropriate for them to computerize this knowledge by building and maintaining the promotion branch of the KnTree. This branch would contain material such as the following.

1. Promotion facts.
   a. Coupon redemption rates.
   b. Promotion cost factors.
2. Promotion events.
   a. Objectives and strategies.
   b. Starting date: planned and actual.
   c. Ending date: planned and actual
   d. Costs: fixed and variable.
   e. Test plan.
   f. Results.
3. Promotion research studies.
4. Promotion vehicles.
   a. Strengths.
   b. Weaknesses.
5. Strategy/promotion checklist.
6. Tutorials.
   a. How to Write a Promotion Plan.
   b. How to Evaluate a Promotion.
   c. Corporate Promotion Philosophy.

A Promotion Management System of Advisers

The concepts of advisers and expert systems can be applied to the set of activities involved in devising a promotion plan. The following is a conceptual model of the promotion-planning process that decomposes the process into a series of linked steps. Each step is considered from the perspective of the required information and knowledge and the resulting conclusion. The conclusion of one step becomes the information in the next step.

Step 1. Summarize the available data into measures of the brand's historical performance.

Information: Raw data, for example, SAMI data.
Knowledge: Data reduction algorithms.
　　　　　　Models.
　　　　　　Statistical procedures.
Conclusion: Brand performance measures.

Step 2. Review the brand performance measures to arrive at an understanding or classification of the brand situation, that is, short descriptions of the brand's situation in a market at a particular point in time. Examples of brand situations includes description such as the following: "Under-attack-by-superior-brand"; "They-don't-know-us-but-they-love-us"; "High-trade-inventory-levels."

Information: Brand performance measures.
Knowledge: Situation classification rules.
Conclusion: Brand situation.

Step 3. Given a brand situation, identify the most appropriate brand strategy for correcting that situation. For example, if the brand situation were "they-don't-know-us-but-they-love-us," then an appropriate strategy would be to increase brand awareness.

Information: Brand situation.
Knowledge: Situation-to-strategy rules.
Conclusion: Brand strategy.

Step 4. Based on the selected brand strategy, choose an appropriate promotion type. For instance, sampling would be an appropriate promotion vehicle for increasing awareness of a brand's features.

Information: Brand strategy
Knowledge: Strategy to promotion rules.
Conclusion: Promotion type.

Step 5. Use a promotion performance model to estimate the performance of the promotion type.

Information: Promotion type.
              Brand performance measures.
Knowledge: Promotion performance model.
Conclusion: Estimated performance.

Dynamic Promotion Reports

The promotion specialist would prepare a system that analyzes data to identify the impacts of promotions on the firm's brands as well as those of competitors. This system would present its conclusions to the manager via traditional computer output format, or it could be programmed to write its conclusions in narrative form. The following is an example of such a narrative in the form of a memo to a product manager.

```
                       Memorandum


To:      Jan Jennings, K2R Product Manager
From:    Promotion Monitoring Agent
Subject: Unusual Activity in Omaha


I believe you should look into the situation in
Omaha. Glory brand is gaining share, at the expense
of P&G's Bissel, which is off seven share points
compared to the same period last year. Your brand,
K2R, has only been impacted slightly. Glory has
been gaining market share (measured by case
equivalents), although its unit sales are constant.
It is accomplishing this by switching consumers
from the 16- to the 24-ounce package. The primary
marketing elements are coupons supported by ''A''
ad features. I estimate that during the past three
weeks, their net revenue has increased 11 percent.
Do you want to examine the supporting information?
```

SUMMARY

Marketing people spend their time developing marketing strategies and plans, designing programs and campaigns, implementing the programs, and reacting to environmental events and deviations from the plan. Currently these are *nonreusable activities*; the plan is executed and the cycle starts over with very little change in the resources available for doing the intellectual work. The idea behind the KSEM is that the firm should spend part of its time creating *reusable* resources. The firm should view its knowledge as reusable and should recognize that capturing that knowledge so that it can be leveraged throughout the organization is a kind of capital formation.[21]

This need to leverage knowledge becomes increasingly important as firms (1) deal with the data explosion caused by widespread use of scanner and scanner-panel data, and (2) continue the trend toward regional or local-focus marketing.

The knowledge support environment for marketing (KSEM) provides the following facilities: a KnTree for organizing and displaying the firm's knowledge; agents for using the knowledge for computer-based reasoning; and facilities for preparing documents. The KSEM should be closely linked to the firm's information system because of the need to couple information and knowledge to trigger the reasoning process of the human or the computer.

The generation of such an event offers a significant challenge to the marketing community. Wegner observes that construction of a knowledge support environment

> involves educational technology, cognitive science, and human factors research. The technology of managing the modular presentation of complex knowledge structures . . . must . . . consider the human factors associated with animation, user interface, multiple windows, and other techniques for improving man-computer communication.[22]

Brown feels that these technologies and capabilities "provide the opportunity to construct cost-effective, electronically based learning-by-doing environments" in which a manager could learn how to perform a task while actually performing it.[23]

These facilities would be available in the KSEM's user interface module. Other components include the actual knowledge base and the agents. The Japanese conceptualization of this type of system calls for a knowledge base machine that holds the

---

[21] Wegner, "Software Technology," p. 8.

[22] Wegner, "Software Technology," p. 34.

[23] John Seely Brown, "Learning-by-Doing Revisited for Electronic Learning Environments," in *The Future of Electronic Learning*, ed. M. A. White (Hillsdale, N.J.: Lawrence Erlbaum Associates), Pending publication.

knowledge in a structure that permits easy access to all knowledge items.[24] When the knowledge base machine receives a demand from an inference engine, it retrieves the needed knowledge and passes it to the inference engine. It also has facilities for updating the knowledge base with new knowledge sent from the inference engine. Of course, in the KSEM the inference engine could be either an expert system or a human.

The KnTree component of the KSEM can be thought of as a knowledge perusal system in that it lets the manager peruse the available knowledge. This perusal system is envisioned as having considerably more knowledge than is used by the agents. The system collects existing knowledge and puts it in one location, makes that knowledge readily available, and gives the user the opportunity to become accustomed to obtaining knowledge from a computer. Capturing knowledge in the perusal system may be a necessary first step toward the creation of agents.

Knowledge can be represented many ways, particularly in the marketing field where so many "product" marketing activities involve advertisements, promotions, products, and packages. Therefore, the KSEM should have the facilities for managing and displaying information and knowledge in many different forms: text, numbers, graphs, images, video, and voice.

---

[24] M. Amamiya, K. Hakozaki, T. Yokoi, A. Fusaoka, and Y. Tanaka, "New Architecture for Knowledge Base Mechanisms," in *Fifth Generation Computer Systems,* ed. T. Moto-oka (New York: North Holland, 1982).

PART THREE

Tomorrow's Computing Environment

This last section of the book provides an in-depth discussion of the marketing workbench and explores the experiences in two firms as they develop the specific marketing workbench that meets their organizational and cultural needs. Chapter Nine begins where Part Two ended—by exploring the implications of computer systems for the new marketing world as presented in Part Two. Chapter Ten discusses the evolution of marketing management information systems and the different approaches a firm can adopt in building its marketing workbench. Chapters Eleven and Twelve are case studies of Frito-Lay and General Foods, firms that are quickly and seriously developing a marketing workbench.

The final chapter summarizes the key points in the first 12 chapters and presents a sample agenda that a firm can and should follow in designing a philosophy and architecture for supporting its marketing managers with a marketing workbench.

CHAPTER NINE

Future Computing Needs

This chapter explores the implications of the emerging situations, as described in Part Two, for the design of future computer systems.

IMPACT OF SPECIFIC TRENDS AND DEVELOPMENTS

Data Explosion

Most firms anticipate a data explosion and are studying their choices for dealing with it. One firm, Procter & Gamble, has designed a corporate data architecture as a means of dealing with the issues surrounding the masses of data. This data architecture specifies (1) the types of data the firm will collect, (2) the locations of the data, and (3) the types of application programs needed to manage and analyze the data. This firm has discovered that the currently available technology must be improved, and it has published its data architecture so that vendors will provide the necessary hardware and software solutions. This architecture uses a five-block model.

Block 1. *Transactional systems and operational databases.* This is the input block that brings the data to the corporate database from the firm's internal transactional systems or from operational databases such as customer or brand data.

Block 2. *Historical databases.* This block represents the transactional and operational data stored at the lowest level of detail ever anticipated. For instance, shipment data may be stored at the level of brand code, customer, and day. Since there may be over 100 brand codes for each brand, this database could contain billions and billions of bytes of data. These databases must be flexible enough to permit unstated aggregations, those that may arrive in the future. This second block is the focus of corporate data.

Block 3. *Algorithms or extraction programs.* This block represents the facilities for transforming and/or extracting subsets of the historical data. It corresponds to a "data utility," which provides data to the application programs.

Block 4. *Application databases.* Either on demand or on a scheduled basis, the data in the historical databases are extracted, aggregated, and/or transformed in ways that are appropriate to the current set of business problems. These data are stored in application databases and are managed in a distributed fashion by users and their supporting organization.

Block 5. *Ad-hoc reporting and analytics.* This block represents the end-user oriented software used to support managerial activities and decisions. Examples are PC-based systems like Lotus 1-2-3 or mainframe applications such as EXPRESS.

The designers of this architecture believe that it helps to clarify the needs of companies such as Procter & Gamble, and should provide guidance to vendors in designing software and hardware products. This five-block model differs from the traditional DSS environment in that it recognizes the need for block 2, the historical databases.

The authors of this architecture offer the following viewpoint on the five-block model:

> The key advantage of this new DSS architecture is its ability to respond quickly to provide historical data to institutionalized systems which are used to solve a broad range of changing business problems. This advantage is subtle, but can best be seen when management stops using the orientation of "What information do I

have to solve this problem?" and begins to adopt a posture of "What information do I need to solve this problem?"[1]

They feel that the advantage of their approach will become obvious when a firm has an MMIS serving 200 to 400 managers working on a variety of business problems, and a computer support staff of about 10. This small group must be supported by such an architecture to provide the multitude of data aggregations required by the large number of users.

The authors of the architecture give an example of the need for the historical databases in block 2.

> *Brandsize Conversion.* To save on the cost of distribution, a brand now packs 12 boxes of product to a case versus 10 boxes of product previously. Management wants to analyze product movement, keeping the old and new quantities equivalent. The changeover is expected to take many months and it will be a gradual conversion with each district receiving shipments of both sizes for overlapping periods. The problem is to restate the volume increase of product in a manner that is consistent with the past history. Maintaining a consistent product measure is important in the analysis of the business.[2]

When the data architecture designers look at available hardware and software, they find that most of the MMIS systems work in the block, 3, 4, and 5 arenas, but do not address the problems associated with block 2. They see the need for a hardware and software system optimized for the storage and retrieval of vast databases. They identify several technical issues that must be resolved before this data architecture can be implemented.

1. The economies of scale of storing and processing large volumes of data (e.g., in the billions of bytes) need to be lowered by at least an order of magnitude.

2. Performance issues arise when realizing that to deliver meaningful data to users as represented in the fourth and fifth blocks, large operational and transactional databases must be "joined." Using hardware and software available today, the join-

---

[1] Laurence J. Laning, Gary O. Walla, and Larry S. Airaghi, "A DSS Oversight: Historical Databases," in *DSS–82 Transactions*, ed. Gary Dickson, San Francisco, 1982, p. 89.

[2] Laning et al., "A DSS Oversight," p. 89.

ing of very large databases with acceptable performance results is questionable. To implement a corporate data architecture to deliver large volumes of corporate data, significant advances in software dealing with very large database processing need to be made.

3. It is imperative that efficient "networking" capabilities exist for the delivery of data in a distributed network represented by blocks 4 and 5.

4. "Better ways to deliver data to users and to perform analyses must be found. Advanced user languages must be developed to fill the gap between the current fourth generation languages and the ultimate goal of providing natural language capability. Fourth generation languages today, while providing enormous productivity gains over previous third generation languages for system designers, still require users to understand and deal with syntactical constraints and processing logic not inherent in their thinking. Without expecting natural language capability in the short term, user languages that provide for natural extensions of management styles need to be recognized and developed."[3]

Implicit in this view of the data architecture is the idea that the data will reside in three different locations, thus providing a degree of data redundancy. The firm's transactions systems will keep the most current transactional data in various files and databases, which will feed the historical databases, thus providing the first level of data redundancy. (However, it is possible that the transactional systems will interact directly with the historical databases, thus eliminating this source of redundancy.) The block 3 extract programs will produce the block 4 application databases, which will be managed by the end-user or his or her supporting staff. These data will be subsets of the data in the historical database, providing the second level of data redundancy.

Thus, this conceptual view of an MMIS seems to call for several new entities:

- A computer optimized for storing and retrieving large databases.

---

[3] Laurence J. Laning, "Corporate Data Architecture: The Key to Supporting Management," *DATA BASE*, Summer 1983, p. 15

- An organizational entity (person or small group) to manage the historical database.
- A scheme for distributing the application databases throughout the user organization.
- An organizational structure that facilitates such management of distributed data by operating and staff departments.
- Advanced user languages or interfaces that provide for "natural extensions of management styles."

Expanded View of Data

The expanded view of data has two aspects. First, the computerized data will contain a combination of time oriented tracking data, event data, and static data on the brands and market participants. Second, the event and static data are currently in the hands of marketing professionals and specialists who may be best qualified to computerize and manage the databases.

The implication is that the firm should move to the concept of database management systems (DBMS) rather than file management, which is used in the currently available marketing systems. And this DBMS should accommodate the notion of distributed management of the data. Further, as marketing people acquire and use desktop computers, they are showing interest in building and maintaining their own databases. Fortunately, software products are available that make it possible for the user to build a database by answering simple questions about the structure of the information to be stored and retrieved.

In addition, more powerful packages are available for the development of information systems and applications. These personal computer packages include dBASE II, KnowledgeMan, and R:base, all of which use the relational database model. The relational model was invented at IBM in the early 1970s and has been implemented on IBM mainframes in the form of the SQL query language.

The relational model is particularly appealing to personal computer users because it offers a simple view of the underlying data structure. Data are conceptualized as being in two-dimensional tables, which is a natural way for most people to view data—most books and reports contain data in tabular form. Data can be extracted from two tables if the developer of the database has included a common column name in each table. Further, the developer does not have to specify the structure of the data relationships other than to build tables with common field names and to make sure that the same names are used to indicate entities in the database.

Another enabling development is the widespread adoption of the SQL retrieval language developed by IBM. The announcement of IBM's DB2 product, which uses the same language as SQL but runs under the popular MVS operating system, gave the market a signal that IBM was serious about the relational approach to data management.[4] Three database management packages, Knowledge Manager, Oracle, and R:base, use SQL. Oracle is an interesting product because it runs on all classes of machines: the IBM PC, minicomputers, and mainframes where it is compatible with IBM's SQL and DB2 software.

Having the same database retrieval languages on desktop computers, departmental computers, and mainframes will facilitate the development of a distributed database environment in which data reside at locations on a network and can be retrieved without the user having to be concerned with its location. Another form of distributed database environment is provided by retaining a central version of all the data on a mainframe and downloading "specific views" of the data to workstations. The data will be downloaded to the workstation with a "specific view generator" that can be activated at the workstation by the user or on a timed basis; that is, the data are downloaded at preset times.

Regional Marketing

The move to regional marketing is causing a drastic increase in the amount of time the brand groups spend with their data. When national marketing was practiced, the regional data were only examined to locate the areas of the country that were causing the national results to deviate from expected results. With regional marketing, a plan and set of marketing programs are

---

[4] C. J. Date, *A Guide to DB2* (Reading, Mass.: Addison-Wesley Publishing, 1984).

devised for each region, resulting in the replication of the old-style national analysis for each region. Each region must have its own "story" and marketing program.

This increased need for data analysis is causing the brand groups to demand that they be provided with tools that are easier to use. They want to be able to do their work more efficiently; they recognize that with the current systems, the analysis of 25 regions may require almost 25 times the effort allocated to analyzing the national market. One of the keys to this jump in efficiency involves the user interface, that is, that aspect of the computer system that the brand group itself uses to do its work.

In fact, the evolution of the existing MMIS has tended to center around the interface between the computer and the marketing managers. Most technical computer problems were solved in the first generation, and advances in subsequent generations have primarily involved changes and/or improvements in the interface between user and computer. The importance of user interfaces is not unique to the MMIS area. An IBM study of 22 interactive business packages found that display generation and management constituted the majority of the computer program code in the typical application.[5]

Most user interface changes have involved a move away from the command oriented interface. The following quote offers one reason for this phenomenon:

> Traditionally, command-driven software is identified by the appearance of a dot or a prompt on the screen and little else. This type of software is rich with hundreds of commands that are usually invoked by pressing the control key and a series of additional alphabetic or numeric characters. Software of this family is advertised as being "complete, full of features, and very powerful."
>
> But there's a problem with this method. Imagine walking into your favorite gourmet restaurant one evening and having the chef come to your table and say, "Good news, we have changed the way

---

[5] Jimmy A. Sutton and Ralph H. Sprague, "A Study of Display Generation and Management in Interactive Business Applications," in *Display Generation and Management Systems for Interactive Business Applications*, eds. E. D. Carlson, W. Metz, G. Muller, R. H. Sprague, and J. Sutton (Braunschweig, Wiesbaden: Friedr. Vieweg & Sohn, 1981), pp. 1–16.

that you order food. Now you can have anything that you want. Just tell me what you want and I'll make it for you." And there you sit, trying to remember what sort of sauce the veal came with last time and whether it was pepper or peppercorns that you liked in your green beans. Imagine a command-driven restaurant. Then mourn for it when it fails because no one knows what to order. The same is true with software. Users don't want to be able to order anything that they can imagine. They don't, in the main, even want to imagine. They only want to get a job done. Open-ended, command-driven software is dead.[6]

This quote forecasts an end to command-driven interfaces in which the user, presented with a blank screen, must compose a command for or give an instruction to the computer. If the computer does not understand the command (i.e., it is not a "legal" command), it will display an error message and invite the user to try again. Designers of end-user software have long recognized that such an approach is not desirable for occasional users. The traditional approach of software designers has been to devise a series of menus that guide the user to the desired result. But users soon evolve to the point where they want combinations of data that are not available in the menus. Or they become so proficient that working through a series of menus becomes a waste of time and thus inhibits the use of the MMIS.

One way to overcome the blank-screen problem of command-driven software is to use natural language front ends that translate the user's natural commands into the system's command language. But the user is still presented with a blank screen and must still compose a request. Research at Xerox Corporation's Palo Alto Research Center indicates that this type of interface (the blank screen) may be a difficult concept for most people to grasp. A blank screen requires the user to work in the abstract, to be creative, to generate a request. Xerox's research led the corporation to the following classification of easy versus hard concepts or interface attributes.[7]

---

[6] Martin Dean, "Simplify, Simplify, Simplify," *Byte*, December 1983, p. 163.

[7] David Cranfield Smith, Charles Irby, Ralph Kimball, Bill Verblank, and Erick Harslem, "Designing the Star Interface," *Byte*, April 1982, p. 248.

Easy	Hard
Concrete	Abstract
Visible	Invisible
Copying	Creating
Choosing	Filling in
Recognizing	Generating
Editing	Programming
Interactive	Batch

One can easily see that a blank-screen interface has most of the "hard" attributes. This research indicates that natural language interfaces may not be the ultimate in direct usage.

Xerox's designers call for a totally different approach; instead of the blank screen, make all the relevant material visible on the screen.

> A well-designed system makes everything relevant to a task visible on the screen. It doesn't hide things under CODE + key combinations or force you to remember conventions that burden your memory. During conscious thought, the brain utilizes several levels of memory, the most important being the "short-term memory." Many studies have analyzed the short-term memory and its role in thinking. Two conclusions stand out: (1) conscious thought deals with concepts in the short-term memory, and (2) the capacity of the short-term memory is limited. When everything being dealt with in a computer system is visible, the display screen relieves the load on the short-term memory by acting as sort of a "visual cache"! Thinking becomes easier and more productive. A well-designed computer system can actually improve the quality of your thinking.[8]

These ideas were the foundation for the design of the Xerox Star computer, which heavily influenced the design of the Apple Macintosh computer, as well as the Metaphor system.

The concept underlying this approach is to overcome some of the user's limitations in accessing and processing information. Designers are just beginning to build systems that consider the cognitive compatibility between the system and the user's attentional, perceptual, and knowledge representation systems. Each successive generation of the MMIS is better at enhancing the

---

[8] Smith et al., "Star Interface," p. 258.

information-processing characteristics of the user.[9] For instance, in a study of how people integrate several pieces of information into a final decision, Goldsmith and Schvaneveldt examined the role of computer presentations on the decision process. Their research indicates that

> Most often, the information displayed on computer terminals is presented in a numerical, piecemeal fashion that requires the user to process it sequentially. Substantial improvements in decision performance may be possible by having the computer arrange multiple sources of information in an integrated output configuration. In this way, a user's general ability to transform information into decisions can be enhanced by capitalizing on the inherent characteristics of the human information-processing system.[10]

The Xerox designers go on to explain the impact of providing all the relevant information on the screen.

> A subtle thing happens when everything is visible: the display becomes reality. The user model becomes identical with what is on the screen. Objects can be understood purely in terms of their visible characteristics. Actions can be understood in terms of their effects on the screen. This lets users conduct experiments to test, verify, and expand their understanding—the essence of experimental science.[11]

This ability to understand what to do by simply viewing the screen explains why electronic spreadsheets such as VisiCalc and Lotus 1-2-3 were so successful. Since a financial spreadsheet is a "user model," there is a one-to-one mapping of the user's objects and the screen's objects. The user knew about spreadsheets from previous exposure to financial calculations. Since the electronic spreadsheets "worked" similarly to the paper-and-pencil spreadsheets, the user was able to transfer existing knowledge to the computer environment. Carrol and Mack refer to this transfer of substantive prior knowledge from one domain

---

[9] A. Freedy and E. M. Johnson. "Human Factor Issues in Computer Management of Information for Decisionmaking," *IEEE Transactions on Systems, Man, and Cybernetics*, SMC-12, no. 4, (July/August 1982), pp. 437–38.

[10] Timothy E. Goldsmith, and Roger W. Schvaneveldt, "Facilitating Multiple-Cue Judgments with Integral Information Displays," in *Human Factors in Computer Systems*, eds. John C. Thomas and Michael L. Schneider (Norwood, N.J.: Ablex Publishing Co., 1984), pp. 243–70.

[11] Smith et al., "Star Interface," p. 260.

to understand another domain as "learning by knowing" or "metaphor."[12] The paper-and-pencil spreadsheet is a metaphor for the electronic spreadsheets; knowledge about using the first could be transferred to the second.

Thus, these research and design efforts have led to the idea of putting a lot of information on the computer screen, displaying it in a manner that matches the user's existing mental model, and allowing the user to work with his or her information-processing abilities in a natural way. But, once the information is on the screen, what is the best way for the user to indicate the desired computer actions? The Xerox researchers indicate that people are good at copying, choosing, recognizing, and editing. Thus, an easy-to-use MMIS interface would be one that allowed the user to perform one or more of the following activities:

- Choose a command (or a segment of a command) from a list and copy it into a final form.
- Recognize an existing command and select it for execution.
- Edit an existing command so that it performs the desired task.

The Acustar system provides a recognition type of interface in that the user is asked a question and can be presented with a list of the legal responses. S/he simply selects the appropriate response.

Texas Instruments Incorporated has created a development package called The Technology Package. With this system, a programmer can develop a package that allows the user to issue commands by constructing a sentence from sentence fragments displayed in different windows on the computer screen. The user builds a command by choosing items from various lists.

The Metaphor system's interface allows the manager to build a database query by choosing the appropriate items from a list of possible items. The new data can be displayed in a report by editing an existing report format to accommodate it. The user simply points to items on the screen.

---

[12] John M. Carroll and Robert L. Mack, "Learning to Use a Word Processor: By Doing, By Thinking, and By Knowing," in *Human Factors in Computer Systems*, ed. John C. Thomas and Michael L. Schneider (Norwood, N.J.: Ablex Publishing Co., 1984), p. 35.

The ability to be able to select, i.e., to point at, material currently displayed and cause it to be treated as input is extremely useful, and situations when such a facility can be used occur very often during the course of an interactive session. Why is such a facility useful? Because most interactions with a programming system are not independent, i.e., each "event" bears some relationship to what transpired before, usually to a fairly recent event. Being able to point at (portions of) these events effectively gives the user the power of pronoun reference, i.e., the user can say use this expression or that value, and then simply point. This drastically reduces the amount of typing the user has to do in many situations, and results in a considerable increase in the effective "bandwidth" of the user communications with his programming environment.[13]

This pointing and selecting interface could very well become popular because its metaphor is the existing process of manually editing a rough draft of a letter or document. The manager uses a pencil to indicate the sections (words, sentences, paragraphs) that should be rearranged on the page. The process is one of moving objects around on the page until a finished document is prepared. This is similar to the pointing and selecting process used in some of the mouse and icon computer interfaces.

These types of "pointing and selecting" interfaces tend to use a mouse for moving the screen pointer. A mouse has several key attributes:

- It is a "Fitts Law" device; that is, you can point with a mouse about as fast and easily as you can with your finger.[14]
- It stays where you leave it and does not have to be picked up like a light pen.
- It has buttons that allow the user to interact with the screen objects in a number of ways.[15]

---

[13] Warren Teitelman, "A Display-Oriented Programmer's Assistant," in *Interactive Programming Environment*, ed. Howard E. Shrobe and Erik Sanderwall (New York: McGraw Hill, 1984), p. 242.

[14] P. M. Fitts, "The Information Capacity of the Human Motor System in Controlling Amplitude of Movement," *Journal of Experimental Psychology* 47, (1954), pp. 381–91.

[15] Smith et al., "Star Interface," p. 246.

Sales Force Computerization

The computerization of the sales force involves the placement of computer systems in the regional offices throughout the country and even into the hands of the sales representatives (SRs). Hence, a small portable unit is required for the SRs and perhaps larger units are needed in the offices. These units should be able to communicate and exchange data and documents with units within the sales organization as well as throughout the company. They should also be compatible with the brand groups' computer systems; as applications are developed in one organization, there will be a desire to share them with the other organization.

Most importantly, the firm needs a plan and architecture for distributing computing throughout an organization that can also be spread throughout the United States. Discussions with the firms in the survey revealed two distinct approaches to this issue. Centralized systems call for the data and their processing to occur on one, large, mainframe computer. Each office has a terminal or personal computer that communicates with the central mainframe. The data can be extracted from the central database for viewing and printing at the local office, or they can be downloaded to local personal computers for viewing, graphing, printing, or use in PC-based programs.

In decentralized system, the data would reside in the computers located in the sales offices. Such systems build on the idea that the data should reside with the people who use and understand it. Thus, if division managers were to use the sales-call data collected by their sales people, those data would remain on the computer in the division office. Aggregations of the data could be routinely sent to the other computers throughout the sales hierarchy.

Merger of Sales and Marketing

One possible aspect of future marketing is the merger of the sales and marketing organizations, or at least a blurring of the distinction between the two. If this occurs, the firm must develop a new organizational structure that does not have the strict and separate hierarchies found in most of today's consumer packaged goods firms. The resulting organization could very well involve the concept of networking, which has been espoused by John Naisbitt and others as the natural replacement for hierarchies.[16]

The result will be an increased need for communications between the brand groups and the people in the field. This need will be particularly pressing if a network-based organizational structure is adopted. Tactical and strategic decisions involving a brand in a region will be made by brand and regional marketing managers. This change could create a communications problem because these people are separated by both time and space.

Future computer systems for the marketing/sales organization will need to solve this problem, perhaps by offering computer conferencing, electronic mail and messages, and facilities for exchanging documents across a possibly wide range of computers.

Ford Motor Co. reports having successfully used such a system for its sales organization.[17] Ford has installed 2,000 voice mailboxes (with a goal of 30,000) as a means of eliminating telephone tag. In addition, a company in the survey reported experimenting with a computer mailbox for exchanging messages within the sales force and with the brand groups; the results were so positive that the company is considering using this procedure throughout the company.

These communication needs mean that office automation may become as major an aspect of marketing and sales computing as data query and analysis are today.

New Ways to Understand and Exploit Information

As marketing people collect more information and go the regional marketing route, they will have to find new ways to understand the information. One of today's trends is to use graphical display and analysis as an adjunct to the traditional numerical display and analysis of data. This trend suggests a need for workstations that provide better graphics resolution than most of today's personal computers. Further, better graphic tools are needed for analyzing the data. Most of today's tools for graphical analysis are similar to those used for presentation

---

[16] John Naisbitt, *Megatrends* (New York: Warner Books, 1984).

[17] "Office System Tunes Up Automaker's Communications," *ComputerWorld*, December 12, 1984, p. 35.

graphics; these tools use bar, pie, line, and scatter charts to display the data. These representations are limited in their ability to display a lot of data at once or to permit the user to ascertain complicated causal or lead/lag relationships in the data. Therefore, a new generation of graphical tools is needed.

Marketing Group Computerization

As marketing managers become more computerized, their workstations need to accommodate the differences among the group members. As long as the detailed data analysis is relegated to the assistant brand manager, the analysis tools (graphical and numerical) can be concentrated in his or her workstation, which means that the other members of the group play more of a managerial than an analytical role. They are more involved in the design, decision-influencing, and diplomacy aspects of brand management. Since data analysis involves communication with people throughout the company, the office automation aspects of information systems become very important.

Knowledge Management

The data explosion and the merger of marketing and sales are creating a need for systems that can help the firm manage its marketing knowledge. Two types of needs are becoming evident. First, computer agents or expert systems are needed to assist the brand groups and the field organization in data analysis. It is possible to develop a system that would constantly examine and analyze the scanner, scanner-panel, retail sales-call, and marketing event data. Such a system could identify abnormal situations and look across the brands and marketing programs to ascertain relationships among the various outcomes (sales, market share, distribution) and their causes (promotions, ad features, advertising, sales events, and so on).

A more advanced system would assist the manager in analyzing and modeling the data. For instance, it is possible to develop a system that would advise the manager about methods for measuring the impact of a marketing event such as a promotion. Or a system could lead the manager through the steps involved in estimating a brand's sales response.

The second need is for a method to share one person's knowledge with others. As brand groups and regional managers gain experience and knowledge, it will be important for these people to share this knowledge with other managers and professionals involved in the marketing effort. This will be especially true when the responsibility for tactical marketing is diffused throughout the marketing and sales organization.

SUMMARY

Several needs for future computing systems are identified in the above discussion. They include:

1. Hardware for storing and processing large databases.
2. Software for joining large files and extracting small subsets of data.
3. Efficient networks for delivering extracted data to application programs.
4. Efficient networks for linking brand groups to the field organization.
5. Better ways to perform analysis.
6. User languages that are a natural extension of management styles.
7. An organizational structure that facilitates the management of distributed data and individual computing.
8. Data models that accommodate the expanded view of data.
9. Small portable computers that are compatible with desktop units.
10. A means of exchanging messages and documents and conducting computer-based conferences.
11. Agents or expert systems for assisting in the analysis of data.
12. Methods for managing the knowledge of the brand groups and the marketing specialists so that it is accessible to the expanded field organization.

Thus, the next generation of systems for use by marketing and sales managers should

- Recognize and solve the issues identified in P&G's data architecture.

- Recognize the existence of time-series, event, and static data types that may be distributed throughout the marketing organization.
- Provide a networked solution to the communications and office situation caused by the computerization of the field organization.
- Provide a user interface that matches the marketing managers' metaphors.
- Provide better ways to analyze data, either by the manager or by a computerized agent.
- Provide a knowledge management facility for sharing individual knowledge with the entire marketing and sales organization.

This computer solution must be matched by an organizational structure and philosophy that recognizes

- That data are distributed throughout the organization.
- The need for marketing managers and professionals to use the computer as an intellectual resource and tool.
- The importance of "feedback learning" in the analysis of marketing data.
- The data analysis implications of regional marketing.
- The potential role of the computer in the management of the firm's knowledge.

These are the challenges involved in the next round of hardware and software for use in marketing management. The speed of the developments makes it desirable for the firm to have a strategic plan that allows it to expand its current facilities and grow with the forthcoming technologies. The next chapter discusses some of the organizational and managerial issues involved in developing a strategic plan for marketing management information systems.

CHAPTER TEN

The Marketing Workbench

EVOLUTION OF THE MWB

This chapter discusses the evolution of the MWB by focusing on the marketing management information system (MMIS), the key component on the MWB. This evolution is described by exploring three generations of the MMIS.

First Generation

Marketing management information systems are the systems that usually run on mainframe computers and give the brand groups access to their shipment and market performance data. These systems run on either an in-house computer and/or external time-sharing computers. In most cases the early version of an MMIS was not an integrated information system; the shipments data were on an in-house system and the market performance data were on an external, time-sharing system, usually operated by the primary data vendor. This is the case in a number of companies where the brand groups use the INF*ACT system to access Nielsen retail sales data, the MAJERS computer to access ad feature data, and an in-house system to access the shipment data.

First-generation MMIS tend to use a command oriented language in which the user types commands or instructions on a terminal. The following is an example of such a command:

GET 140 BOST-NAT S229 S.VOL-S.SOM

This computer interface requires that the user memorize or look up instructions (e.g., GET) and codes (140 refers to a particular product, BOST refers to a region, S229 refers to a time period, and S.VOL refers to a fact). This approach requires that the brand group learn a new language—the language of the MMIS.

Command oriented MMIS are very efficient for the heavy user who memorizes the codes. However, this type of interface is frustrating for the new or intermittent user who does not use the MMIS enough to remember the codes from one usage to the next. Such intermittent use characterizes brand groups. To overcome the problem, firms have adopted one of two approaches. The most common approach is to assign the use of the MMIS to an intermediary who uses the system at the request of the brand groups and provides them with printed reports. Putting an intermediary between a brand group and its data tends to slow down the data access process and prevent "feedback learning" in which a person retrieves a set of data, examines it, recognizes the need for more or different data, retrieves them, and so on.

The second approach is to assign a systems person to work with the brand groups in preparing a series of standard report formats. These reports use a facility for grouping the MMIS commands into a file or "macrocommand" that is assigned a new name. The brand groups build a library of these report formats, and access new data by first examining hard-copy versions of sample reports and then entering the name of the report into the computer.

First-generation marketing management information systems made three major contributions. First, they solved the data structure problem by matching the user's conceptualization of the data with the data retrieval methods. Marketing people need to retrieve data along various dimensions and at different levels in the product and company hierarchies. Second, they solved the data extraction problem by providing the facility for the manager to extract and display the needed data from a large database. The third contribution involved the combination of data query and reporting with analysis capability, which varied from simple descriptive statistics to powerful statistical techniques. This analysis facility made it possible to perform diverse analyses, described as follows by John Quelch in a discussion of the planned use of an MMIS by the consumer department at the Mobil Chemical Corp.:

Promotion

- Evaluate trade deal impacts on Nielsen or SAMI shares.
- Test alternative promotion schedules for profit impact.
- Examine on-deal cannibalization among your own brands and competitors.
- Set realistic objectives for coupon redemptions and profit impact.
- Find out who's buying on-deal, and how it has changed their buying habit.
- Monitor your newspaper exposures and rank your programs by effectiveness.

Advertising

- Plan spending based on market response.
- Design and monitor ad tests to maximize advertising effectiveness.
- Learn more about your competitors' advertising than they know.
- Examine differences in regional response to advertising.
- Defend ad budgets intelligently or reallocate to other needs.

Price

- Monitor relative price movement for your brand to spot competitive changes.
- Analyze the profitability of price changes.
- Spot and evaluate price thresholds.
- Evaluate pricing policy across sizes and brands and test alternative prices.
- Track pipeline effects of price changes from shipping dock to consumer.
- Model material prices and production plans to prepare for inflationary pressures.

Distribution

- Determine the impact of distribution on sales.
- Examine the profitability of achieving greater distribution.
- Identify order patterns of major wholesalers and retailers to spot buying strengths and weaknesses.

Test Market

- Develop realistic test-market objectives using past test data more effectively.
- Prepare more accurate long-run forecasts with only three to six months of test-market data.

- Diagnose sales results based on measures of consumer attitudes and behavior.
- Determine the impact of alternative marketing plans.

Sales Force

- Determine the optimal call level for each sales representative for each account and prospect.
- Establish sales territories to maximize total sales potential.
- Identify the best size for the sales force.[1]

Second Generation

The second-generation MMIS exhibits more intelligence in that it has been programmed to carry on an intelligent dialogue with the user. This dialogue involves either a question and answer session or a series of menus that produces the desired results by leading the user through a series of choices. If the user does not know the answer to a question or cannot remember the form of the answer, s/he types a question mark (?) and the MMIS responds with the legal answers to the question. Further, if the user happens to type a response that is ambiguous to the MMIS, the system indicates the set of answers that could legally match the user's response and asks the user to select from the list. Acustar is an example of such a system.

This question and answer approach is cumbersome for the heavy user but good for the novice or intermittent user. This trade-off seems to have been recognized by the designers of the EXPRESS package when they added a second-generation front end to their first-generation EXPRESS package. EXPRESS EASY-TRAC has a menu oriented interface that eliminates the need for the user to memorize EXPRESS commands. EASYTRAC handles the dialogue with the user, and then generates a set of EXPRESS commands. The user selects items from a series of hierarchical menus. These menus are flexible in that the user can set his or her own pace by telling EASYTRAC to shorten (or lengthen) prompts and descriptions.

These second-generation packages are sufficiently "user friendly" to enable a marketing person who is motivated and

---

[1] John Quelch, "Mobil Chemical Corporation," Case no. 9-583-024 (Boston: Harvard Business School, 1982), Exhibit 1, Applications of a Marketing Decision Support System, p. 9. Copyright © 1982 by the President and Fellows of Harvard College. Harvard Business School Case 9-583-024. Reprinted by permission.

takes the time to understand the concepts being used by the system to break away from reliance on standard reports. Brand groups can use their MMIS for creative data analysis in an intensive feedback-learning mode. Such an MMIS removes most of the barriers to direct data retrieval and report writing.

Third Generation

The third-generation MMIS is still evolving. It is moving in various directions, including the evolution of both first- and second-generation systems, as well as an integration of mainframe data into personal computer spreadsheets.

First-Generation Evolution. One growth path involves a return to the command orientation of the first-generation MMIS. However, instead of the user learning the system's language, the system learns the users' language. Data retrieval methods have been developed that use "natural languages," that is, languages the user considers natural. These packages have three major components. First, they have a lexicon that contains a mapping of common or "natural" words or phrases to the set of systems words or commands. For instance, the system may use the command GET to retrieve data from a file. The lexicon would know that the commands SELECT, RETRIEVE, GIMME, I WANT TO SEE, GIVE ME, and LETS LOOK AT mean the same as GET.

The second component is a "parser" that allows the user to type whatever sentences or phrases s/he chooses. The parser reads this input and breaks it down into words or phrases that the lexicon can use. The third component is a program generator that writes or generates the set of system commands that produces the desired result. The INTELLECT system from Artificial Intelligence Corp. provides a natural-language front end to different file and database systems on IBM mainframes.

General Foods is experimenting with a natural language approach. They are working with Cognitive Systems Corp. to develop DESI, a natural-language front end to Analect, a command oriented system from Dialogue Systems Corp. This approach is an attempt to overcome the deficiencies of their first-generation MMIS.

> To query the systems, managers initially used two traditional, time-tested—and unsatisfactory—methods. Most stuck with pre-

formatted reports developed by data processing. An application that is simple to use: pick a report from a menu, fill in the blanks, and the program will do the rest. But managers kept thinking of combinations of data that the existing reports did not cover, and bothering data processing to create new applications for them. Delays and miscommunications with DP produced among managers what internal consultant George O. Williams describes as a growing desire to "roam freely through the database." The second General Foods option, Analect's query language, offered managers the freedom preformatted reports denied, but its powerful commands were difficult to learn. . . . Users must also remember the names of all database files and fields pertaining to a subject area.

General Foods hopes to resolve this impasse by giving its managers DESI, a natural language interface to Analect. . . . When the system is up and running at General Foods (April 1985 is the current target date), managers fresh out of business school will be able to create multidimensional models of marketing data—like changes in sales of pork-flavored Stovetop® Stuffing in the Northeast during the past 12 months—after only a couple of sessions at the terminal.[2]

Second-Generation Evolution. Another direction for third-generation systems is a further evolution of the second-generation approaches to user interfaces. Several manufacturers and software vendors are developing graphically oriented systems that use on-screen icons and a "mouse" instead of the keyboard for interacting with the system. The Xerox Star computer and the Apple Macintosh are examples of such systems, as is the Top-View package from IBM. Instead of learning commands, the user selects functions and data "icons" with the mouse (an icon is a small drawing on the computer screen that represents a system function or file). To activate or select the function, the mouse is used to move the cursor into the icon, which the user selects by pushing a button on the mouse. Once an icon has been selected, the system opens a window on the screen that contains a menu or more icons. The user then selects from the menu with the mouse.

Metaphor Computer Systems, Inc. has introduced Metaphor (a system targeted at brand groups), which uses this approach. Its

---

[2] Elisabeth Horwitt, "Natural Languages Improve the User-Computer Dialogue," *Business Computer Systems*, November 1984, pp. 32–33.

designers have provided a graphical programming environment in which the user can build an entire program by selecting a series of icons and menu items.

Complex procedures involving multiple database queries, spreadsheet calculations, plotting and printing, and even lengthy data reduction programs written in BASIC can be designed graphically as sequences of generic icons. When "opened," each icon offers a series of windows and interactive "option sheets" that help customize the icon's function to user needs. The spreadsheet icon, for instance, opens to reveal a standard spreadsheet display. Many of the sheet's elements, however, are "active" in that when pointed to with the mouse, menus and help screens appear in order to guide the user. Once defined through such menus, applications can be "encapsulated" and from then on called into action by invoking a single application icon.[3]

Another unique aspect of the Metaphor approach is that it does not include or directly involve a mainframe. The data are kept on a file server (i.e., a large disk drive), and are accessed via a local area network. However, software and facilities are provided for extracting data from large IBM mainframes and storing them in the file server.

While Metaphor is the first company to provide an approach involving the development of systems for specific professional groups (e.g., brand managers and financial analysts) using icon and graphical programming icons running in a network, the hardware and software are available for using this approach on computers from other manufacturers. In particular, IBM has developed a language called Office-By-Example (OBE), a two-dimensional language and system that is an attempt to mimic manual procedures of business and office systems. OBE is described by its developer as

an attempt to combine and unify aspects of word processing, data processing, report writing, graphics, and electronic mail. With such a language, end users are able to specify and store complex OBE programs, thus developing their own applications. In addition, end users can set up menus (which in essence are stored OBE programs) for their use or for others who are not motivated to learn details of the OBE language. An executive can specify to an assis-

---

[3] John Verity, "Metaphor Unveils Network," *Datamation*, October 1, 1984, pp. 40–50.

tant the menu(s) he would like to select from and the results to be displayed by the execution of the particular program selection. As an example, the executive may want a menu in order to see his mail and various summary reports (which aggregate data from a data base), together with the ability to send messages. Others may wish to see their calendars or to reserve a room automatically. In all cases, the assistant or secretary can set up an appropriate stored program based upon the executive's specifications. The novelty of this approach is that the menus are not preprogrammed by the system developers; rather, they are customized according to specification and set up by end users for end users. The programming style of OBE is the same as that of QBE: direct programming within two-dimensional pictures of business objects.[4]

A major difference between the second-generation menus and the third-generation user interfaces is that the second-generation system was designed to operate in a time-sharing environment in which the questions or menus were sent over communications lines to a terminal. The slow speed of this arrangement limited the amount of information on the screen at any one time. Third-generation systems tend to be developed with a personal computer as the interface. Screen "painting" is one of the strengths of a personal computer because there is little communications delay between the central processor and the screen. Also, some personal computers are being developed with a separate processor dedicated to managing the screen.

PC and Mainframe Data

In most firms the MMIS is separate and distinct from the personal computers. The MMIS is used to retrieve data that are manually loaded into a Lotus 1-2-3 spreadsheet. The next step is to retrieve the data in the appropriate form for direct placement into the PC application package. Such facilities are becoming available from the vendors of the mainframe MMIS packages. Management Decision Systems, Inc. provides EXPRESS-mate/link, a software package that runs on an IBM PC and allows the user to extract data from an EXPRESS database and convert it to a format compatible with most PC application packages.

---

[4] M. M. Zloof, "Office-by-Example: A Business Language That Unifies Data and Word Processing and Electronic Mail," *IBM Systems Journal* 21, no. 3 (1982), pp. 274–75.

Artificial Intelligence Corp. offers INTELLECT MICRO-TO-MAINFRAME LINK, which allows users of an IBM PC to use natural language to retrieve and download data from the mainframe to the personal computer. The downloaded data can be incorporated into PC-based programs for analysis and graphing.

In addition, the increasing power of the personal computer is motivating some companies to shift applications from mainframes to PCs. David Ferris, chairman of Ferrin Corp., has described the impact of the newer electronic spreadsheets on the form and location of managerial computing: "An important new development in Symphony, among others, is the providing of a modeling language that goes far beyond the capability of previous spreadsheets. There's more control over screen definition, data entry, and data validation."[5]

Ferris feels that this facility will allow personal computer packages to replace mainframe-based planning packages because applications can now be built that guide the user through a series of formatted screens. One implication of this new power is that spreadsheets are becoming a programming tool or environment for data processing professionals. Hence, the firm could begin to allow the workstation to play a more central role in the overall MMIS, which is the central theme of the next-generation MMIS.

NETWORK-BASED MARKETING WORKBENCH

It is largely a matter of convenience whether the components of a computer system are housed in one box or widely separated. If the users of the system are themselves dispersed, the separation—given an efficient communications network—is much more cost-effective than concentration. . . . Users have extensive computing resources immediately available at their own locations and will normally be able to treat them as personal. However, when additional resources are needed, they borrow them from elsewhere in the network, just as their resources may be borrowed by others. The resources in question might be hardware (a faster or better printer) or software (a specialized editing program). Together these hardware and software resources give the aggregation of machines in

---

[5] Mike Major, "DSS Outlook: Micros, Links, AI, Integration," *Software News* 4, no. 12 (December 1984), p. 26.

the net or ring much of the power and sophistication of a large mainframe computer.[6]

The Network Philosophy

Before the personal computer, almost all business computer services were supplied by mainframe or time-shared minicomputers. The PC allowed users and managers to understand that a desktop computer could do certain things better than a very powerful, but remote, mainframe. High-speed networks will allow people to extend their awareness of distributed computing and to recognize that a combination of computing devices, connected by high-speed networks, may offer better service than one central computer center.

The Data Architecture Viewpoint

Several companies are beginning to take an integrated view of their market data and to study the implications of this view on the design of computer systems for supporting their marketing managers. Procter & Gamble has studied the problem extensively and has developed the corporate data architecture concept to help the firm's managers conceptualize the needs of the next generation of computer equipment.[7]

Implicit in Procter & Gamble's view of the data architecture is the idea that the data will reside in three different locations, thus providing a degree of data redundancy. The firm's transaction systems will keep the most current transactional data in various files and databases. These data will feed the historical databases, thus providing for some data redundancy. (However, it is possible that the transaction systems will interact directly with the historical databases, thus eliminating this source of redundancy.) Extraction programs will produce application databases, which will be managed by the end user or his or her supporting staff.

---

[6] Gordon Pask, *Micro Man: Computing and the Evolution of Consciousness* (New York: Macmillan, 1982), pp. 57–58.

[7] Laurence J. Laning, Gary O. Walla, and Larry S. Airaghi, "A DSS Oversight: Historical Databases," in *DSS-82 Transactions*, ed. Gary Dickson, San Francisco, 1982.

Thus, this conceptual view of an MMIS seems to call for several new entities:

- A computer optimized for storing and retrieving large databases.
- An organizational entity (person or small group) to manage the historical database.
- A scheme for distributing the application databases throughout the user organization.
- An organizational structure that facilitates such management of distributed data by operating and staff departments.
- Advanced user languages or interfaces that provide for "natural extensions of management styles."

The Data Warehouse

One of the key components of this architecture is the historical database and its associated computer retrieval system. The implementation of the hardware depends on the development of hardware and software systems that achieve orders-of-magnitude increases in the speed of retrieving data from the database.

A number of research and development projects are investigating the feasibility of significantly increasing the speed with which a computer can access data from its storage devices. Current computers are based on vonNeumann design principles, which call for the execution of one instruction at a time—sequential processing. In addition, there is a single channel between the processing element and main memory through which all instructions and data must flow. This bottleneck restricts the ultimate speed of conventional computers.

A number of the projects involve an attempt to move from this sequential-processing computer to a parallel-processing device, that is, one with several processors operating in parallel fashion rather than a single processor. In addition, some of the designs provide parallel channels and memories, as well as parallel disk drives. The idea is to eliminate the bottleneck between the processor and secondary storage device by distributing it over a large collection of processing elements and their local memories. Such a machine is one of the goals of the fifth-generation computer projects in Japan, Europe, and the United States.[8]

One reason for interest in this type of design is the emergence of relational databases as the preferred database structure in end-user computing environments. A relational database is one "that is perceived by its users as a collection of tables (and nothing but tables)."[9] Since all users and programmers are comfortable working with tabular data, they tend to welcome and appreciate the relational model. Moreover, most recent versions of the relational model provide a user interface that makes it easy to formulate a complex query without writing a complex program. These features have led to their rapid adoption. In fact, some database researchers believe that this model will become the dominant one.

> Most database professionals now believe that relational technology is the way of the future—so much so that new users have no need even to be aware of the older technologies—and just about every product announcement in the database field these days is either for an entirely new relational system or for relational enhancements to one of the older systems.[10]

The relational model is particularly appealing in an end-user computing environment because it is oriented toward ad hoc application system design, thus permitting quick building, modifying of prototype applications, and the maintenance of application systems whose data requirements change often.[11] These functions characterize the world of the marketing manager in his or her end-user computing mode.

The relational systems are well suited for parallel-processing computers because queries that require data from multiple tables can take advantage of multiple processors and storage devices if the tables are on different processors. Consider a database containing information on the firm's salespeople and their retail

---

[8] Lubomir Bic, "The Fifth Generation Grail: A Survey of Related Research," in *The Fifth Generation Challenge*, ed. Richard L. Muller and James J. Pottmyer (Proceedings of the 1984 Annual Conference of the Association of Computing Machinery, 1984), pp. 293–97.

[9] C. J. Date, *A Guide to DB2*, (Reading, Mass.: Addison-Wesley Publishing, 1984), p. 7.

[10] C. J. Date, *Database: A Primer* (Reading, Mass.: Addison-Wesley Publishing, 1983), p. x.

[11] Clyde Holsapple, "Uniting Relational and Postrelational Database Management Tools," *System & Software*, November 1984, p. 183.

calls. The data could reside in two tables: a sales-call table with a record for each sales call, and a sales-rep table with a record containing personal information for each sales representative. If a manager wanted the number of sales calls for all sales representatives over 45 years of age, the computer would first look in the sales-rep table for the names of all the salespeople over 45. After it had extracted all the names, it would turn to the sales-call table and find all the sales calls for each of the over-45 salespeople. This could be a slow process because the computer has to do its work sequentially; it must first find the names of all of the over-45 sales representatives before it can find their sales calls.

A parallel-processing computer could do the two activities at the same time. After finding the first name from the sales-rep table, it could begin locating that person's sales calls in the sales-call table while it was also finding the next over-45 salesperson in the sales-rep table. The advantage of such a parallel approach grows stronger as the complexity of the query increases, that is, when the computer has to extract data from several tables.

This parallel processing approach may call for the replacement of the general-purpose computer with machines that are optimized for specific purposes. An example is the IBM System 38, which was build around a relational database and is thus optimized for database work. More recent introductions include database computers from Teradata Corp., which uses hundreds of microprocessors operating in parallel fashion as opposed to one central processing unit, and computers from Britton Lee. The Britton Lee machines permit direct access to the data from personal computers.

Researchers at IBM's Thomas J. Watson Research Center have issued a call for hosts growing toward "the development of generalized extract programs. Such host programs would perform sophisticated host database requests and merely provide the workstation with the end results to be incorporated into reports" and into applications running on the workstation.[12] Such extract programs could be based on currently available software. For instance, the developers of the FOCUS fourth-generation language package believe that it can be used for such an extract

---

[12] B. C. Goldstein, A. R. Heller, F. H. Moss, and I. Wladawsky-Berger, "Directions in Cooperative Processing between Workstations and Hosts," *IBM Systems Journal* 23, no. 3 (1984), p. 243.

program because in addition to having its own relational database, it can access data in all of IBM's file systems. As such, it could be used as a "front-end driver to provide data to the more specialized packages."[13]

Network Design Approaches

This section describes two conceptually similar, but physically different, approaches to designing and implementing a network oriented MWB. Both of these approaches recognize the data, software, and user activities inherent in the P&G five-block model. The first approach assumes that the network is oriented around a traditional mainframe; the second uses the local area network concept.

Traditional Network. P&G's corporate data architecture calls for the existence of a historical database, extract programs, application datasets, and decision support software. A network-based MWB could be built that uses the mainframe for the historical database, extract programs, and the application datasets, while leaving the decision support application programs on the workstation. In addition, the communications aspect of the network could be managed by the mainframe.

A view of such a system can be gained by examining the Tempus-Link and Tempus-Data products offered by Micro Tempus, Inc., of Montreal, Canada, to run on IBM mainframes. These products provide a facility for connecting personal computers to the mainframe so that the mainframe/personal computers combination appears to form a closely knit network. The key aspect of this combination is the way the data are stored on the mainframe, making it appear to the user that they are stored on one of the PC's disk drives.

This feat is accomplished by creating "virtual" disks on the mainframe. Virtual disks, which can be almost any size, can be shared simultaneously by multiple micros. An application program interface provides the user with the ability to mount and dismount virtual disks from programs written in languages such as BASIC or from application programs such as dBASE. In addi-

---

[13] Donald Wszolek, quoted in 'DSS Outlook: Micros, Links, AI, Integration," Mike Major, *Software News*, December 1984, p. 26.

tion, a host application program interface allows the PC application to request action by a mainframe application. Hence, a PC application can use the mainframe as a "slave" or peripheral device.

A network based on Micro Tempus's products offers the following features.[14]

1. Corporate database access is provided by Tempus-Link, which has four modules.
   a. Mainframe virtual disk system that manages a limitless number of microcompatible disks in sizes from 32 kilobytes to 15 megabytes.
   b. Mainframe access method that provides access from mainframe programs to the virtual disks.
   c. Communications module that makes the system independent of the teleprocessing monitor, and communications devices used to tie the personal computers to the mainframe.
   d. Microsoftware that provides the micro with concurrent access to four mainframe virtual drives in addition to its physical drives. Any request from programs or from DOS commands are automatically routed to the mainframe where they are processed by the virtual disk manager.
2. Tempus-Data is a data management system that allows end users to select, extract, and update mainframe data while operating in the personal computer environment. Tempus-Data is comprised of three modules:
   a. The batch portion, which allows data extraction from most popular databases and read/write from/to any mainframe file. Output can be written to mainframe files or to Tempus-Link virtual disks in flat-file format or in PC oriented formats such as DIF.
   b. The on-line portion, which performs the same functions as the batch version but allows for on-line access.
   c. The micro portion, which communicates with the on-line portion to allow requests to be formulated on

---

[14] Material in this section is based on "Tempus-Link, Tempus-Data: Their Place in Your Corporate System," Micro Tempus, Inc., April 1984.

the micro from a full-screen editor or from within applications written in Assembler, BASIC, or C languages.

3. Once the data are in the virtual disk, the personal computer user can copy them by using the DOS COPY command, or s/he can read the data directly from the virtual disk into any micro program.

4. Since the distributed data (the block 4 application data) are on the mainframe, the files can be updated at any time by the central database management system (block 3 extract programs), regardless of what the personal computer is doing.

5. Data, program, and application sharing among personal computer users are done through the virtual disks. A PC file stored in a Tempus-Link disk is immediately available to all other users on the mainframe network. Users can exchange a wide variety of files, such as spreadsheets, graphics, and word processing files.

6. Backup of user data stored in Tempus-Link Virtual disks can be made automatically with the firm's normal mainframe backup procedures. In addition, data that reside on the personal computer can be backed up at slack time (i.e., at night) by having the personal computer "wake up" at a prescribed time, execute a user-written program, establish a link to the virtual disks, and initiate a backup by copying the PC-based data to the virtual disks.

One firm in the survey was planning on installing Tempus-Link and Tempus-Data to provide networked access to its marketing research survey data. The researchers were doing extensive analysis on several IBM XTs, and they needed a common database and communication system.

The Tempus-Link and Tempus-Data products offer an attractive introduction to networking because they permit the firm to ease into networking by using its existing computers and communication equipment. This transition is facilitated by the Host Application Program Interface (HAPI), which provides the programmer with a transport system allowing personal computer applications to request action by a mainframe application. This feature seems to be one of the key "selling points" for Micro Tempus, Inc.

As clients become more experienced with HAPI, they start salvaging large portions of programs written in the past 20 or 30 years. The objective is to slowly shift part of the mainframe applications to micros while keeping the core running as before. Thus they can write a small application on the micro which uses the central dinosaur as a slave. In most cases, there is no need (and worse, no manpower) to convert entire systems to a brand new language when the old one can be salvaged in pieces. The return on investment could be much greater and earlier.[15]

Adopting a network framework leads to an interesting twist in the way people think about mainframes and personal computers. Currently, firms connect personal computers to mainframes by using hardware and software that convert the PC into a terminal, thus making the PC a peripheral to the mainframe. The quote above describes a setup in which the mainframe is a peripheral (a slave) to the personal computer. In this arrangement, the mainframe is just another network device that can deliver computing services to the workstation. From the individual user's viewpoint, the computer is the *extended* workstation, that is, the workstation is extended via the network.

Building a networked MWB around the Tempus-Link and Tempus-Data products requires the development of a software package for the personal computer. This package could be written in a high-level language such as BASIC or C, or it could be developed by using a package such as Symphony, Framework, or KnowledgeMan. The last product is an integrated package build around a relational database that uses SQL as its query language.[16] It includes facilities for database management, screen management, interactive forms painting, report writing, text editing, graphics, spreadsheets, and a structured programming language. Access to Tempus-Link could be achieved via KnowledgeMan's DOS access method, which permits any DOS program to be accessed from within the KnowledgeMan session.

A similar approach to a mainframe-based, network oriented MWB is available via the IBM Personal Decision Series (PDS) and the related host attachment products. PDS is a modular se-

---

[15] Bob Lemay, "Tempus-Link Is Unique," *Tempus*, Micro Tempus, Inc., Summer 1984, p. 3.

[16] Shawn W. Bryan, "Two-Level, Flexible DBMS Offers Hefty Decision Support," *Business Computer Systems*, May 1984, pp. 137–40.

ries of integrated software products that can

- Access data created by other programs and systems as well as their own data.
- Analyze or edit data in data files or text documents as well as in spreadsheet formats.
- Produce queries, customized reports, spreadsheets, graphs, and correspondence.
- Build complete applications, ranging from simple reports to sophisticated database updates, that can include user-written BASIC routines.
- Exchange tasks and information between host systems and personal computers.

The Personal Decision Series is actually modules that can be mixed or matched to produce an integrated system, particularly when used with the TopView multitasking and windowing addition to the DOS operating system.

The networking aspect of PDS is provided by Attachment/ 370 for sharing data and resources with mainframes, or by Attachment/36 for interfacing with the IBM System/36 minicomputer. Both products interact with the data edition module running on the PC. These products offer several features. They

- Access data created both inside and outside the PDS environment.
- Use host disk space as virtual diskettes.
- Archive PC programs and data at the host.
- Send and receive messages between PC users.
- Save series of tasks as data edition procedures; these tasks can be accomplished unattended and can include host connection.

One advantage of the PDS series of products is that a firm can build a host-based network around a small, relatively inexpensive System 36 by using the Attachment/36 product. As use of the network grows, the firm can switch to a mainframe host by substituting Attachment/370 for Attachment/36.

Local Area Network.   The second approach, a local area network (LAN), provides most of the capabilities of the mainframe-based network but does not depend on a mainframe being at the center or core of the network. Instead, central data are stored in file servers, which store data in a manner similar to the virtual disks on a mainframe. Access to the data is usually provided by an addition to the PC operating system that acts as a shell that filters all requests made to the operating system. This shell passes requests that can be handled locally to the operating system for servicing by the PC. Requests for a remote resource (such as data access from the file server) are sent directly to the network and never get to the local machine's operating system. The network routes the commands to the file server, where they are executed by the server's operating system.[17] Some LANs dedicate a hard-disk PC as the file server; others use the concept of distributed servers in which all workstations on the network can act as file servers in addition to performing local computing.

The LAN approach has been implemented by Metaphor Computer Systems Corp. to produce the Metaphor application package for consumer goods marketing management. Metaphor shares a common attribute with the Acustar system: they were both designed specifically for marketing managers and professionals in packaged goods firms. Since they are "tailor-made" for brand groups, both packages enable a marketing manager to start using the systems with very little training.

Metaphor has built a network and workstation system around Xerox's Palo Alto Research Center's research and products. The product designers and managers are "graduates" of the center and have built a system that operates much like the Xerox Star. The major components of the system are workstations, file servers, network, and access to outside, host computers.

1. Metaphor workstations employ a mouse for interacting with software that has data retrieval, spreadsheet, analysis, graphics, and text-processing tools. Icons are used to represent items and applications (e.g., product mix analysis, 1985 forecast, brand financial history). The user employs a mouse to select a particular icon and then uses a set of five keys on a small keypad to direct the activities with the chosen icon.

2. The database server stores and accesses the large central files. This server, similar to a Britton Lee database machine, is a relational database computer that uses the SQL language for data

---

[17] Nat Goldhaber and Winn L. Rosch, "Networks at Your Service," *PC Magazine*, February 5, 1984, pp. 125–34.

access. The workstation software interprets the user's data needs and writes the necessary SQL commands. These commands are then sent to the database server where they are executed, after which the extracted data are sent to the workstation and incorporated into a spreadsheet.

3. The file server stores data, programs, applications, and icons that are specific to individual workstation users. This centralized file server replaces floppy or hard disks at the workstations (which do not contain disk drives).

4. The communications server permits connection to IBM host computers and to remote computing services. Mainframe data are downloaded via the communications server to the database server.

5. Printers are available for printing reports, spreadsheets, and graphs from the workstations.

6. A LAN ties the components together via the Ethernet networking system.

7. An IBM PC can be connected to the LAN by installing an Ethernet board in an unused PC adapter slot. PC-based programs can then be run from the Metaphor workstation, which acts as a terminal to the PC.

COOPERATIVE PROCESSING APPROACH

Perhaps the end result of a network approach to the MWB will be an environment in which all of the networked devices cooperate with each other without the user being involved. Hardware and software components are evolving to the point where a single integrated system can be developed containing one session that uses the capabilities of both the mainframe and the personal computer.

Cooperative Processing Concept

Such an integrated system uses the concept of cooperative processing, which has been defined by Pope as the last of five stages of growth in the workstation connection with a host.[18]

---

[18] Bucky Pope, "A Study of How Users of Programmable Work Stations Can Effect VM/CMS Usage," Working paper (Yorktown, N.Y.: IBM Thomas J. Watson Research Center, 1984).

Stage 1. Independent microcomputer with no host connection.

Stage 2. Microcomputer used as a terminal.

Stage 3. Serial synchronized with the host. The user does PC work on the PC and mainframe work on the mainframe, with occasional file transfer between the two. The user cannot be active on both systems at once.

Stage 4. Parallel synchronized. The user flips back and forth between the PC session and the host session, with both sessions being active at once.

Stage 5. Cooperative processing. There is asynchronous activity on the PC and the host in that the PC and the host are working on the same problem or function at the same time. An example is cooperative data analysis in which a host program is summarizing data from a database while the user is manipulating the summarized data on the workstation.

The basic notion behind cooperative processing is that one system takes advantage of the strengths of both the host and the workstation.

The services offered by a host should be made available to the workstation without the host's complexities being brought to the workstation. The key challenge is that the workstation user not be required to learn three command languages—that of the local workstation to which the user has already adapted, the network command language, and the host command language. In general, the user wants to work with the language to which s/he has already adapted.

The way to meet this challenge is to let the user continue to work in the workstation's application package or command language and to let the cooperative processing interface provide links to a set of virtual services and data in such a way that their local and remote locations are obvious to the requester.

The application perceives all services and data as local, even if they actually exist on a remote processor. The user would issue workstation commands for services and the system would get a given service from either the workstation or a host without the user having to be concerned about the location of the service.

In this way, the concept of "downloading" data from the mainframe would become obsolete.

George Williams at General Foods (GF) has written an application that is based on the philosophy of cooperative processing. His application, a decision support system (DSS) generator, allows the user to generate a Multiplan spreadsheet on the PC while interacting with the MMIS on a host computer. The GF MMIS uses the ADDATA database package from Applied Decision Systems—a first-generation MMIS based on the user entering commands. The DSS generator appears to the user as an extension of the ADDATA system because s/he uses the same types of commands to indicate the brands, regions, geographies, and time periods to be included in the spreadsheet.

The DSS generator (1) reads or "parses" the user's commands, (2) converts the commands into the appropriate Multiplan language specifying the spreadsheet, (3) determines what data are needed in the spreadsheet, (4) extracts the needed data from the proper ADDATA database, (5) logs on the user's PC, (6) downloads the data and the spreadsheet specification to the PC, (7) logs off the host, and (8) places the user in Multiplan with the loaded spreadsheet. All of this happens within seconds after the user has entered the appropriate commands.

An Evolutionary Approach to Cooperative Processing

A system that, when given a goal, could carry out the details of the appropriate computer operations and could ask for and receive advice, offered in human terms, when it was stuck. An agent would be a "soft robot" living and doing its business within the computer's world. . . . What might such an agent do? Hundreds of data retrieval systems are now made available through computer networks. Knowing each system's arcane access procedures is almost impossible. An agent acting as a librarian is needed to deal with the sheer magnitude of choices. It might serve as a kind of pilot, threading its way from database to database. Even better would be an agent that could present all systems to the user as a single large system, but that is a remarkably hard problem.[19]

---

[19] Alan Kay, "Computer Software," *Scientific American* 251 (September 1984), pp. 58.

Multiple Systems

If it were feasible to build an agent that presented different systems to the user as a single large system, a firm could pick and choose the elements of each that were the most appealing to its situation, and then merge these elements into an integrated system. This combination approach is highly appealing to a firm that wants to evolve to a final system by experimenting with different approaches; or to a firm that does not want to "put all its eggs into one basket" (i.e., one software product).

The following is a sketch of a possible evolutionary approach to the MMIS that builds on combining different applications and systems. Consider the firm that uses the following data sources:

- Nielsen store audit data for tracking purposes.
- TRIM scanner data.
- Scanner-panel data from IRI.
- Ad feature data from MAJERS.
- Shipment data from the in-house, time-sharing computer.
- Events database in an IMS database on the in-house system.
- Budgets and P&L statements on individual personal computers.
- Sales-call reports stored on an IBM System 36 in the sales department.

All of the above data suppliers offer on-line access to their data through their own time-sharing service. Currently, the brand groups that use these time-sharing services to prepare a detailed report on the brand's performance must use a terminal to interact with each system.

A common data analysis procedure encountered in the survey involved the scanning of "top-line" or high-level figures from these databases to detect any abnormalities. When a number that was out of range or unexpected was spotted, the manager tended to stop the scanning and search for the cause of the abnormality by looking at the numbers and figures behind the top-line number. This approach can be termed the *onion* approach to data exploration in which the user "peels away" layers of data to get a finer view of the problem.

Let's envision such an onion system. It would have top-line numbers on the screen and a mouse for obtaining various top-line views from a menu. By selecting items from the menu, the user is able to pull top-line reports to the screen. When an abnormal number is spotted, the user selects the number with the mouse and then picks an onion icon, which activates a menu listing available paths to finer analysis. These paths involve looking at finer data aggregations by regions, brand items, time periods, or measures (e.g., category volume and market share). When a path such as regions is selected, the computer displays the top-line number for all the regions. For instance, the user may have spotted an abnormally high return rate in the national average. By selecting the regional path to finer analysis, s/he would produce the return rates for each of the regions.

An example of this form of analysis is provided by the process that brand people at Borden use every four weeks when SAMI releases new data. Their goal is to locate problems in the sales regions, determine the underlying cause of the problem, and write a memo to the appropriate sales manager asking for assistance in solving the problem. The following is a typical analysis.

1. Use an on-line system to retrieve sales in each district for each product UPC code in percent of quota and percent of last year's sales. Examine these data to locate problem districts.
2. Use the same on-line system to retrieve the corresponding data for all the accounts within the problem districts. Examine these data to locate the problem districts.
3. Use a different database to see if the problem lies in the distribution level or in the number of items stocked by the account.
4. Use a third database to see if the item's prices are in line with competitive brands in the account.
5. Use this same database to determine whether the shelving arrangement meets the planogram requirements agreed to by the account.
6. Summarize the problem and the possible causes in a memo to the sales manager who handles the account. Ask him or her to fix the indicated problem.

The labor-intensive nature of this type of work has caused the firms in the survey to move the data off the outside vendor's computers and onto an in-house MMIS. To achieve this MMIS, the firms have had to make a major, all-at-once commitment to one approach (e.g., Acustar on the mainframe). Another approach would be to build a workstation that has sufficient intelligence to extract data from the various time-sharing systems and combine them into spreadsheets, graphs, or reports. This workstation would be able to "mimic" the steps an analyst or brand manager might use in going through the various data extraction processes and building the spreadsheets and graphs. It might even be able to mimic some of the decision rules the analyst uses in the extraction and combination processes. A really advanced workstation could even perform the onion type of data analysis discussed earlier. That is, it could examine top-line numbers and use various triggers or decision rules to direct it to more numbers that provide a detailed view or explanation of the top-line numbers.

To achieve such a workstation, the workstation would have to be able to "mimic" the same process a user goes through with his or her eyes and hands. Consider the process of logging onto the INF*ACT computer and extracting some Nielsen data, moving the data to the PC, logging off the system, loading Lotus 1-2-3, positioning the cursor in the appropriate spreadsheet cell, transferring the data into the spreadsheet, examining one particular cell to determine if a condition is met (e.g., year-to-date sales below plan), logging onto the in-house computer, running the shipments program, downloading the needed data to explain the condition in question, logging off the in-house computer, reloading Lotus 1-2-3, locating the appropriate cell in the spreadsheet, transferring the new data into the spreadsheet, graphing the combined Nielsen and shipments data, and printing the graph.

If a way could be found to program the workstation to mimic these steps without excessively complex programming effort, then the MWB could grow with the user; that is, it could take over some of the tasks the user was accomplishing with different software packages and/or computers. It would provide a means for accessing data and programs anywhere on the network without the manager having to go through the time-consuming and intellectually difficult task of knowing the intracacies of all the required applications: s/he would be able to use "agents" to do the work.

The Key Element: Program-to-Program Communication

How can we *easily* produce agents that run in a workstation and make all the needed systems appear to the user as a single large system? For instance, how can a firm produce a workstation that allows the manager to extract and combine Nielsen data via the INF∗ACT system and MAJERS ad feature data via the MAJERS computer? The answer lies in the concept of program-to-program communication. If we could develop a program that runs in the workstation and talks to the INF∗ACT program, the workstation program could then extract the needed data just as if a person were using a terminal to do the same thing. The INF∗ACT program would not need to "know" that another program was talking to it. Rather, for this to be a viable approach, programs such as INF∗ACT *must not* have to be modified to achieve program-to-program communication.

This relatively new concept is being implemented by IBM as part of their Systems Network Architecture (SNA) in a construct called Advanced Program-to-Program Communication (APPC).[20] APPC provides general-purpose, program-to-program protocols that could be implemented on any SNA product. The first implementation seems to be in the area of document exchange.

> With the office workstation . . . the operator interacts with a program in the workstation itself, and the documents created are stored locally. When the workstation communicates with the host, it does so in a program-to-program manner. The operator directs a local program, for example, to distribute a document or to have a document stored in—or retrieved from—the host library. Then the local program takes over and communicates with the host program to accomplish this task.[21]

However, APPC seems particularly well suited for "transparent access to remote databases."[22]

The concept of program-to-program communication is important in the design of a MWB because it allows the designer to

---

[20] J. P. Gray, P. J. Hansen, P. Homan, M. A. Lerner, and M. Pozefsky. "Advanced Program-to-Program Communication in SNA," *IBM Systems Journal* 22, no. 4 (1983), pp. 298–318.

[21] Robert J. Sundstrom, "Program-to-Program Communications—A Growing Trend," *Data Communications*, February 1984, p. 87.

[22] Ibid., p. 92.

produce a single user interface that can be used to access any program or data. Without such an interface, the user would have to learn all the access procedures of all the systems s/he wanted to use. Or one, single, large application program would have to be used for all of the manager's work. This workstation-based interface would have, for instance, a common way of making a request for data in the four database dimensions: measure, time period, region and brand item. The same commands or procedures would be used to extract ad feature data from MAJERS databases, or retail sales data from Nielsen databases. The workstation-based program would know how to translate these requests into the appropriate commands for the systems containing the data. It would then communicate with the appropriate programs on the Nielsen and MAJERS computers. The MWB and the other computers would cooperate to produce the needed result, with the MWB in control of the cooperative processing.

CURRENT IMPLEMENTATION OF COOPERATIVE PROCESSING

IBM has implemented the cooperative-processing concept via its 3270 PC and its application processing interface.

Cooperative Processing Hardware: 3270 PC

One way the cooperative-processing concept is implemented is via the IBM 3270 Personal Computer (3270 PC), which combines the 3270 Information Display System's ability to perform host interactive functions with the IBM PC's computing capability. The user can concurrently establish up to four 3270-type sessions with possibly four different hosts, two local notepad sessions, and multiple PC DOS sessions.

From a cooperative processing perspective, the IBM 3270 PC addresses three distinct alternatives.

By utilizing its highly sophisticated window system, the user can easily move information between any of the 3270-type sessions and/or the notepad areas. Thus, information that is being displayed by one session may be moved to the display of another session, without the modifications of any host/workstation application.

Explicit commands are provided for in the PC DOS session to import (receive) and export (send) files between the PC DOS sessions and the host session. The user learns a single (albeit new) set of commands for the movement of files irrespective of the host environment. That is, the IBM 3270 PC does not require the user to learn a new set of commands for file transfer (or window data movement) for each different set of host environments.

The IBM 3270 PC also provides the ability to establish concurrent sessions with up to four different hosts. This means that the user may be requesting heavy computations or data-intensive activity to be performed on four different systems, while running a PC DOS application or while transferring data between the PC and one of the sessions.[23]

The 3270 PC is also a good device for the workstation in an environment that uses a broad view of information, particularly one that uses image data. A unit equipped with the IBM 3270 PC host graphics adapter can display images sent from a mainframe in the form of drawings, signed papers, forms, and handwritten notes.

Program-to-Program Communication: API

A program-to-program workstation is possible if it is built around the IBM 3270 PC, which offers a feature called the Application Program Interface (API) that allows programs running on the workstation to send "keystrokes" to programs running on other computers. For instance, the workstation program could send the necessary keystrokes to the INF*ACT computer for logging on, extracting data, downloading the data, and logging off. In fact, the entire session described in the Multiple Systems section of this chapter is possible with the 3270-PC API, which allows workstation programs to call for data when needed from any source. It uses IBM's SNA network procedures to acquire data on IBM computers, and the workstation's ASCII interface to acquire data from remote computers that are not part of an SNA network.

The key advantage to this type of approach is that it permits the firm to build on existing systems without having to buy an entirely new mainframe package and/or rewrite all the existing systems. Also, by continuing to use the computing services of the software vendors, the firm will take advantage of these vendors' efforts in providing on-line access to their data. The firm

---

[23] Goldstein et al., "Directions in Cooperative Processing," p. 242.

need only commit to developing the workstation program that uses program-to-program communications to build a unified user interface. The workstation program will handle all the interactions with the various computers and software packages and provide a single interface to the user.

Further, this approach would allow firms to build a sophisticated workstation while using a "pay as you go" arrangement with data suppliers. Whenever their use expanded beyond a break-even point, they could bring the vendor's data in-house and change a few instructions in the workstation program. The user would never have to know that the data had changed locations.

Another feature of this approach is that the firm could build the MMIS by mixing and matching computing services among the following locations: outside time-sharing computer, in-house mainframe or departmental minicomputer, and personal computers. Again, these locations could change over time without disrupting the user. Such changes would be inevitable as the new data sources arrived and the firm found it had to adopt a different type of database philosophy to handle the new data combinations.

STAND-ALONE MWB

Another approach to the MWB is to accept the idea that current computer trends are really based on the notion of one machine per person. In his keynote address at the 1984 National Computer Conference, John Akers, IBM president, predicted that workstations will be on every desk of almost every professional and administrative employee in industry, government, and academia, as well as in their briefcases and their homes.[24]

These desktop units are becoming more and more powerful. The units available in 1985 from major computer firms are based on 16-bit microprocessors that provide (1) a speed of about 0.5 MIPS (million instructions per second), (2) a main memory of about 0.5 megabytes, (3) a screen resolution of about 0.25 megapixels (700 by 350 pixels), and (4) external storage in the 20- to 100-megabyte range. The next generation of personal computers will be based on 32-bit technology that should permit the emer-

---

[24] John Akers, quoted in *Infosystems*, September 1984, p. 20.

gence of the Meg³ machine:

One megabyte of main memory.

One-megapixel screen (1,000 by 1,000).

One megabyte of random access memory.

Such a unit has been called a "mainframe on a desktop."[25]

A first step away from the IBM PC's technology, which limits the user to 640 kilobytes of memory, was the introduction of Intel's Above Board add-on accessory that allows use of up to four megabytes of random-access memory; such a configuration would permit a Lotus 1-2-3 spreadsheet to contain half a million cells.

As personal computers become more powerful, the need to perform computations on large shared machines decreases. In the marketing management environment, the data are relatively static in that they are updated infrequently. Although shipment data may change daily, the other data are updated weekly, monthly, or bimonthly. Hence, systems for use by marketing managers do not have to operate in a transaction-based environment that requires large shared computers.

The primary reason for sharing computing resources in marketing management is the need to access a common database. However, the marketing database is highly partitionable because the practice of marketing is partitioned into brand groups and regional sales divisions. Hence, all the data about a brand and its competitors can be put on a brand manager's desktop unit, and all the data about a market can be put in the appropriate field office.

Such partitioning results in redundant data because part of a brand's data will be in the field office's database and because different brands share a common set of competitors. This redundancy calls for central control over the distribution and updating of the data. A large historical database could be maintained by a central organization, with extract files generated on a periodic basis for distribution to the appropriate desktops.

Another reason for having a database on a mainframe is that the programs and systems that generated the data run on the

---

[25] Wendy Lea McKibbon, "A Mainframe on a What?" *Infosystems*, August 1984, p. 27.

mainframe. Hence, there is a natural tendency to leave the data at their source so that they can be accessed by the generating program, as well as by other programs that use them. Marketing data are different from most corporate data in that they do not originate within the firm; they are not generated as part of the firm's normal business activities. Rather, they are bought from an outside supplier. Thus, placing them on a desktop computer does not involve a move from the place of primary residence.

Technology is moving rapidly toward having the ability to put very large databases on very small media. For instance, new optical-disk technologies make it possible to put a gigabyte of data on a 5¼-inch optical disk. Such a disk could hold data on 100 measures on 100 brand items in 100 markets for 100 time periods—a very large brand database. These disks could be prepared by the central database administrator and distributed to the brand groups and the field offices through the firm's normal mail system.

A driving force behind a move to stand-alone personal computers will be economics. Some studies have indicated that the firm should select the smallest computer that will perform the task. Ein-dor, in a study of the cost effectiveness of computers available in 1981, concluded that

> It is most effective to accomplish any task on the least powerful type of computer capable of performing it. The observed tendency of firms to decentralize and distribute computing power is the apparent practical application of this conclusion. Since Grosch's law holds within the appropriate category, it is also advantageous for an organization to use the most powerful computer within the appropriate category. So, one powerful microcomputer is preferable to two less powerful micros, even though a number of microcomputers are preferable to a minicomputer which has the combined power of the micros.[26]

Grosch's law states that the average cost of computing decreases with the square root of the power of the system. This law could be interpreted to mean that the most cost-effective arrangement would be to concentrate all computing on the largest available computer. However, Ein-dor's study indicates that Grosch's law

---

[26] Phillip Ein-dor, "Grosch's Law Re-visited: CPU Power and the Cost of Computation," *Communications of the ACM*, February 1985, p. 151.

holds within each of five distinct classes of computers and that the average cost of computing varies significantly among the classes, measured in MIPS per $100,000 of purchase price.

Computer Classes	MIPS per $100,000
Microcomputers	8.00
Minicomputers	0.50
Small mainframes	0.25
Large mainframes	0.22
Supercomputers	0.25

These numbers have to be interpreted carefully because (1) they only apply to the CPU and hence ignore the channel and disk speeds, and (2) a MIP on a microcomputer does much less computational work than a MIP on a large computer due to the difference in word size. However, the numbers do point to the desktop units playing an increasingly important role.

Another reason for going to stand-alone units is their simplicity of design, construction, and operation. The firm does not have to worry about, or incur the expense of, communications equipment. This is particularly important because there are no clear standards for building a networked communications environment.[27] The firm can bypass or postpone the communications decisions by initially installing stand-alone units and then adding communications capabilities as the networks become standardized.

Simplicity for the user is yet another reason for moving toward stand-alone units. The widespread acceptance of Lotus 1-2-3 as the primary analysis tool for management means that most user-developed applications will be on the PC. In an environment of mainframe and PC application packages, the user must learn and use two different operating systems and interface philosophies. With all applications and data on their personal computers, users can become proficient in the PC environment without having to worry about changes made in the firm's mainframe environment.

---

[27] William P. Martorelli, "SNA: After 10 Years, Something to Think About," *Information Week*, April 22, 1985, p. 23–29.

SUMMARY

This chapter has identified four distinct hardware approaches to providing data, applications, and decision support systems to marketing managers. All of these approaches differ from the standard hardware system of the 1960s and 1970s—a time-shared mainframe. The advent of the personal computer and packages such as Lotus 1-2-3 have ended the time-shared mainframe's reign: it is no longer the *only* vehicle for managerial computing. The alternatives include:

- Separate computing on the mainframe and PC, with the capability to download data from the mainframe to the PC.
- Cooperative processing in which system designers arrive at the optimal assignment of computing tasks among the appropriate computers.
- A mainframe-based network in which mainframe disk space emulates PC-based disk drives, or local area networks with the data centralized on a file server.
- Stand-alone personal computers.

It is not possible to foresee which alternative will become the dominant one. In fact, a single approach may not universally dominate the others because a firm should select the approach that matches its culture and philosophy. However, one approach seems to make sense for firms that have different computing needs throughout the organization: this approach calls for a computing environment that has four primary components—the mainframe, departmental computers, network, and workstations.

- The mainframe will be a central "data warehouse," a repository of data for use by managers and professionals.
- Departmental machines will play a major role. In some firms they will do most of the transaction processing that is managed by departments within the firm. They are also envisioned as playing a "police officer's" role in controlling the flow of information between micros and mainframes. For instance, an IBM System 36 could be used as a distributed resources controller to which information queries originating at the desktop would be sent to determine where that information resides in the network. Departmental computers are beginning to be used in market-

ing as machines dedicated to the marketing management information system. It is becoming an acceptable practice to purchase an IBM 4300-class computer and dedicate it to EXPRESS or Acustar. This "marketing mainframe" contains shipment data that has been downloaded from the firm's central mainframe, as well as environmental data from outside data suppliers.

- High-speed networks tie the workstations, data warehouses, and departmental computers into an integrated environment in which the workstation user can access data and run programs located anywhere on the network.
- The workstation is a display-intensive device that manages the user's interface with the network and provides for personal computing. A great deal of intelligence is built into the workstation to allow it to format and display information sent from the other network devices. The workstation will have considerable power, which will permit it to meet most of a manager's computing needs.

In such an environment, the network is the computer!

Frito-Lay, Inc.

INTRODUCTION

A new group, Market Analysis, was formed in July 1984 to support the brand groups by providing data, systems, and analytical tools for studying the markets for Frito-Lay's products. A key function of this group is the translation of the brand groups' information and analysis needs into system needs, and strategies for meeting these needs. One reason for forming this group was a recognition that developments within and outside the company could have strong impacts on marketing and product management at Frito-Lay.

The Management Services department was implementing a new systems strategy that would provide a state-of-the-art computer system throughout the company. The Sales department was using a hand-held computer program as a major component of the systems strategy. This program would dramatically change the information base with which the brand groups worked.

Externally, developments in the capture of market data by store scanners will provide a much richer view of the retail environment. Further, scanner panels offer the potential for in-depth analysis of consumer behavior through consumption and response to marketing programs. These systems would increase the available market data by several orders of magnitude.

The data explosion arrives at a time when the brand groups have numerous things to do. They need systems and frameworks for helping them deal with all the data; now, they are barely able to stay on top of the existing data. What will happen in the future, when they have the ability to know what is going on in every small market and chain, or even in every store?

MANAGEMENT SERVICES

Frito-Lay is a centrally controlled, functionally oriented company. Consistent with that philosophy, the data processing function had traditionally been highly centralized; all computing was centralized in the data processing organization. However, recent studies have resulted in significant changes in the philosophy for providing systems support to the user community.

The Systems Philosophy

A new philosophy for providing computer-based management services has emerged that is based on four related ideas.

Integration is key for economics.
Control is key for integration.
Leadership is key for control.
Vision and execution are the keys to leadership.

Integration. Although Frito-Lay's business is relatively simple, its product mix and multibillion-dollar size means that the operation of the business must generate a large number of small transactions. Hence, computers are extremely important in running the business. To provide the necessary services at a reasonable cost, an integrated system of computers and software is necessary, with network communications important to achieving the integration.

Control. To achieve the integration, the management services department must be in control. But the company recognizes that the old, totally centralized approach does not fit the current world of technology and systems. Management realizes that they cannot get the information and reports needed by the people in the company with an army of programmers, so they began to "unravel a strong central government into a strong federation."

The central department will design the technical architecture, operate the mainframes and the network, build and maintain the transaction systems, specify the types of distributed hardware and software that will be networked, determine the appropriate data structures, and provide access to the data via end-user languages and packages. The functional departments (marketing, manufacturing, finance, and so on) will use end-user languages to access, analyze, and report the information. These departments will use Management Service's "information and computing utility" for their end-user application development.

Leadership. The Management Services department must establish a leadership position by stating their current and future systems path. They must be out in front. "We are going this way. You may go that way, but we are going this way." Such leadership will result in a clear path toward the computing utility, and a structure through which the departments and individuals can develop their own analysis and reporting systems.

Vision and Execution. To successfully lead, a clear vision of the future computing environment is necessary, along with a view of its impact on the practice of management. Execution of this vision involves selecting and managing people, devising appropriate processes and controls, developing the technical architecture, and choosing the appropriate funding strategy.

The View of the Future

Management Services' view of the future computing environment has the following elements:

1. Most of today's computing roadblocks will be overcome with the coming generation of mainframes, workstations, data management systems, and fourth-generation languages.
    a. The new mainframes and storage devices will have sufficient speed and capability to permit the firm to capture, store, and access item-specific data at the account (i.e., store) level.
    b. Relational database systems will make it possible to manage these data and to integrate them with data from other sources (e.g., externally purchased marketing data).
    c. The workstations will have sufficient power to assume most of the managerial analysis and reporting of these data.

      d. The new languages will make it possible for end users to do their analysis and reporting without extensive training.

2. Networks and the new workstations will make it possible to combine voice, text, image, and numerical data.

3. Since computing costs are falling while professional and managerial salaries are rising, technology must be used to "get on top of salary and head count." Firms such as Frito-Lay have been able to contain their manufacturing costs via automation, which substituted capital investment for labor. Today, a major manufacturing cost is equipment depreciation. This same philosophy of using equipment to augment human labor must now be adopted in the other functional areas to improve their efficiency.

4. The effectiveness of these business areas can also be strongly increased by providing timely information and systems for assessing the information. Several insightful, information-based business decisions could pay for the cost of the computerization.

5. Functional area managers and professionals are the appropriate people to specify and build the end-user applications.

6. Given the current and anticipated salary levels, it is advisable to invest $4,000 to $5,000 in computing and communications services per year on most of the professionals in the functional areas (not including the mainframe costs). Hence, each desktop could be supplied with $12,000 to $15,000 in computing and communications equipment. Such investment will reduce the need for support people and assistants, and increase the productivity of the managers and professionals.

The Strategy

The development of a systems strategy based on this philosophy of using technology to increase managerial productivity was part of Frito-Lay's recognition that data processing has remained essentially the same since its inception. It involves three steps: input, processing, and output. However, there have been three phases in the use of data processing in support of management, particularly when viewed from a systems' output perspective. Phase one involved the computerization of the firm's transaction systems, and the output consisted of reports and tables summarizing these transactions—a large volume of computer printout. Phase two arose out of the volumes of output that caused data overload and resulted in the development of both standard and exception reports. Because, with this data overload situation, everyone was forced to receive the same standard reports on a fixed timetable, a need arose for ad hoc or individual access to the data on an as-needed basis. Phase three involved the use of inquiry languages to provide this type of access, the so-called fourth-generation languages such as FOCUS and IFPS.

Management believes that Frito-Lay is now in phase three, and has been there for several years. For example, a marketing management information system allows managers and analysts to access data at any time and in almost any format.

While the output side of data processing has changed, the input and processing parts have remained essentially the same at most companies, including Frito-Lay. Transactions are recorded on paper and are input into the computer via clerical keying from the paper forms (or by optical scanners that read the handwritten forms). These data were processed by batch programs in which the input data were accumulated for a period of time and then processed in a batch computer run. These batch oriented programs were designed during phases one and two to produce printed outputs. The need for direct data access during phase three required the modification or "patching" of the programs so that the original input data and the program output could be routed to files for use by the query systems.

The computer industry is now entering a new era, phase four, and Frito-Lay has developed a corporate systems strategy for taking advantage of the new technologies and accomplishing the necessary work. This strategy recognizes that technology and costs have changed to the point where the company should make significant changes in the input, processing, and output aspects of data processing. The elements of the strategy include:

- Hand-held computers for data capture.
- Common programmable terminals.
- Common base of processing programs.
- Office automation.

- Distributed processing.
- User education and support.

Hand-Held Computers. The primary inputs to Frito-Lay's transaction system are the sales orders submitted by the salespeople who sell and deliver products to retail stores. Currently, each salesperson submits large sheets of paper containing handwritten sales orders. These pages are read by optical scanners that convert the handwritten data into digital data. Technological developments are beginning to make it cost effective to capture these data electronically at the point of sale. Each sales representative will use a hand-held computer to input the sales orders. Further, computers and disk drives are entering a cost/performance area that permits the storage and retrieval of masses of data to support managerial decision making.

This approach is being implemented in one sales division, the Model division. Each salesperson will use a small computer to take an order in a store. A printer in the salesperson's truck will be used to print sales tickets and reports. At the end of the day, the salesperson will call an IBM Series 1 computer and send the data on the day's transactions. These regionally located Series 1 computers will store and transmit their data to the IBM mainframe in Dallas. The system has facilities for sending information from the host computers to the individual computers used by the sales representatives.

This system will be used as a prototype in the Model division. At the same time, the systems people are working on a whole new architecture for using and looking at these data. They are asking the question, "How do we turn data at the account and line-item level into information?"

Common Programmable Terminal: the IBM 3270 PC. In keeping with this distributed-processing philosophy, Frito-Lay is making a commitment to use personal computers that are integrated with the host systems. The vehicle for this integration is the IBM 3270 PC. The philosophy behind this choice is given in the July 1984 issue of the *iRc Newsletter*, the publication of the Information Resource Center.

> The 3270 PC is IBM's introduction to a workstation that combines the features of a personal computer with a hard disk, a host (mainframe) terminal, and desktop "scratch pads" into a single

unit. In fact, this unit provides up to seven sessions at one time; one personal computer session, two notepad sessions, and four mainframe (TSO or IMS) sessions. The viewing screen can be set up according to the individual user's preference, displaying any combination of those seven sessions. For example, on a daily basis you might heavily use the personal computer and access TSO for some mainframe data. You could set up one of the screens on the 3270 PC to contain the personal computer session and one mainframe session. Additionally, you could include one notepad session on which to record scratch-pad type information.

But what are the capabilities of the 3270 PC? Most importantly, the 3270 PC combines equipment. That is, this one unit will provide BOTH personal computer and mainframe capabilities. The most exciting feature is the 3270 PC's ability to QUICKLY and EASILY transfer data files from the host down to the 3270 PC for processing in the PC session.

Common Base.   The common base aspect of the strategy involves rewriting the company's base systems with one major assumption in mind: each person will have a terminal on his or her desk. These base systems will handle the firm's transactions and provide data to the databases. They will use IBM's Information Management System (IMS) for data management, thus creating a standard method for storing and accessing all the firm's data.

The adoption of the 3270 PC has impacted the rewrite of these systems because this workstation contains a feature called Application Program Interface (API) that makes it possible for one computer program to communicate with another. Programs can be written to run in the PC part of the 3270 PC, which communicates directly with programs running on the host computer. These PC-based programs can "mimic" the actions the user would take if s/he were directly working with the host computer. With this type of facility, it is relatively easy to program the PC so that the user does not have to learn or understand how to operate the mainframe-based programs. The API will act as an interface between the user and the host application.

Office Automation.   The automation of the office is a key element in the move to leverage computing technology for the support of managerial and professional personnel. It is being implemented because of the needs for access to the large internal and externally purchased databases. As a side benefit, the firm will acquire the means for automating the text management, time management, and electronic mail aspects of traditional OA.

From the users' perspective, office automation is the backbone of the system because it is the vehicle through which they do their work. Office automation is broadly defined to include MIS, decision support systems, word processing, and traditional office automation activities. It includes personal computing, text preparation, electronic mail, electronic filing, professional services, host applications, and attachment to foreign computers. The data in the mainframe files will be available via a data utility that is part of the office automation aspect of the strategy.

Distributed Processing. This strategy recognizes that networking and personal computers are making it possible to distribute computers throughout the organization. So every time a common base system is rewritten, the systems people analyze the proper location for it. Such analysis has led to the placement of IBM 8100 computers in each of the manufacturing plants. These machines are networked so that the actual location of the application is transparent to the user.

Distributed processing means that a small host computer could be placed in a "closet" in the marketing area. But the marketing systems will probably remain on the large IBM mainframes because of the sizes of the databases and the need to constantly update the data and redefine the hierarchies in the data structures. However, the overall system is being built so that it can accommodate such a distributed-processing approach.

User Education and Support. This overall strategy involves (1) centralized control and operation of the transaction systems and the data utility, and (2) end-user computing for reporting and analysis. Unfortunately, the current databases and programming languages require that the user know a lot. Management believes: "We need another generation of languages and databases in order for people to easily use computers. We can't wait, so we are overkilling with training."

To provide the training, an Information Resource Center has

been created at Frito-Lay. Its role and how it operates are explained in the first issue of its *iRc Newsletter*, published in January 1983.

Increasing end-user productivity during the 1980s is a major goal of Management Services. To ensure this, a major component of our system architecture is to provide an effective way for management and staff to directly access the information they need without having a systems analyst intervene in each occasion. The opening of the Information Resource Center (IRC) at headquarters in Dallas should enhance both Management Services and end-user productivity by providing customized data manipulation and ad hoc reporting. If the functional user has the ability to retrieve and organize data for his specific analytical purposes, then the programmer/analyst can concentrate on developing the databases for the functional user to access. The key is to encourage and facilitate the utilization of end-user computer tools by nonprogramming personnel. This will greatly increase the productivity of the company, not only within Management Services, but throughout all functions.

The IRC has been established to provide consulting, educational, and direct help services to the general end users. IRC staff do not code specific programs or applications. The IRC provides the place, equipment, and staff to allow you to learn user-friendly computer tools. The IRC staff can be consulted to help you choose the best computer solution for any particular problem. After the method of attack has been identified, the IRC can schedule you for formal classes in the new tool. Use of these tools will enable you to convert many of your existing manual analytical methods into computerized information-handling systems. Data can then be retrieved, manipulated, and reformatted by you as your needs dictate. Thus, you are in control. You will not only be able to easily build and maintain your own data files, but also access many public databases. These public databases will be created for information that is needed by many groups within Frito-Lay. Possible public databases are sales, stales, unsaleables, and General Ledger.

IRC tools emphasize time-sharing and personal-computer products. Time-sharing products on the Headquarters computer are SAS, IFPS, FOCUS, BASIC, and VS APL. FORTRAN is offered, but no programming assistance or classes will be offered by the IRC. Selected personal computer hardware and software is available for your review and use in the Center. Stand-alone, time-sharing, and personal-computer graphic systems are also available. In addition, subscription services such as *Legislate, Ami,* and *New York Times* are available for information searches.

Specific Growth Paths

The implementation of this strategy has placed Frito-Lay on the cutting edge of technology. To keep from floundering in such an exposed position, the company has elected to follow the lead of the major companies who "make the market" in their industries.

This philosophy has led to the adoption of IBM's MVS operating system, IMS data manager, and the DISSOS communications and office automation facility. With this base, Frito-Lay is adopting and/or experimenting with the new technologies when they become available. For instance, MVSXA (the new IBM operating system) and DB2 (IBM's relational database system) are being installed. One of the senior managers states that the basic idea is to "put in place the infrastructure for these advanced technologies by staying with IMS and MVS. We should be ready for IBM's next mainframes, which will run MVSXA and have the speed, channel capacity, and price performance to allow us to extend the advantages of DB2 to our users."

INFORMATION FOR MARKETING MANAGEMENT

Two groups have evolved for providing information and analysis for marketing: Marketing Research Department (MRD), which focuses on the consumer, and Market Analysis (MA), which focuses on the marketplace.

Marketing Research Department

The MRD has two primary functions. The first is oriented toward looking at information on a brand basis, with the marketing researchers aligned with their counterparts in the brand organization. The second function has several goals.

- Study and understand the market structure of the Frito-Lay product categories.
- Develop modeling tools.
- Manage the scanner data from Burke and Behavior Scan.
- Develop an on-line system with which the brand managers and researchers can design their market-testing activities.
- Develop a library of test-marketing information that contains a database of the histories of the company's test-marketing experiences.

The test-marketing library would contain computerized versions of the reports from all past studies. A brand manager who is contemplating running a study could ask "Have we done studies of Type X before?" and the computer would provide a history of such studies. The goal is to provide a facility for "transferring knowledge" from one study to another. In addition, providing on-line access to each study's database is being considered.

Market Analysis

The second group, Market Analysis, has three functions. The first involves working with the systems people to develop software for managing data from the major suppliers such as Nielsen and MAJERS; the second is to "understand how well we are performing relative to the programs we execute in the market"; and the third is to search out and analyze information on the trade and competitors.

Marketing Management Information System

The primary system for accessing the marketing data is the marketing management information system (MMIS). Its development started about six years ago when a systems analyst went and "lived" in the marketing area for one year to study the information needs of the brand groups. The result was an architecture for supporting ad hoc queries to produce rapid retrieval of data. It is used by the brand groups and the professionals in Market Analysis.

The MMIS, which was written in COBOL and uses IMS for data management, provides the following functions:

- Graphics.
- Flexible report writing in which the user's inquiry produces a dataset of rows and columns for a given topic. That is, the three-dimensional dataset is "cut" along one dimension to produce a "two-dimensional matrix of data.
- Language similar to BASIC that runs in the IMS environment and permits analysis of the datasets obtained by the query.
- Predefined analytical routines, for example, a pipeline analysis routine.

- Statistical forecasting routines.

This system was first implemented in 1980, and continues to evolve. The initial data included weekly shipment data and the Nielsen bimonthly retail sales data. The MAJERS ad feature data are being added, along with retail display data.

To augment the capabilities of MMIS, the systems people are experimenting with alternative software approaches. They have been using FOCUS for prototyping and quick systems development. FOCUS was used to develop an inquiry system for a scanner database purchased by one of the brand groups. This system was developed in two weeks. One systems person estimated that it would have taken 6 to 12 months to do it using traditional methods.

CURRENT SITUATION

The managers of Market Analysis face two major problems. First, they must gain an understanding of how the company's systems strategy and the new data sources will impact the practice of marketing and product management. Second, they must develop a strategy for marketing systems that recognizes the new data.

When considering this challenge, several thoughts and questions run through their minds.

- Our biggest challenge is to make the information we have easy to use.
- We should look at information as a management resource.
- We currently have reams of data—we have some tapes that are not being used. So simply acquiring more data is not the answer.
- Once we get all of these data on-line, how do the brand groups handle them?
- Brand groups currently develop strategies, design programs for achieving the strategies, implement the programs, and evaluate the results. What systems and modules do they need to support this work?
- Is our current brand management structure of product manager, associate product manager, and assistant product manager the best organizational design for such a data and systems explosion?

- What type of training should be provided to the brand people?
- What type of support should our organization provide?
- What should be the background and talent of the people in our group?

With these questions as guides, the management of Market Analysis devised a three-part approach. First, they developed the following procedure for arriving at a marketing systems strategy:

- Determine the business objectives of the corporation and the functional objectives of sales and marketing.
- Determine the marketing actions and activities required to meet these objectives.
- Determine the information needed to conduct these activities.
- Determine the systems that must be in place to access, analyze, and report the needed information.

Concurrent with this planning activity, they conducted a hardware review. They found that the marketing managers had access to personal computers and terminals for accessing the MMIS. This equipment was in special rooms near the brand groups. The personal computers were the most heavily used, except at the close of each four-week period, when the brand groups used the MMIS to determine what had happened during the period and to forecast performance during the next few periods. Whereas the MMIS was used to access data, the data analysis was done on the IBM PCs and XTs, which were used to

Integrate data from different sources.

Display, graph, and analyze the data.

Perform calculations that were not possible with the MMIS.

Perform simple simulations.

The Market Analysis group had been working with the Management Services people in the development of a program for downloading data from the MMIS to a Lotus spreadsheet. The resulting program made heavy use of the application program interface feature on the IBM 3270 PC.

Based on this survey and Management Services' systems strategy, the Market Analysis group recommended that the personal computers and dumb terminals be replaced with IBM 3270 PCs. In addition, they recommended that the equipment rooms be augmented by placing individual 3270 PCs on the desks of the heavy users in the brand groups, and that the long-run goal be one 3270 PC on each desk.

The third activity involved an evaluation of the available software for doing market analysis, particularly forecasting and promotion evaluation. One approach was to work with selected brand groups to develop prototypes that used software that seemed to meet their needs. For instance, a promotion evaluation package offered by Management Decision Systems, Inc. was being considered by using the software running on the vendor's computer. In addition, alternatives to the existing MMIS were examined. There have been significant improvements in hardware and software since the MMIS was developed six years ago. The Market Analysis group was particularly interested in providing a better user interface than the command oriented MMIS interface; the necessity for the user to learn a lot of codes made it difficult for the new user to learn that system. The Market Analysis group wondered if other types of interfaces were more suitable for people in the brand groups.

In summary, the Market Analysis group had to develop a marketing systems strategy, recommend specific software and hardware for use by the brand groups, and devise a strategy for improving or replacing the current MMIS.

CHAPTER TWELVE

General Foods[1]

Bob King, manager of Marketing Information Systems (MIS), had just completed reading George Williams' review of the department's current computing situation and an assessment of its software and hardware needs. Bob believes that George is a rare individual who works at the cutting edge in a number of areas: computer hardware and software, marketing data, statistical modeling, and the practice of marketing. Therefore, Bob King was prepared to accept George's evaluations and to work through their implications for the management of marketing information at General Foods.

Bob and George realized that the MIS group had come a long way in the last 18 months; the divisional approach to computing had resulted in over 3,000 hours of computer use each month by the brand groups. But they were aware that much more was possible. The notion of leveraging information technology for the support of product management had become a "religion" to

---

[1] This case is designed to illustrate the decision process leading to a departmental computing approach to marketing information systems. The focus is on the individuals involved in the design and implementation of the management structures, philosophies, and systems. The approach is to center on one person, Bob King, who was involved in all phases of the development and who now must make recommendations about the company's future directions in its management of marketing information and technologies. The author feels that the reader can best understand both the history and the current situation by studying Bob King's role and the roles of other "founders" of the Marketing Information Systems Department.

Bob King and the other founders of MIS, and they wanted to make sure that the next moves were the proper ones.

The MIS group has become part of a new organization, the Information Management Department (IMD), formed in January 1984 to closely link two existing departments—Information Services (ISD) and Marketing Research (MRD). By jointly applying marketing research methodologies and information technologies, management believes that GF will be better able to anticipate and respond to consumer and customer trends. IMD is headed by Vice President Ed Schefer. IMD's vision is that:

> In 1990, GF will be recognized as the premier food and beverage company in the world. IMD's support efforts will have contributed to this preeminence, and GF will also be known as the most effective user of its information resources in achieving its operational goals and improving its competitive position.
>
> This vision requires that IMD make the transition from a data management orientation to one of information management. During the remainder of the 1980s, two central themes will dominate:
>
> - Information will be increasingly important in helping to achieve a competitive advantage and in facilitating the decision-making process throughout the company.
> - An array of information technologies will be available to help solve a broad range of business problems. These technologies will become increasingly cost effective, easier to use, and easier to implement.
>
> During the remainder of the 1980s, the food and beverage company with the best and most current information will have the competitive advantage.[2]

With this vision serving as a challenge, the MIS group realized that they faced strong challenges during the rest of the decade.

THE FORMATION OF MARKETING INFORMATION SYSTEMS

The MIS department had its roots in work performed by the Marketing Advisory Committee, which prepared a marketing information systems plan in early 1981. This committee was

---

[2] *1985 Strategic Plan.* General Foods Information Management Department, fiscal year 1985.

formed because the problem of information management was of growing concern to senior management and had been addressed at the corporate level. An outside consulting firm had evaluated GF's use of computers, and a principle author of the report, Ed Schefer, had joined GF to manage the Information Systems department and to implement the consulting firm's recommendations.

One of the early questions addressed by Ed Schefer was "How do we leverage information technology for marketing?" To find an answer, Schefer was instrumental in forming the Marketing Advisory Council, which was composed of Ed Schefer, vice president of Information Services, and Kent Mitchel, vice president of marketing staff, key members from both their staffs, and line-marketing and finance representatives. A consulting firm was hired to assist the council. The council's plan consisted of four basic activities:

- Make marketing information more readily available to product management via databases and the associated user-friendly retrieval systems.
- Conduct ongoing prototype development, test, and evaluation of new data types, analytical methods, and information technology.
- Make use of this information in supporting marketing decisions through quantitative tools, decision aids, models, and by providing and performing special analyses.
- Undertake an ongoing educational and training effort with the users of the systems and models.

The council recognized that ISD had the hardware and the software, and that MRD had the data and the data expertise. To bring these elements together, they recommended the creation of a new department, Marketing Information Systems. Bob King was made director of MIS; he reported to Kent Mitchel. Bob also retained his position as director of Data Research, where he reported to Jack Andrews, director of the Marketing Research department. In addition, Bob had an informal, or dotted line, reporting relationship to Ed Schefer. A key element in getting the MIS project off the ground was the strong support of General Foods' divisional marketing managers.

Several people were assigned to MIS: Vic Grund came from

ISD, George Williams and Pete Callaghan from MRD; and Bob Judge, who was assigned to act as a liaison with ISD. MIS got going in the summer of 1981. The initial approach was to build prototypes. Since they did not know what would work, they tried various approaches and projects. One such project involved commissioning ISD to build an information system for use by the Maxwell House Coffee division (MHD). The result was the Integrated Coffee Data Base (ICDB) system, a menu and screen oriented system that ran on GF time share, an in-house time-sharing system. By making a selection from a menu, the user got predefined screens and reports. This system gave MIS a chance to experiment with the menu-driven approach and provided a base for the evolution of future systems.

Other projects were underway in MIS. George Williams had built a similar system for the Main Meal division on a time-sharing system outside the company. It was a success in that the marketing people used it so much that by October 1981 they had exceeded their computing budget. The Beverage division started using the INF*ACT database management system to manage the Nielsen data; this system was accessed by connecting to the Nielsen time-sharing computer. King's group worked with Management Science Associates (MSA) to build the MARIS system through which product people could access SAMI data on the MSA computer.

In early 1982, Bob King and George Williams met to review the situation. They observed that several systems had been built and were in use by a few people. They classified the overall use of the systems as "decent." However, they thought something was wrong, and that they had about six months to figure out what the problem was and to devise a strategy for MIS.

IN SEARCH OF A PHILOSOPHY

The new MIS group was faced with a multitude of decisions. It seemed as if they were making these decisions in an ad hoc manner, without any underlying theme. All decisions were difficult, and a look at the alternatives did not result in clear, easy-to-see next steps.

In reflecting on the situation in MIS, Bob King sensed that the industry's generally accepted procedures for the development of computer system applications were based on notions that were simply not appropriate for ongoing marketing information problems. When a marketing manager needed an information system, an analyst would be sent to ascertain the user's needs. This practice was based on the assumption that the analyst could understand the marketing manager's needs, and that these needs were static, not dynamic. The result was an information management system that was report oriented; the user would interact with the system by specifying what report s/he needed. The processes to generate these reports were preprogrammed into the system.

The MIS group's major problems with this approach involved the assumptions that (1) marketing managers know (in advance) what information they are going to need, (2) a systems analyst can understand these needs, and (3) the needs will remain static for a relatively long period of time. But the use of information in marketing decision making seems to involve considerable learning by the decision maker. S/he gets some information, then learns to ask for more or different information. Perhaps such an iterative process is necessary for building successful information systems for marketing management. But it seemed that the user should play a far more prominent role in the development and management of his or her information.

These considerations led to the realization that a strategy for MIS had to be based on an underlying philosophy designed specifically for the management and analysis of marketing data. In searching for such a philosophy, two programs were initiated. First, the MIS group was seeded with Apple computers. The purpose of this program was to experiment and learn how such computers would be used; people could use them in any way they wanted. Second, Bob King started to read books and articles describing the changes that were occurring in society. His reading list included *Soul of a New Machine*,[3] *Future Shock*,[4] *The Micro Millenium*,[5] *Nine Nations of North America*,[6] and *The*

---

[3] Tracy Kidder, *Soul of a New Machine* (New York: Avon Publishing, 1982).

[4] Alvin Toffler, *Future Shock* (New York: Random House, 1970).

[5] Christen Evans, *The Micro Millenium* (New York: Viking Press, 1980).

[6] Joel Garreau, *Nine Nations of North America* (New York: Avon Publishing, 1982).

Third Wave.[7] The last two books were particularly instrumental in Bob arriving at a philosophy for information management in marketing.

The *Nine Nations of North America* describes the United States as a collection of nine distinct regions, with each region having unique characteristics. Bob tested the implications of this notion by examining differences in product and brand usage across the nine regions. The results were somewhat startling, and convinced Bob that GF must find ways to take advantage of these differences. In fact, further analysis pointed to an even larger number of regions. Thus, marketing management in such an environment called for regional programs based on extensive analysis of regional differences and brand performances in the regions. This type of management requires easy access to a wide range of information about consumers, competitors, and the trade in the regions. The importance of this "local-focus" marketing led Bob to believe that the MIS group must succeed in bringing information technology into wide use by marketing people.

Books such as *The Micro Millenium* indicated that the world of computer hardware was changing rapidly. The Apple computers that Bob's group was using were the forerunners of an entirely new technology, one that would make it possible to move computer hardware from the "glass rooms" to the desktop. The rapid acceptance of the Apple computer indicated that such a possibility could become a reality.

Alvin Toffler's book *The Third Wave* put all of this into perspective and provided the core of a philosophy for the MIS group. King summarized Toffler's view in the following manner.

Wave 1. The consumer was the producer and the chief economic resource was land. This situation of consumer-as-producer was a wave of agriculturalization that began thousands of years ago.

Wave 2. The second wave was the recent industrial revolution, which relied on the availability of inexpensive energy. The consumer was separated from the producer and the producer was in control. The chief assets were capital and labor. People con-

---

[7] Alvin Toffler, *The Third Wave* (New York: Morrow, 1980).

sumed the products and services that were produced by firms of ever-increasing size. They tended to accept the notion that the producer was in some way "responsible" for meeting their needs. The electric utilities were responsible for providing electricity and could make all necessary decisions. IBM was responsible for providing computers. The American Medical Association was responsible for health care. The schools were responsible for education. In the United States, the consumer's view of success was obtained from other people and institutions, perhaps in part from Norman Rockwell and the *Saturday Evening Post*. This era was at its height during the Eisenhower years—around 1955.

Wave 3.   Here the consumer is in control. Information technology plays the role that energy played during the industrial revolution. We will see the demassification of production—short-run, perhaps even customized production—based on computers and numerical control. Certain mass-marketing concepts are being replaced by market segmentation, direct marketing, specialty stores, and individual teleshopping via home computers tied into electronic sales networks. During the second wave, national economies and markets replaced highly localized communities. During the third wave, a reversal will occur. New technologies are making it possible to produce goods and services localized for regions smaller than a nation. As we move toward demassification and the economy becomes differentiated, more information must be exchanged and used to manage systems and processes.

The MIS group was particularly struck by the notion of the consumer being in control. For example, the consumer was taking responsibility for his or her health care through nutrition programs, exercise programs, and by taking the initiative in situations such as getting a second opinion on a medical diagnosis. People were no longer allowing responsibility for their lives and well-being to rest with other people or corporations. The way this notion impacted on the MIS group is illustrated by the question, "Who has or should have the responsibility for the information management needs of an individual manager?"

To Bob King, the answer was clear. The product manager was also a manager of marketing information. S/he was going to insist on being in control of that information. The implication for MIS was clear: put information and information technology in the hands of the marketing groups. This idea became the cornerstone of the emerging philosophy for the management of marketing information.

When Bob began reading articles about the current trends in information technology, he found that similar viewpoints were being expressed by certain people in the computer industry. He was particularly impressed with Haeckel's ideas; Haeckel is director of Advanced Market Development for IBM. In the opening sentence of an article titled "Decade of Transition,"[8] Haeckel wrote: "The individual—as 'end user' in the office, and as 'consumer' in the home—motivated by the need for specific information, and enabled by the falling cost of information technology, will become a primary focus of strategic planning in the 1980s." Haeckel went on to paint a picture of the transition from the industrial revolution to the information revolution that agreed with the MIS group's interpretation of *The Third Wave*. Further, they both seemed to agree about the implications for information management.

THE MINICOMPUTER PROGRAM

With a philosophy in place, two objectives were set for Management Information Systems: (1) make data available to whoever wanted it, and (2) make decision aids available to the users of data.

The belief that the individual manager was responsible for information management led the MIS group to go to each manager and ask, "What do you want"? King and the others in the group were not going to try to define the information and usage needs of the company's eight different divisions.

Another important aspect of the emerging plan was the acceptance of George Williams's recommendation to physically locate computers in the marketing groups. The group believed it was important for the marketing manager to recognize that s/he had *total control* over the information resources.

---

[8] S. H. Haeckel, "Decade of Transition," *New Zealand Interface*, October 1983, pp. 20–23.

Based on discussions with the marketing managers, MIS recommended a program for placing a minicomputer in each division that wanted one. The program was approved in December 1982. It involved selecting one computer brand, buying software packages (as opposed to writing software applications in a language such as COBOL or PL/1), and using "hired guns" to work with the managers on the computers.

After evaluating several proposals, MIS recommended the adoption of Prime minicomputers. The group chose Prime because of price and several product attributes: size, noise level, and the need for computer "techies" to support the machine's operation. Since these machines were going to be placed in the product groups' office areas, they had to be small and quiet. To foster a sense of computer ownership, Bob ruled out machines that required a lot of service and attention by "high-tech types."

MIS went to each division with a plan that involved a first-year commitment of $100,000. The initial $25,000 was for leasing the computer and was nonrefundable. The remaining $75,000 was to be spent on an outside consultant (hired gun), who would assist the division in using the computer. These consultants would eventually become system administrators. A division could terminate the consultant by giving one month's notice.

The total MIS program went from an annual cost of $2.3 million to $1.7 million with the adoption of the minicomputers, to less than $1 million in fiscal year 1986.

The key actor in the minicomputer program is George Williams. The design and execution of the program required a multitalented, multidimensional person who understood data, computers, and marketing theory and practice. George possessed these talents and was therefore able to specify the technologies necessary to implement the program. He continues to work on strategic planning issues involved in the evolution of the computer systems at General Foods.

George Williams believes that the reason for the success of the minicomputer program is that GF broke one large problem into seven smaller, more manageable problems. Specifically, by putting the computers, data, and a systems administrator into the seven divisions, the proper level of information management was achieved. A minicomputer was chosen not only because of its functionality but also based on its "fit" with the organization.

THE DATA

Ed Schefer asked Bob King the question: "Why are marketing data different from all other corporate data?" Bob said that the answer lay in the fact that they were not "corporate data"; that is, they were not information about or generated within the corporation. Marketing people were interested in seeing how their products related to and competed with other companies' products. This information cannot be found in the transaction oriented information systems within the company. Marketing data are collected by outside agencies and sold to the marketing groups. At General Foods, Pete Callaghan supervises and coordinates the data acquisition activities as manager of Data Systems. Each division has a system administrator who keeps the data system running and oversees the division's data.

The marketing databases contain information about product and performance in different markets in different time periods. Performance is measured by several factors: shipment from wholesalers to retail stores, consumer purchase at the store, and shelf space in the store. In addition, the databases contain information about advertising spending levels, promotion activities, in-store display activities, coupon redemptions, and in-store inventory levels. Typical suppliers of such data are Nielsen, SAMI, and MAJERS. A typical database may have 30 pieces of information on 20 brands in 40 regions for 36 months—or about one million numbers.

To manage such data, a data utility (i.e., a software package that would allow them to organize, retrieve, print, and update the data) was needed. Such a package did not need to have extensive analytical capabilities because many other packages were available for this purpose. The MIS group selected ADDATA, which is sold by Applied Decision Systems.

The ADDATA system is used to store the data and for ad hoc queries. The data are organized by four categories: (1) measures—volume, price, share, and so on; (2) regions—nation, regions, districts, market areas; (3) products—categories, brands, sizes; and (4) periods—year, quarter, month. They are obtained from suppliers and stored at the lowest level of aggregation (e.g., dollar volume of small containers of Cool Whip in Seattle during January 1984). They are also stored in higher aggregate levels according to the four categories.

Data can be obtained from the system via a series of commands issued at an interactive terminal. The user gives commands that tell ADDATA to extract a subset of the data from the disks and to bring it into an active work space in the minicomputer for analysis and display. To extract the data subset, the user specifies the desired levels of the four categories—measures, regions, products, and periods. An example of this process is shown in Exhibit A at the end of this chapter. The ADDATA user can also run one of several standard reports. Exhibit B describes four of these reports.

The databases require periodic updating when the outside services collect new information. Historically, these data were shipped to GF on magnetic tapes, which were read by mainframe programs and incorporated into the database. The MIS group initiated discussions with the suppliers about obtaining the data via direct computer-to-computer links. Although the suppliers were initially resistant to this idea, most of them eventually agreed to such an arrangement. For instance, Nielsen data are now obtained via telephone links between the GF Prime computers and the suppliers' mainframe.

The direct transfer to the marketing divisions' computers has created a new problem because the data are not always accurate and must be "cleaned." When computing was centralized, data analysts would deal with such problems. Now, the user must be aware of any potential problems and deal with them as they arise.

The installation of the minicomputer-based systems uncovered the fact that different divisions want their data in different formats. For instance, one division wanted "raw" SAMI data; that is, they wanted the data in the same form as those produced by SAMI. SAMI data are reported every four weeks and aggregated into SAMI regions (regions defined by SAMI). Another division, however, wanted their data converted to monthly time intervals and aggregated to its sales territories. An analyst in MIS wrote a program that would make the necessary conversions of the raw SAMI data before they were put on the minicomputer.

Another member of MIS, Vic Grund, has concentrated on developing training programs for the brand groups. Vic brings a "user perspective" to MIS and works to ascertain how a product manager can use the various systems. Training and education are extremely important because of the high turnover rate among assistant and associate product managers; they move from one brand to another about every nine months. Since such moves occur across divisions, the brand people must be retrained on each division's system. New recruits from the college campuses also require training.

To eliminate the need for such training, MIS is looking into alternative ways for users to interact with the computer. Included among these alternatives are a natural language interface and the use of a human voice instead of the keyboard.

PRODUCT MANAGEMENT USE OF COMPUTERS

Product groups use a combination of personal computers and minicomputers. Data oriented work is done on the minicomputer, and user-developed programs tend to be on personal computers. The following are examples of the uses by three people in the product groups.

Manny Calvin is an assistant product manager who uses a shipments database on his department's minicomputer. Currently, his system has only data on shipments from GF warehouses. Manny uses the customized reports and does not do ad hoc queries. He uses the computer about 12 times per month; each session lasts less than 30 minutes.

Manny anticipates much heavier usage when SAMI data are added to the system. He plans to divide the United States into regions depending on the local nature of the competition for his brand. He is beginning to see the market differently from his brand's predecessors—he views the world as regions. "We need to develop spending principles that recognize regional difference." SAMI data will be aggregated by "competitive regions."

In addition, the PRIZM system, which has survey data on consumers, with each consumer identified by zip code, is being used to support such regional analyses. PRIZM allows regional segmentation by clustering zip codes by product usage, demographics, attitudes, and media usage. The system is accessed from a time-sharing service via a terminal.

Grant Thomas is an assistant product manager who has a personal computer in his office that also serves as a terminal on the minicomputer. Grant believes that his "class" of assistant product managers (those who joined GF in the summer of 1983) is the first to feel comfortable with computers.

Grant uses the customized reports feature for most of his database work. Major use is made of the SAMI database to do historical analyses of brand performance and to assess the effectiveness of the various marketing programs.

Lotus 1-2-3 is used on the personal computers for consumption analysis and forecasting. Weekly reports are prepared that analyze his brand's consumption. Grant developed a "template" in Lotus for this type of analysis.

Brad Darnell is an associate product manager who has used computers for several purposes during his two years at GF. He uses the SuperCalc electronic spreadsheet on an IBM PC for his personal computer applications. He has developed the following PC-based applications:

1. Monthly volume updates and forecasts.
2. A 25-year, historical, brand database containing quarterly data on volume, earnings, market share, media spending, and promotional expenditures. This system brought all the brand data to one spot, and facilitated the use of regression analysis to determine the key driving factors.
3. A trade promotion system for evaluating the efficiency and effectiveness of trade spending.
4. A regional market database containing volume indexes for brand and category volume (Brand Development Indixes [BDI] and Category Development Indixes [CDI]). Brad used this database to determine how "regionalized" his business was becoming. His analysis led to an increased emphasis on regional segmentation for his brand. "The SuperCalc database made it crystal clear."

Brad has also used the PC for nonrecurring activities. For example, a competitor recently entered the market, and Brad's group needed to prepare a trade promotion program that had the best regional breakdown for countering the competitor's activities. This program had to recognize 52 regional market areas and had to be designed, costed, approved, and implemented in two weeks. (This work normally takes 10 to 12 weeks.) Brad set up a SuperCalc template containing BDIs and CDIs for his brand and the competitor in each market. He input his estimate of the competitor's activities and the costs for various trade promotions in each market. From this system, he was able to determine the most cost effective program. Further, Brad's extensive analysis led to rapid approval that resulted in his meeting the two-week deadline.

Brad uses an integrated database on the minicomputer containing SAMI, company shipment, distribution, and advertising data. One use of this database is to ascertain the brand's situation in shelf movement by market area. From this system, Brad can determine each brand's profit per linear foot of shelf space.

A DECISION SUPPORT SYSTEM GENERATOR

When the people in the brand groups started to use personal computers, George Williams saw that they were spending a lot of time learning to use the spreadsheets (such as VisiCalc, Super-Calc, Lotus 1-2-3, and Multiplan). These programs were being used to develop decision support systems (DSS), which in turn were used to simulate the effect of various marketing programs on a brand's performance. George observed that the many DSSs had common features and that the common practice was to build the DSS first, then get on the ADDATA system to extract some data, and finally to enter these data into the spreadsheet by typing on the PC keyboard. George decided to write a program that would generate the spreadsheet and automatically load the data into it from the ADDATA disk files. His program is a DSS Generator.

The DSS Generator runs on the minicomputer and creates a Multiplan model that can be downloaded to one of five different microcomputer brands. It allows the brand manager to generate a model into which s/he inputs information about a marketing program. The models produce estimates of market share, volume, profits, and so on. The user specifies the inputs, the outputs, and the model. The DSS Generator reads and interprets the user's commands and creates a Multiplan model.

The DSS Generator is compatible with the ADDATA commands. Thus, a user who is familiar with ADDATA can easily build a simulation model of a brand's performance in one or more regions.

An interesting feature of the DSS Generator is its use of regression equations for the total market volume and the brand's market share. The user obtains the regression formulas from a statistician in the Forecasting and Planning group. The DSS Generator leads the user through a procedure for inputting the formulas that may contain lagged values for the variables. A different regression equation may be used for each region or group of regions. The DSS Generator has four parts:

1. A "parser" that decodes the user inputs to determine what s/he wants.
2. A procedure for writing a FORTRAN subroutine to extract the data from the ADDATA files.
3. A routine for inputting the regression formulas.
4. A procedure for writing formulas in Multiplan data format (the so-called SYLK format).

CURRENT SITUATION

In terms of statistics like level of use or number of users, the minicomputer program is a big success. The marketing groups are using the systems and are becoming self-sufficient.

But the MIS group is not satisfied because (1) they know there is so much more that could or should be done, and (2) they are aware that future developments in the marketing research industry are going to have a strong impact on marketing information.

Information technology is moving rapidly. Bob King is often asked: "When are you going to upgrade from the minicomputers to a mainframe?" His usual response is: "I see us downgrading to micros." The primary reason for adopting minicomputers was that the microcomputers were not ready for the marketing applications.

When Bob was reviewing his situation in early 1985, he noted several significant developments. A disk drive manufacturer had come out with a disk drive based on optical disk technology as opposed to the magnetic technology of floppy and Winchester disk drives currently in use. This new drive attaches to an IBM PC, stores 1,000 megabytes of data on a 12-inch removable platter, and costs about $15,000. Such a device would give the PC a storage capability exceeding that of the minicomputers now in use. Technologies that were demonstrated at a trade show in Atlanta, Georgia, indicated that it would be only a matter of months before the current personal computers were replaced by ones using the next round of 32-bit microprocessors. John Akers, IBM president, made the following observation in his keynote speech at the National Computer Conference in Atlanta:

> For the price of today's personal computer, one will be able to buy a 32-bit workstation operating at 10 MIPS [millions of instructions per second], with up to 16 megabytes of main storage and 400 megabytes of disk storage. We'll see electronic mail among enterprises, file sharing among nonsimilar workstations, [and] software that integrates systems across the network and data portability.

These machines would exceed the internal processing power of the minicomputers. AT&T had announced local area networks that would permit microcomputers from different manufacturers to communicate and share common data and peripherals. These developments pointed to a situation in which a marketing manager could have a workstation containing all the necessary data and computing power to support his or her computing activities; and this computing world would arrive soon.

Another problem was arising from the coming "revolution" in the marketing research industry. As a major customer of most marketing research suppliers, GF learned of pending developments in the marketing research industry. It was becoming increasingly clear that the types of data available to marketing managers would undergo drastic changes in the next 18 months. The reason for most of these anticipated changes was the rapid adoption of UPC scanning equipment by the retailers in the supermarket and drugstore industries. These scanners would impact on

How a retail store is run.

How the chains and manufacturers buy and sell.

How consumers shop.

How marketing research is conducted.

How brand and competitive volumes and activities are measured.

This new marketing research industry would expand the amount of accurate information about competitive performance in small geographic areas of the country. Given the differences presented in the *Nine Nations of North America*, firms were going to focus their attention on smaller regions. The timeliness of local information would permit market testing (to understand the unique aspects of each area). Given this information, localized marketing programs could, and would, be developed for each area. Such "local focus" had dramatic implications for the management and use of the new marketing information.

Bob King was concerned about the ability of the technologies then in use to support the marketing manager who must deal with such a local focus. More graphics were needed. Bob was enchanted by the idea that advanced graphics could be used by the product manager to "weed through" the masses of data that would soon be available. He was not interested in "presentation graphics," but rather in graphical techniques that support analysis and decision making. He believed that the command orientation of current applications would have to give way to "icons" and flexible menus, as more processing would be shifted to the workstation. Smart systems like the DSS Generator by George Williams were needed to support the managers.

George Williams, in reviewing GF's current situation, reported that there were seven areas where improvement was needed.

> A major weakness is in graphics, particularly in our ability to move data from ADDATA into various PC-based graphics packages.
>
> A more friendly and integrated user interface is needed for all user modules. Friendly is specified as the ability to phrase requests in the user's own language (natural language interface) and to summon help when needed in an unobtrusive manner.
>
> Ad hoc reporting should allow greater functionality for the user, especially in his or her ability to manipulate individual rows and columns in a dataset. Greater emphasis should be placed, perhaps via education, on the user's ability to generate attractive reports.
>
> The micro should be more truly integrated into the systems environment as a workstation rather than a dumb terminal. It should be obvious to the user which environment s/he is in. In this operating mode, graphics, DSS, and some analysis could be downloaded to the PC, and the Prime would become a sophisticated file server. Ideally, on the PC end, the user would already be accessing the Prime in an integrated environment such as Symphony or OPEN ACCESS.
>
> The user should have easy access, either on the Prime or in the PC environment, to a functional statistical package allowing corre-

lation, multiple regression including pooled regression, scatter, and time-series plots.

Some kind of intermachine communication has to be set up to allow machines without tape drives to back up easily to tape and to enable the smooth transmission of data coming into the central MIS machine to go to the divisional machines.

The updating/housekeeping routines need significant streamlining and improved data checking—for instance, flagging data elements or aggregations that were updated last period for this data set, but not this update.

In doing his review, George saw that

There are two paradoxes that bother me in this review. The first is that as the micro generates more and more integrated and genuinely user-friendly software, so the mini and mainframe software packages seem to maintain their relative unfriendliness and inability to be flexible enough. The second is that as we increase the amount of data that we put on the Primes, so there is more and more need of a more classical database solution.

Yet the classical database programs are not well suited to marketing's aggregate-type data but are much better suited to transaction-type data. Yet such things as a Natural Language interface are now available for database packages.

When I couple these things with the relatively high cost of the Primes, I wonder whether a totally different configuration might not be preferable.

In addition, the emerging systems would be part of GF's technical architecture, a framework for planning GF's computing and communications facilities. These systems would serve as a model for the development of technical principles and standards, help to ensure that the many different components of the facilities could be connected and linked together, and ensure systems access and high-quality service to ISD clients.

All technology installed or planned at GF fits within one of seven components, each with its own particular hardware and software.

- The base facility includes two IBM computers, front-end communications controllers, and related software and hardware. The production services are executed in the base facility. The Prime computers access this facility for sales, financial, and other data.

- The CMS facility provides time-sharing services via a variety of user-friendly software suitable for interactive problem solving, business analysis, and user development.
- The message-switching facility offers store-and-forward communications for GF's administrative network and acts as a translator of information among a variety of machines, including personal computers and word processors.
- Special-purpose subnets include single or networked systems that perform specialized functions such as word processing, process control, or graphics. The Prime systems are networked using Primenet.
- Terminals are the input and output devices attached via cable or telecommunications to a host computer.
- Remote computers are those on-site computers in the plants and distribution centers whose purposes are local processing and telecommunicating information to the base facility.
- The data network includes communications controllers, modems, leased lines, and switching equipment that transfer data from one component of the architecture to another.

Pete Callaghan observed that the placement of the computers in the divisions has created a demand for a person with several skills or areas of expertise: marketing data, hardware, software, and knowledge of the particular business (e.g., coffee). Since these people do not exist today, a team approach would be employed. This team could be composed of the assistant or associate product manager, the system administrator, and a marketing research specialist.

Although enormous strides have been made during the last 18 months, considerable work lies ahead. But King believes General Foods have no choice: "For this company to achieve its objectives, it must go to local focus and learn how to better manage marketing data."

EXHIBIT A   EXAMPLE ADDATA SESSION

GOAL: Print data on Cool Whip volume (dollars and pounds), price, and market shares in all of the geographical areas for SAMI period 229.

A. The system contains a menu that is used to initiate a task or process.

```
 1  . . . Electronic Spread Sheet.
 2  . . . Ad Hoc Query.
 3  . . . Customized Reports-SAMI.
 6  . . . Down Load To Micro.
 7  . . . Statistical Analysis.
 8  . . . Prime Operating System.
 9  . . . End Your Session.
10  . . . Data Base Status.

WHICH ITEM DO YOU DESIRE?:  2
```

B. The user has selected the ad hoc query feature for retrieving and possibly transforming data. ADDATA asks for the name of the database and the user enters the name TOP to indicate the Toppings database.

```
DATABASE NAME?  TOP
```

C. ADDATA asks for the next command by typing "What Next"? The user asks for a listing of the measures, or facts available in TOPS. The user asks for a listing of the geographic, time period, and product codes in the database. S/he will use these codes to compose the data retrieval command.

```
WHAT NEXT?  SHOW MEASURES

  S.VOL          S.DOL          S.PRI          S.SOM

WHAT NEXT?  SHOW PER

   S161.011279       S162.020979       S163.030979
   S164.040679       S165.050479       S166.060179
   S167.062979       S168.072779       S160.082479
   S170.092179       S171.101979       S172.111679
   S173.121479       S174.011180       S175.020880
   S176.030780       S177.040480       S178.050280
   S179.053080       S180.062780       S181.072580
   S182.082280       S183.091980       S184.101780
   S185.111480       S186.121280       S187.010981
   S188.020681       S189.030681       S190.040381
   S191.050181       S192.052981       S193.062681
   S194.072481       S195.082181       S196.091881
   S197.101681       S198.111381       S199.121181
   S200.010882       S201.020582       S202.030582
```

```
S203.040282        S204.043082        S205.052882
S206.062582        S207.072382        S208.082082
S209.091782        S210.101582        S211.111292
S212.121082        S213.010783        S214.020483
S215.030483        S216.040183        S217.042983
S218.052783        S219.062483        S220.072283
S221.081983        S222.091683        S223.101483
S224.111183        S225.120983        S226.010684
S227.020384        S228.030284        S229.033084
S230.042784        S231.052584
```

WHAT NEXT? SHOW PRO

```
001.TOT.TOP        002.TOT.DRY        003.TOT.AERO
004.TOT.FROZ       031.TO.FZ.S        032.TO.FZ.M
033.TO.FZ.L        034.TO.FZ.X        050.GF.FZ.T
051.GF.FZ.S        052.GF.FZ.M        053.FG.FZ.L
054.GF.FZ.X        110.TLFZDY.T       112.TLFZDY.M
113.TLFZDY.L       120.GFFZDY.T       122.GFFZDY.M
123.GFFZDY.L       124.GFFZDY.XL      130.TTLCW.T
131.TTLCW.SM       132.TTLCW.M        133.TTLCW.L
134.TTL.DW.XL      140.CWND.T         141.CWND.S
142.CWND.M         143.CWND.L         144.CWND.X
150.CWEC.T         152.CWEC.M         153.CWEC.L
160.DF.FZ.T        162.DF.FZ.M        163.DF.FZ.L
175.BEWC.M         200.LC.FZ.T        202.LC.FZ.M
203.LC.FZ.L        210.PT.FZ.T        310.PL.FZ.T
311.PL.FZ.S        312.PL.FZ.M        313.PL.FZ.L
314.PL.FZ.X        315.PL.SM.FZ       316.PL.LX.FZ
330.PL.DR.T        410.AO.FZ.T        411.AO.FZ.S
412.AO.FZ.M        413.AO.FZ.L        414.AO.FZ.X
415.AO.SM.FZ       416.AO.LX.FZ       501.TO.DR.S
502.TO.DR.M        503.TO.DR.L        510.DW.DR.T
511.DW.DR.S        512.DW.DR.M        514.DW.DR.L
630.LW.DR.T        640.AO.DR.T        650.DZ.DR.T
670.AO.DIET        998.DEMOG.HH
```

WHAT NEXT? SHOW GEO

```
BOST            NY              PHIL
BALT            ALBY            BUFF
SYRA            CLEV            PITT
DETR            DIN             INDI
CHI             MIL             KC
STL             MINN            DMOI
CHAR            MEMP            NORL
ATL             BIRM            JACK
MIAMI           DAL             OKL
HOU             SAN ANTO        SF
LA              PORO            SEA
DENV            PHOE            EASR.TOT
CENR.TOT        SOUR.TOT        WESR.TOT
NATIONAL
```

D. The user retrieves data on product 140 (DWND.T) for all the regions between BOST and NAT, for period S229, and wants data on the measures between S.VOL and S.SOM.

WHAT NEXT?   GET 140 BOST-NAT S229 S.VOL-S.SOM

E. The user obtains a printout of these data with the PRINT command.

WHAT NEXT? PRINT

———————————— 140.CWND.T ————————————

	S.VOL	S.DOL	S.PRI	S.SOM
BOST	55459.0	294575.0	5.3	49.1
NY	65186.0	399276.0	6.1	41.4
PHIL	33007.0	211080.0	6.4	36.6
BALT	34302.0	199723.0	5.8	46.9
ALBY	10758.0	64973.0	6.0	27.3
BUFF	22759.0	130601.0	5.7	43.7
SYRA	11148.0	64062.0	5.7	29.6
CLEV	27486.0	150755.0	5.5	49.5
PITT	23025.0	130711.0	5.7	39.5
DETR	25365.0	124884.0	4.9	44.6
CIN	42113.0	229444.0	5.4	49.2
INDI	17077.0	96362.0	5.6	43.5
CHI	52144.0	292451.0	5.6	51.0
MIL	20392.0	109181.0	5.4	44.8
KC	20616.0	124032.0	6.0	47.0
STL	20466.0	114490.0	5.6	41.7
MINN	37338.0	228134.0	6.1	57.7
DMOI	23287.0	139052.0	6.0	41.6
CHAR	14104.0	78151.0	5.5	36.2
MEMP	26302.0	153051.0	5.8	47.6
NORL	22133.0	132947.0	6.0	38.1
ATL	18497.0	104151.0	5.6	36.8
BIRM	14489.0	86459.0	6.0	32.3
JACK	41261.0	231433.0	5.6	26.5
MIAMI	17758.0	105282.0	6.0	32.6
DAL	35109.0	198404.0	5.7	41.6
OKL	27523.0	158105.0	5.7	50.2
HOU	31100.0	176892.0	5.7	51.5
SAN ANTO	20648.0	123870.0	6.0	41.5
SF	47358.0	282234.0	6.0	39.5
LA	59143.0	296609.0	5.0	30.0
PORO	23241.0	146752.0	6.3	42.4
SEA	25394.0	144152.0	5.7	46.3
DENV	19896.0	105744.0	5.3	46.0
PHOE	23239.0	140095.0	6.0	38.9
EASR.TOT	283130.0	1645756.0	5.8	41.9
CENR.TOT	258798.0	1458030.0	5.6	47.7
SOUR.TOT	268724.0	1548745.0	5.8	38.0
WESR.TOT	198271.0	1115586.0	5.6	37.4
NATIONAL	1384550.0	7893882.0	5.7	41.5

EXHIBIT B   AVAILABLE REPORTS

BRAND REPORT (Multigeography Single Product)

1. Generates an n-week report with areas down the side and measure within a brand across the top of page.
2. Report combines various measures into one report:
   - % Change
   - SOM
   - Price
   - BDI
3. Report is useful in analyzing a brand within multiple geographies.

TOPLINE REPORT (Multiproduct/Single Geography)

1. Generates an n-week report with brands down the side and measures within a geography across the top of page.
2. Report is useful in analyzing the performance of multiple brands within specific markets.

GEOGRAPHIC TIME: SUMMARY REPORT (Volume Summary—Multiproduct)

1. Generates a report with brands down the side. Measures appear within the brands. Across the top, the report displays n-week headings for the latest four-year period.
2. Report is useful in analyzing the performance of brands within a specific geography over a period of time.

BRAND VARIABLE: TIME REPORT (Volume Summary—Multigeography)

1. Generates a report with geographies down the side. Measures appear within the geographies. Across the top, the report displays n-week headings for the latest four-year period.
2. Report is useful in analyzing the performance of one brand within multiple geographies over a period of time.

CHAPTER THIRTEEN

Summary and Agenda

In the first 12 chapters, we discussed the current use of computers in marketing management and identified the trends and developments that will impact on such use. At this point, the reader should consider the question: "What should I do to take advantage of this situation?" This chapter presents one agenda that an individual or a company can follow to capture the emerging technologies and to leverage them for the support of marketing. Before discussing this agenda, we will review and summarize the material in Chapters One through Twelve and present some additional material that is important in such an agenda.

SUMMARY

Current marketing practice can be supported by a mainframe and personal computer combination built around packages such as:

- Acustar or EXPRESS for the marketing management information system.
- Lotus 1-2-3 or Framework for the PC-based analysis and reporting.
- Multimate or Display Write for word processing.
- PROFS for communication and office automation.

These and similar components are evolving in the direction of better user interfaces. This evolution will permit more and more computer-naive marketing managers and researchers to incorporate the MMIS into their daily activities.

But the marketing and computer worlds are dynamic; thus, major changes are imminent. The following developments in information technology will have a profound effect on the practice of marketing research:

- Random access memory (RAM) chips for use in desktop computers are becoming ever-more powerful. The table below is a forecast of how the size of these chips is expected to increase.

Year	RAM Chips
1980	64k
1985	256k
1987	1024k
1990	4096k
1995	16384k

  And, the chips will be relatively inexpensive. In July 1985, a 2-megabyte memory expansion board for the IBM PC (which uses 256k RAM chips) had a list price of $500.
- The same firm is building an 8-megabyte version using 1-megabit chips for the IBM AT.
- The microprocessor in the IBM AT, the Intel 80286, can address 16 megabytes of memory versus 1 megabyte in the IBM PC. And the successor to the 80286, the Intel 80386, can address 4 gigabytes of real memory and 64,000 gigabytes of virtual memory. Hence, it is not hard to agree with the projections that by 1990, "one chip will be able to do the work of today's mainframe."[1] Workstations will be loaded with memory and have processors that can address the memory at reasonable speeds.
- The manufacturers of minicomputers and mainframes are producing desktop versions of their machines in the form of the IBM 370 AT, IBM Desktop 36, and DEC MicroVAX II.
- The decreasing costs will continue to affect the affordability of the advancing technology. With prices for small

---

[1] "Superchips: The New Frontier," *Business Week*, June 10, 1985.

computers continuing to decline at about the historical rate of 20 percent per year, 1990 prices will be about one third of 1985 prices. So an IBM XT workstation that cost $5,000 in 1985 would be $1,600 in 1990; a $16,000 workstation like the IBM 3270 AT/GX would become a $5,000 item; and a 300-megabyte relational database machine costing $50,000 in 1985 should sell for less than $20,000 in 1990. Five hundred dollars bought 2 megabytes of memory in 1985; it should buy at least 6 megabytes by 1990.

- New high-resolution color graphics cards will lead to increased use of workstation-based graphics.
- Database management packages that use the relational and network models can handle large and diverse databases. Personal computer versions of these packages are opening the door to the development and management of local or departmental data on personal computers.
- Fourth-generation languages are making it possible for end users to produce mainframe-based applications.
- Marketing oriented decision support system packages are migrating from the mainframes to the personal computers. For example, the EXPRESS package was migrated to the IBM PC as pcEXPRESS.
- Electronic spreadsheets are leading to the rapid deployment of personal computer throughout most corporations.
- Advances in links between mainframes and personal computers are leading to the optimal partitioning of computing tasks between the two devices.
- Local area networks promise to be one of the major computing developments during the last half of the 1980s.
- Office automation advances suggest a new office environment that will allow strong participation by mainframes, minicomputers, and the personal computer. This environment will contain data in all forms: text, coded, image, video, and voice.
- Artificial intelligence philosophies and tools are migrating from university laboratories to the corporate world. This migration is being hastened by the "Fifth-Generation Computer Challenge" from Japan. Its results will include advances in the human-computer liaison and the acceptance of the notion that knowledge can be managed via the computer system.

- End-user computing and end-user application development are emerging as the dominant forms of computing.

The technological developments listed above parallel a number of technology-based marketing developments.

- Data from UPC scanners are augmenting the traditional sources of market-tracking data. The richness of these new data may lead to their dominance as the primary means for tracking markets and competitors.
- Scanner panels are growing rapidly and offer a new way of tracking and understanding the underlying consumer dynamics of aggregate market performance data.
- These scanner panels are being equipped with in-home devices that measure a household's exposure to television commercials. The result is a database that provides information on both consumer purchases and advertising.
- National Decision Systems (NDS) is offering a desktop market research tool that includes a 1-gigabyte laser disk connected to an IBM XT containing six national marketing and demographic databases. The data, stored at the ZIP-code or census-tract level, include 480 demographic items from the 1980 census with current year estimates and five-year projections; the Vision geodemographic database, with NDS proprietary information on 85 million U.S. households; a shopping-center database on 8,000 locations; a consumer expenditure database with information on buying patterns in 10 major retail trade categories; a mapping database with more than 80,000 boundaries for ZIP codes, metropolitan areas, census tracts, counties and states; and a site-location reference database with latitudinal and longitudinal coordinates for more than 24,000 specific locations.[2]
- Data suppliers may begin offering a service that monitors the showing of television commercials in local markets. These suppliers are experimenting with image recognition technology to identify TV commercials according to brand and manufacturer by matching the commercial with a database of about 10,000 commercial images.

---

[2] Corey Sandler, "Market Research Desktop Tool Uses 1G-Byte Laser Disk," *PC Week*, June 11, 1985, p. 12.

- Major banks are working with manufacturers and retailers in using signature-recognition technology to recognize and classify coupons at the point of redemption (i.e., at the retail check-out scanner). This technology will make direct-funds transfer possible from the manufacturer to the retailer at the time of redemption.
- Research firms are merging and beginning to offer an expanded view of the marketplace based on integrated databases.
- Manufacturers are beginning to provide their retail sales force with portable computers and to build a computer network throughout their field sales organization.
- The retailer is beginning to use the UPC scanner data for tactical and strategic decision making.

These technological and marketing trends are likely to change the way computers are used and the way marketing is practiced as follows:

- The data in the MMIS will be expanded to include information on marketing program events, consumer and market data, sales-call report summaries, and data on wholesalers, brokers, suppliers, and competitors.
- Regional marketing will become more pronounced.
- As retail chains learn how to use their scanner data, channel power will initially shift in the direction of the retailer. The retailer will become more proactive in decisions concerning shelf space allocations, product assortments, in-store promotions, and advertising features.
- Recognizing this shift, manufacturers will accelerate the computerization of their sales organizations as a means of increasing their retail oriented information bases.
- Firms will begin to "rethink" their organizational structures, which were designed before the current technology explosion. As a result, there will be a blurring of the organizational distinction between sales and marketing when, for example, first-line sales managers begin assuming more responsibility for tactical marketing.
- The trend toward fragmentation of the media will continue, resulting in an array of different options for reach-

ing smaller and more geographically diverse target audiences. This trend will interact with the move toward local marketing and make it possible for the local marketing manager to apply all the elements of the marketing mix to the development of local marketing plans and programs.

- The existing computerization of brand groups will continue, and these groups will be able to access the sales management information system.

- Knowledge management will become important as firms seek new ways to distribute the marketing function into the field sales organization.

- Brand groups and sales managers will be confronted with a data overload caused by the widespread adoption of the new data sources. Thus, they will begin to search for new and innovative ways to manage their data.

- Expert systems will emerge as a way to gain control over the data overload problem and as a means of solving the educational and knowledge distribution problems caused by the distribution of the marketing function.

- Brand groups, marketing research departments, and other marketing professionals will assume more responsibility for computerization of their own databases and for developing computer applications that use these databases along with the firm's corporate data.

- Networks will begin to play a large role, primarily in communications and in the sharing of data and knowledge.

The activities listed above are likely to occur in a computer environment characterized by the following components:

- From a marketing management perspective, the data processing aspects of the mainframe will play a smaller role. The mainframe will become a data warehouse, and may even be replaced or augmented by a special-purpose database computer.

- Departmental computers may become important in marketing departments, particularly for the marketing management information system.

- The workstation will be the dominant element in the marketing manager's computing environment. It will contain a workstation management program that allows the user to readily acquire computing services from mainframes, database machines, departmental computers, and other workstations.

- Cooperative processing among the various devices, using the concept of program-to-program communication, will be the key to producing a modular and expandable system for use by marketing managers.
- Networks will tie all of these computing devices together and provide an integrated environment known as the marketing management information system.

VISION AND PLAN

The most important items on the agenda are the development of (1) a vision of the future computing environment, and (2) a master plan for using information and knowledge management technologies to enhance the firm's competitive position. Because technologies are evolving rapidly and in multiple directions, the development of a plan for capturing these technologies is dependent upon one having a picture or vision of the future of computing.

Chapter Nine described the evolutionary path taken by the current marketing workbench, along with the following future directions for the MWB: network-based, cooperative-processing, or stand-alone workstations. It also presented the author's personal vision of the future, which includes powerful personal computers in a networked, cooperative-processing environment. This view can serve as a springboard or starting point for the development of other visions. Its key aspect is a recognition that most firms' marketing management computing needs can be separated from their transactional and operational systems; and links can be provided among the systems when needed.

Should such visionary thinking only be expected of (or restricted to) the people in charge of a firm's information systems? Some companies are treating information management as a shared responsibility and one that requires general management involvement.

The information revolution is sweeping through our economy. No company can escape its effects. Dramatic reductions in the cost of obtaining, processing, and transmitting information are changing the way we do business. Most general managers know that the revolution is underway, and few dispute its importance. As more and more time and investment capital is absorbed in information technology and its effects, executives have a growing awareness that the technology can no longer be the exclusive territory of EDP or IS departments.[3]

Once a vision of the future is in place, a master plan can be developed. This plan should include a broad description of the current and future architecture, and the evolutionary path from today's computing world to tomorrow's. The architecture should include a strong concern for each of the five blocks in P&G's corporate data architecture (as discussed in Chapter Nine). In addition, the user interface should be addressed and not left to the whims of a programming staff or the software vendors. The concept of cooperative processing makes it possible for a firm to devise its own standard interface and then "plug" different vendors' systems into that interface.

This plan should also address the role to be played by distributed computing, distributed data, personal computers, departmental computers, end-user computing, end-user application development, and knowledge management. Further, it should deal with the organizational implications of each of these elements. Finally, the plan should recognize that the new technologies have moved computing from an industrial to an intellectual realm. In this new world, concern shifts from control and efficiency to creativity, productivity, and effectiveness.

The planning process will reveal activities and processes that a firm should be implementing over the next five or so years. The remainder of this chapter outlines several of these activities.

Prepare for the Data Explosion

The supply of scanner and scanner-panel data is approaching the level where firms can start to use it, along with their traditional data, to gain new insights into their markets and customers. With this in mind, a firm should undertake the following steps.

- Plan for detailed causal and results data.

---

[3] Michael E. Porter and Victor E. Millar, "How Information Gives You Competitive Advantage," *Harvard Business Review,* July–August 1985, p. 149.

- Plan to combine three types of data—dynamic, event, and static—into one system.
- Recognize that analysis will become increasing important as managers move beyond mere data retrieval and descriptive statistics. This interest in analysis calls for the increasing involvement of marketing scientists.
- Recognize the need for an exploratory systems development process and recognize the notion of "programming under uncertainty," because the evolving nature of the data and their uses means that it is not possible to specify in advance the ways the data will be used.
- Put in place a group of people who are concerned with the management of knowledge, particularly the knowledge and expertise of the analysts. This group should investigate the use of expert system technologies to model the modelers and the more analytical product managers. The group should also concern itself with the use of knowledge-based systems as tutors, advisers, and agents.

Prepare for Regional Marketing

Interest in regional or local-focus marketing was overwhelming among the survey participants. To gain a true local-focus emphasis, certain steps are necessary.

- Computerize the sales force. Sales representatives and managers need computers to capture the details of their sales calls and selling environment, and to prepare tactical marketing plans that use those marketing data that pertain to a firm's regions, accounts, and competitors. The field force will be a key source for the event and static data.
- Build a distributed-computing/data network. Brand groups and marketing managers at headquarter locations must have access to the same data as those being used by the field force. Further, electronic mail will also play an increasing role as a firm goes to local focus because of its expanded communications requirements. Computer-based store-and-forward mail systems solve the "phone-tag" problem caused by people being separated in time and space.

- Expand the office automation environment to include data. Since it is important that the workstation have only one interface, access to the marketing data should not be separate from access to the more traditional office automation features.
- Recognize the role of knowledge management. Distributing tactical marketing responsibility to the field must be accompanied by a distribution of the knowledge necessary to plan, implement, and control marketing programs, campaigns, and events. Knowledge management technologies can be used to disseminate this knowledge via advisers and agents.

Prepare for the Marketing Workbench

The evolutionary nature of the marketing workbench discussed in Chapter Nine calls for a series of research and development projects that will lead to the design and implementation of the most appropriate systems, given a firm's resources and culture.

Networks.   Chapter Nine described different approaches to networking: mainframe-based versus local-area networks. In addition, communications firms are refining their local PBX products so that both data and voice can be "switched" through the PBX, thus providing a third approach to networking. R&D projects are needed in this area because of the broad nature of marketing information: numerical data; text memos, plans, and budgets; images of promotional material, packages, and print advertisements; television commercials and focus group interviews in video form; and voice data for messages as well as radio commercials. Hence, a network designed for marketing managers would include video, image, voice, numerical, and text data.

Database Systems.   The addition of static and event data to the dynamic databases calls for a move away from today's file management systems and toward newer database models. Moreover, the need to incorporate video, image, text, and voice data places severe demands on a database system.

Analysis of Scanner and Scanner-Panel Data.   The new forms of data present a challenge to find the most appropriate analysis techniques and models for gaining insight into markets and customers.

User Interface for Marketing and Sales Management. The discussion in Chapter Six revealed the need to develop a user interface that builds on a manager's natural metaphors and permits him or her to "learn by knowing." Projects need to be initiated that identify these metaphors and build interfaces that are based on them.

Cooperative Processing. Technologies such as the IBM 3270 PC are making it possible to design and implement a network of workstations that uses the concepts of cooperative processing and program-to-program communication. How should these technologies be used in a firm's marketing workbench?

Knowledge Management. The concept of using computers to manage knowledge is so new to most firms that significant R&D projects are needed to learn how to use the new AI technologies.

The projects described above can be conducted along with a series of prototypes that implement alternative MWBs or build components for one MWB. One way to proceed is to identify an "electronic brand group" and an "electronic sales force." These organizations would adopt state-of-the-art technologies and attempt to run their businesses by pushing these technologies to the limit.

Prepare for Organizational Impact

These hard- and software oriented projects need to be accompanied by studies of their organizational impact. These studies might include the following.

Distributed Network Management. How does a firm manage an environment characterized by distributed data and distributed computing?

End-User Application Development. How should a firm manage the development of applications by end users?

Personal Characteristics for the MWB. What are the characteristics of an individual who can thrive in a marketing workbench environment?

Impact of MWB on Marketing and Field Sales Force. What is the most appropriate organizational structure for managing a firm's resources and processes in a world characterized by powerful workstations, distributed data and computing, computer-based knowledge and information management, and the free flow of information?

Information Ownership and Barriers to Flow. What is the most appropriate level of information flow within a firm? What are the issues that need to be resolved to achieve this level?

Role of Advertising Agency and Marketing Research Suppliers. What roles should ad agencies and marketing research suppliers play in an MWB oriented environment?

In summary, the opportunities provided by the notion of a marketing workbench can be captured by a series of R&D projects, prototypes, and studies that permit a firm to (1) design and implement a system that matches its culture, and (2) develop an organizational structure that recognizes the role of technology in marketing management.

ADDITIONAL READING

This book has drawn on the work of other authors and followers of the marketing and computing scene. This section is a guide to some of the books that are useful reading for the individual who is interested in building and/or using a marketing workbench.

Computer Revolution

MARTIN, JAMES. *An Information Systems Manifesto*. Englewood Cliffs, N.J.: Prentice-Hall, 1984. Describes the problems with existing approaches to the development of information systems, presents Martin's views on the current revolution in computing, and issues an information system manifesto to the executives of the modern corporation. In fact, Martin issues manifestos to senior management, end users, DP executives, system analysts, programmers, computing professionals, software houses, computer manufacturers, and entrepreneurs.

VALLEE, JACQUES. *The Network Revolution*. Berkeley Calif.: And/Or Press, 1982. This book, subtitled *Confessions of a Computer Scientist*, explores the author's view of the impact of computer networks on individuals, corporations, and society. It is a very readable account of the potential usefulness of networking via computers.

FEIGENBAUM, EDWARD A., and PAMELA McCORDUCK. *The Fifty Generation*. Reading, Mass.: Addison-Wesley Publishing, 1983. The authors warn of the coming threat from Japan as its industry brings out products developed in the government-sponsored Fifty Generation project. This book is designed to present the following challenge to the American government and people: "A new breed of supercomputer is about to alter the balance of power in the world. Can America rise to the challenge?"

Information Management

MARTIN, JAMES. *An End User's Guide to Data Base*. Englewood Cliffs, N.J.: Prentice-Hall, 1981. Presents the concepts of database management to the end user so that s/he can participate in the design of information systems.

DATE, C. J. *Database: A Primer*. Reading, Mass.: Addison-Wesley Publishing, 1983. A good primer for the person interested in learning about relational databases and the various query languages such as SQL that are used to access data stored in a relational system.

BONCZEK, ROBERT H.; CLYDE W. HOLSAPPLE; and ANDREW B. WHINSTON. *Micro Database Management: Practical Techniques for Application Development*. Orlando, Florida: Academic Press, 1984. A technical book that covers the network database model and shows how to build data oriented application systems that use the database model. A good technical description of the state of the art in information management on small computers.

Knowledge Management

HARMON, PAUL, and DAVID KING. *Expert Systems*. New York: John Wiley & Sons, 1985. A very readable introduction to knowledge-based expert systems that assumes no prior knowledge of the subject.

WATERMAN, DONALD A. *A Guide to Expert Systems*. Reading, Mass.: Addison-Wesley Publishing, 1985. A complete and readable guide to expert systems written by one of the authorities in the field. It catalogs most of the expert system languages, tools, and applications, and contains a good discussion of the various methods for representing knowledge.

HAYES-ROTH, FREDERICK; DONALD A. WATERMAN; and DOUGLAS B. LENAT. *Building Expert Systems.* Reading, Mass.: Addison-Wesley Publishing, 1983. A collection of articles by leading authorities that explores the issues involved in building an expert system. The book is built around a "competition" in which teams of experts were presented with a common problem (crisis management in an oil spill situation) and used their tools to build an expert system for dealing with the problem.

Marketing Analysis and Modeling

LILIEN, GARY L., and PHILIP KOTLER. *Marketing Decision Making: A Model-Building Approach.* New York: Harper & Row, 1983. Discusses the available tools and techniques for building models that assist managers in marketing decision making.

Computers in Marketing

BUZZELL, ROBERT D. *Marketing in an Electronic Age.* Boston: Harvard Business School Press, 1985. This book is a collection of papers presented at the Harvard Business School colloquium "Marketing and the New Information/Communications Technologies" held in 1983–84.

INDEX